Advanced Custom Motorcycle Assembly & Fabrication

Timothy Remus

Published by:
Wolfgang Publications Inc.
PO Box 223
Stillwater, MN 55082
www.wolfpub.com

Legals

First published in 2006 by Wolfgang Publications Inc.,
PO Box 223, Stillwater MN 55082

© Timothy Remus, 2006

All rights reserved. With the exception of quoting brief passages for the purposes of review no part of this publication may be reproduced without prior written permission from the publisher.

The information in this book is true and complete to the best of our knowledge. All recommendations are made without any guarantee on the part of the author or publisher, who also disclaim any liability incurred in connection with the use of this data or specific details.

We recognize that some words, model names and designations, for example, mentioned herein are the property of the trademark holder. We use them for identification purposes only. This is not an official publication.

ISBN: 1-929133-23-5
ISBN 13: 978-1-929133-23-9

Printed and bound in USA.

Advanced Custom Motorcycle Assembly & Fabrication Manual

Chapter One
  Where It All Started 6

Chapter Two
   Planning 12

Chapter Three
   Pick A Frame 20

Chapter Four
   Suspension & Brakes .30

Chapter Five
   Drivetrain 42

Chapter Six
   Wiring 62

Chapter Seven
   Did It Myself Assembly 72

Chapter Eight
  Donnie Smith One-Off Assembly 96

Chapter Nine
   A Dave Perewitz Bobber Assembly 120

Sources/Catalog 142

Acknowledgements

As always, I need to thank the people who allowed me into their shops to photograph their every move. Sometimes the same move two or three times. The list starts with Rob Roehl and Donnie Smith at Donnie Smith Custom Cycles, extends to Troy and Neil Ryan at American Thunder, and ends with David Perewitz and his merry crew of very talented misfits.

For the assembly photos and captions used in Chapter Two I'm grateful to Doug at Dougz in LaCrosse, Wisconsin. And for product photos and insight regarding what people are really buying for their home-built projects, I thank Squiggy from dumbassbiker.com.

Product photos are an integral part of a book like this, thus I appreciate the quick response I received from companies like Cyril Huze, S&S, Rolling Thunder, Kustomwerks, Accurate Engineering and Zipper's Performance Products.

Putting together my own bike, seen near the end of this book, proved a little more work than I planned for. When things got tough I took my own advice and asked for help. Those helpers include Don Tima from the Donnie Smith shop, Ike and Todd at Full Throttle in North St. Paul, and the whole crew at American Thunder. The awesome paint job is the work of master craftsman Jon Kosmoski.

The layout for this fine book is the work of Jacki Mitchell and Deb Shade. Jacki and Deb and I have a place to work because Krista Leary makes sure the rent and the printers all get paid on time. And last but not least, I thank my lovely and talented wife Mary Lanz for proof reading.

Introduction

If all the books I've written and published would sell for as long as the Ultimate V-Twin Motorcycle book, I could be retired by now.

The fact is, Ultimate V-Twin Motorcycle was first published in 1995, and despite a number of revisions, the material was/is due for an overhaul. Rather than publish a really-new Ultimate V-Twin book, we've decided to start over – and bring you Advanced Custom Motorcycle Assembly & Fabrication.

The most obvious difference in the two books is the use of color throughout the new book. Nearly as obvious is the inclusion of bikes that we hope represent a good cross section of the bikes being built right now in garages and small shops all across America.

Over the years the typical Wolfgang book has evolved to include more hands-on assembly sequences and less "buyer's guide" type material. This book reflects that trend, with three start-to-finish bike builds totaling 70 pages. Two of these assemblies come from professional shops, and one from an amateur, yours truly.

The bikes represent opposite ends of the bike-building spectrum. Of the two professionally built bikes, one is a short and simple Bobber built by Dave Perewitz and crew, while the other is a long sophisticated 300 tire custom from the shop of Donnie Smith.

I've always said, "If you want to know how to do something, ask the person who does it all day long." Yet, I think the amateur perspective brings to light some of the mistakes I made, mistakes that another non-professional would be less likely to make after reading the chapter.

As always, it's my hope that the book informs, inspires and (mostly) motivates you to build a bike of your own.

Chapter One

Where It All Started

How We Got Here

The bikes we see on television, at the bar or the local bike show, or (if we're lucky) in our own garage, have changed over the years. I don't mean that a new Softail is different from an old Softail. I mean the bikes we build from scratch, from aftermarket components, have changed dramatically in the past ten or more years.

HISTORY

Bikers have built motorcycles from scratch or from crashed and cast-off parts for as long as

The cover bike for the original edition of Ultimate V-Twin Motorcycle. The first of the scratch built bikes were often just glorified Softails, with better paint and more horsepower than a similar factory bike.

there have been motorcycles. Yet, the phenomenon of one-off custom bikes, built in volume in garages and small shops all over this country, didn't really get crankin' until the mid-1990s. Those were the years when people were forced to stand in line to buy new factory bikes from Milwaukee. What looked at first like a great boon to Harley-Davidson, turned out also to be a great boon to the companies who manufactured things like frames, sheet metal, engines, transmissions, wheels and all the rest of the components necessary to build a "custom" motorcycle.

They weren't all Softails. This custom bike, built for Larry Page by Departure Bike Works, used a rubber-mount Kenny Boyce frame. These popular twin shock frames used FXR-style engine support.

Because of course, the people standing in line at the dealership started to look around. They discovered that they, or the small shop of their choice, could assemble a soft-tail from aftermarket parts, for about the same amount as a new factory bike. No, it wasn't a Harley-Davidson. With demand at an all-time high, however, most people didn't care. Part of the reason they didn't care of course had to do with the extra horsepower and brighter custom paint that came along with the aftermarket bikes.

New companies like Kenny Boyce and TP Engineering, and old companies like Arlen Ness, CCI and Drag Specialties, jumped into the gap sepa-

In the early '90s there were no 113 cubic inch S&S or TP engines. A lot of bikes used hot-rod-80 Evo engines assembled from a combination of S&S and/or H-D parts.

A lot of scratch-built bikes from the '90s were based on the Arlen Ness five-speed frame. This example by Dave Perewitz uses seventeen inch, spun-aluminum wheels from PM and a mix of H-D and hand-fabricated sheet metal.

The Evo-style engine - assembled from Delkron cases, S&S internals and H-D cylinders and heads, displaces 89 cubic inches.

rating supply and demand. Pretty soon every city had a small company manufacturing motorcycles. Some lasted six months, some, like Big Dog and American IronHorse, are still with us.

The bikes, especially those built by individuals at home, tended to be fairly conservative, especially as judged by today's standards. Rear tires went to 200, and rake angles to forty degrees, but a lot of the bikes could be called near-clones of the factory bikes. Even the radical bikes weren't that different from bikes built in Milwaukee.

In response to the growing trend in home-built bikes, we published one of our first books, Ultimate V-Twin Motorcycle. The book was and is a guide to anyone intending to screw together their own motorcycle from a mix of aftermarket and factory parts. Yet, all things change, and the bikes you and your buddies are building today differ a great deal from the bikes being built eight or ten years ago.

Current Technology

Today's custom bikes, even the somewhat conservative ones, are longer and faster than anything we could have dreamed of ten years ago. In 1995 a 89 inch, stroker Evo was a big motor, and when the

96 inch S&S engine came out, that was a big deal. When this phenomena started, a 200 tire was wide, and a right side drive transmission wasn't even a twinkle in Bert Baker's eye.

Today, everybody is running bikes with well over 100 cubic inch engines, 250 and wider tires and right side drive transmissions. Thus we've written the new book in response to the evolution of the hand-built V-twin market.

No, not all the bikes use 300 rear tires. The Bobber deal (with the necessary skinny tires) is hot as well. In fact, farther along, we've included three assembly sequences, everything from a long and ultra modern roadster from the Donnie Smith shop, to a short and simple Bobber built by Dave Perewitz.

What's covered in the pages that follow is a chapter-by-chapter analysis of the things that separate a good frame from a not-so-good frame, and how to pick the best one for your project. We've also included a look at the wide variety of powertrain packages being used on the street. Everything from retro Knuckleheads to factory and aftermarket Twin Cams, mated to a wide variety of transmissions through belt or chain primary drive.

As the offerings from the traditional catalog

Current state of the art, Bill Schwab's project started life as a long, Carolina Customs 300-tire chassis kit. The next stop for the new chassis was the Ted Tine Motorsports shop in Connecticut. Ted and crew assembled the kit – with a few twists. Like the fabricated bars by Paul Gamache with integral speedo housing, and the custom pipes by Cycle Exchange. Paint is the work of Bob Gorske from Roade Studio.

A thoroughly modern drivetrain, Bill's ride is powered by a polished 121 inch V-Twin from TP Engineering, connected to a 6-speed right side drive transmission from Trick-Shift with chain drive to the rear wheel.

The super bright chopper is another Ted Tine project. Up front Ted used a 21 inch tire on a PM rim with matching brakes. Frame is a TTM one-off with single downtube and soft-tail style suspension. Swoopy bars are the work of Paul Gamache, (working with stainless), as are the fenders. 131 inch Kendall Johnson motor makes it easy to burn the 280 rear tire. R. Pradke applied the HofK ultra violet/silver base.

Rob Roehl from the Donnie Smith shop built this ride for brother John. For power Rob installed a 145 inch S&S mill connected to a Baker RSD 6-speed. Sitting on top the Motorcycle Works frame is one of Rob's hand-fabricated tanks. John turned a best of 10.7 seconds on his first day at the strip. Not bad for a show bike.

companies and the new start ups provide more and more options for sheet metal, it becomes harder and harder to have a bike that's truly unique. Which means a lot of people are wanting to fabricate, or have fabricated, one-off sheet metal pieces. And while there isn't enough information here to make you a master fabricator, there is enough to whet your appetite and at least point you in the right direction.

The best thing about custom bikes is the fact that they are, in fact, custom. With the aftermarket providing more and more options it's become easier and easier to build a bike that's your own. As fast, as low, as bright as you want. If your tastes run the other way, there are plenty of Bobber frames and kits. Just bolt on minimal sheet metal and paint the whole thing rattle-can black.

The best part of the whole deal is the fact that our industry, or hobby, or whatever you want to call it, has grown to the point where it can embrace long, expensive billet bikes on one end, and short, cheap Bobbers at the other.

As much as possible, I've tried to put it all in here, advice on what to buy and how to screw it together, whether it's a 300-tire rolling chassis kit from Paul Yaffe or a stubby, skinny tire frame from

Kustomwerks or Paughco.

A final word on the broad range of bikes that are all part of our hobby. There's certain amount of tension between some of the flat-black Bobber riders and the pro-street 250 tire custom bike builders and riders. Some of this tension is fed by parts of the media.

Before you expend too much energy bad-mouthing the riders on the other side of the fence, there are a couple of things to remember. First, when they come to take our custom motorcycles away from us, they won't care if it's a black Bobber or candy apple red roadster. They will only care that they aren't factory built, and that they're too loud and too unsafe.

Second, even if you don't believe we need allies to lobby, remember that even the best of custom bikes do break, and it might be one of those other guys who pulls up to help when you're sitting along the shoulder on a lonely two-lane.

And if none of that works, there's one final argument. All the people on bikes, whether young or old, rich or poor, male or female, experienced or new-to-riding, have one thing in common. They're having fun with motorcycles, and that's what it's all about.

Old Bobbers, and bikes that look like old Bobbers, never go out of style. This particular example is an interesting mix of components, including the hardtail frame and springer fork...

...combined with a Twin Cam Engine disguised as a Panhead.

Chapter Two

Planning & Design

Your Brain, the Best Tool of All

Building your own motorcycle is a tall order – and a lot of plain old work. Yes, it's fun and exciting and something you've wanted to do for years and years, but it's still an undertaking that should include considerable thought and planning. There's that dread word again: planning.

We all know it's easier to just go out and buy parts. Sexy parts like billet wheels and chrome plated six-piston calipers. And a big-ass polished V-twin engine. If what you really want to do, however, is build a motorcycle, you need to back up and think a little first.

Instead of using typical product photos for this chapter, we decided to use real mock up and assembly pictures of a bike recently finished at the Dougz shop in LaCrosse, Wisconsin. The captions (and photos) are Doug's own, explaining why they did it the way they did.

The idea behind the Badfinger was to create a bike that had some elements of the Gasser drag car era. The high neck is reminiscent of motors being mounted high on the chassis for weight transfer. The Weld Racing 'Forgewire' wheels have the look of the old magnesium wheels. The frame is 4 out and 5 up, 42 degrees. We ordered it special from Redneck with the 'wishbone' split. The tank is from KustomWorks, fender came as a blank from Independent.

Design the Motorcycle

As you think your way through the project, you soon realize that you aren't just screwing together a motorcycle, you are in fact designing your own vehicle. Before doing anything else you need to decide what it is you want, and then, what it is you need.

Paul Yaffe encourages his customers to think first about how the bike will be used, and to be sure the bike is comfortable to ride and use on a daily basis. To quote Paul, "It's great to profile, but it's better to ride." If you have a Bagger in the garage then it may not matter as much if the new hardtail is only suited to shorter rides. If this is going to be the only bike in the garage however, then it will need to be a bit more comfortable, a little less radical, and maybe designed so you can occasionally throw a set of soft bags over the two-person seat.

Pick a Frame

Like everything else, this designing process is a compromise. What do you want, what works on a regular basis, and what can you afford. Builders like Dave Perewitz and Donnie Smith ask prospective customers to bring in their favorite motorcycle photos or magazine images of bikes they really like. With those images in hand they (and you) can determine the profile of the new machine.

Once you know which profile you want, the choice of a frame becomes much easier. Do you want it long or short, with a raised or lowered neck? Is this going to be a Bobber with a 130-rear tire or a pro-street bike with a 300 tire from Avon. If a hardtail is what you've got to have, then pick a hardtail frame that matches your overall look, or profile. If you want a measure of comfort with the hardtail look, then a soft-tail type frame is a better choice. For those few who want a true road burner, one that goes through corners as well as it does down the highway, then a twin-shock FXR or Dyna style frame may be the best answer to all those questions.

Not all frames are created equal. In 1995 there were probably less than 30 companies making motorcycle frames. Today that number is well into the hundreds. Every city has multiple frame makers. Yet, the styles, and the quality, range all over the map.

We've said this before, (and will probably say it again) when you buy a frame, purchase the best one you can. You aren't spending extra money, you're

The original pipes we installed were from Eddie Trotta and had the zoomie look but, Dustin could NOT make a right hand turn with them.

So I reworked the pipes by cutting them off and making new ends that are bigger in diameter thereby creating a bit of an anti-reversionary effect.

We fabricated the bars and added 'spikes' on the tops of the risers to mimic the American Suspension Springer, and the sissy bar.

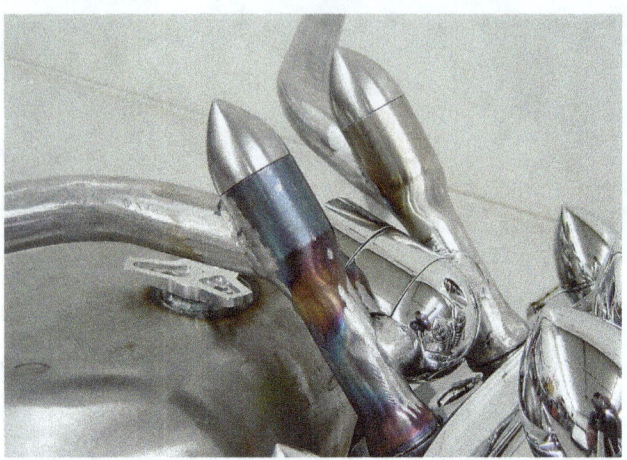

Here you can see the bars with gauge housing. Much of this was painted later, I like to mix paint and chrome.

Dustin likes to have a Maltese cross somewhere on all of his bikes. This one started as a paper template...

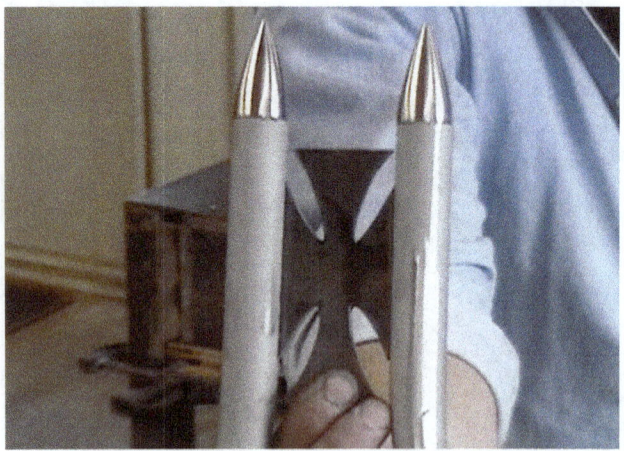

...used to cut out the cross, shown here before being welded to the sissy bar.

actually saving money. To quote Donnie Smith, "whenever the customer brings us a cheap frame for a bike-building project, they end up spending extra money because we have to do so much work to make everything fit right."

High quality frames come with high quality welds that are stronger and neater. More important, high quality frames come from a fabrication shop that uses good jigs, and good welders who follow a sequence that compensates for any movement that occurs as a result of the heat that comes with welding – these are frames where everything fits.

I've said it before. The Frame is the foundation for the entire project, the one component that affects nearly all the others, and that affects how much trouble you do, or don't, have making everything fit.

Your choice of a frame will also determine the choice of certain related components. Obviously, a right side drive frame requires a right side drive transmission. A 300-tire frame will require a w-i-i-i-i-de rear fender.

KITS

The idea of selling the customer most or all the parts he or she needs to build a motorcycle isn't new. Custom Chrome really gave the idea a kick start a few years back with their BYOB (later called HR-3) that included "everything except the paint and labor." Today, every catalog from J&P Cycles to Drag Specialties offers rolling chassis kits. These packages include most of what you need to build a bike, minus the driveline. Complete kits like those manufactured by Big Bear Choppers (Custom Chrome is no longer selling complete bike kits), provide all the parts right down to the last nut and bolt.

There are a number of advantages to buying a kit, be it complete or just a rolling chassis. First, you know what the finished bike will look like, either from looking at the finished kit in photos or at a booth in Daytona or Sturgis. Second, a number of decisions have been made for you. Things like fork length and fender width are no longer a question. Third, the major components are more likely to fit without having to enlarge the holes or install any shims.

EVERYTHING ELSE

Once you know which frame will provide the perfect profile, it's time to think about all the other little details. Things like the engine and transmission, the wheels, brakes, controls and wiring. If you're like the rest of us, the choices are determined by their relative cost. So it's time to put together a budget. Enter a cost for each item and work through the list. This is a lot of work, but well worth it in the end. If you're buying most of the parts from one shop, then they will no doubt provide a cost estimate of the parts or rolling chassis you have your eye on.

Buying most of the parts from one source makes a lot of sense. If it's an experienced shop or outlet they will likely have insights as to what works best, and which parts fit which frame. Buying it all from one store means you have a little leverage in asking for a good deal, and the ability to bring things back without hassle if they don't fit.

You might want to use this same shop for help with parts of the job you don't feel qualified to perform, like the wiring for example. If that's the case, discuss it with the staff and work it into the construction schedule and the budget. Don't, for example, put the whole bike together and then bring it in for wiring.

Financing

It's hard to borrow money against a bike that doesn't exist, or exists only as a pile of parts. Paying as you go only works if you already have a savings account, or the ability to steal money from the weekly paycheck. People have been known to charge the whole thing on a credit card, and that's viable, but you have to be sure you have enough credit and that the floating interest rate doesn't float up into double digits. A local Minneapolis shop reports the sad tale of a man who put it all on a credit card and finished the bike, only to sell it later because he got behind on the credit card payments.

Using saved money, combined with a loan taken out against the house or your truck (the one that's already paid for) is a good alternative for most of us. What you don't want is to run out of money part way though the project. The garages of America are filled with unfinished two, and four, wheeled projects. It's hard enough to keep the momentum going, to get something done every week. Running out of money, or postponing the purchase of a major item because of your cash shortfall, is one more thing that will stall the project.

I did a tank skirt on a build last year and it went over well so I decided to do one on Badfinger. I don't really care for all the empty space left between the rocker boxes and the bottom of the tank...

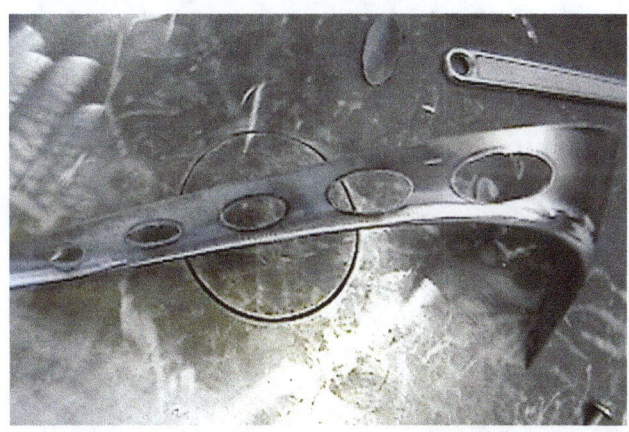

...when the downtubes are stretched and I'd seen lots of bikes with tank drops to fill the space, but then the tanks start looking kind of tall. So this gave me another opportunity to mix color and chrome...

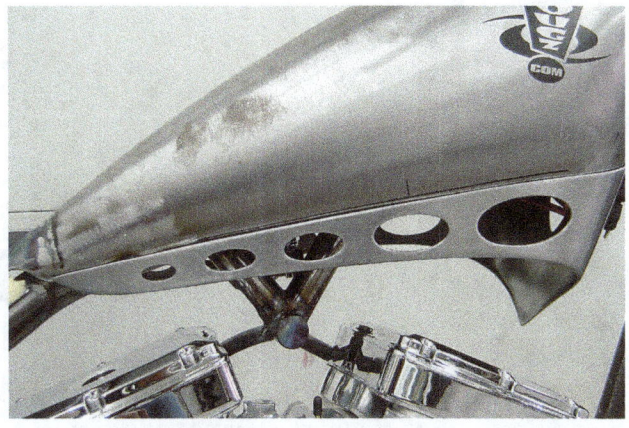

...in a way I hadn't seen before. It takes a lot of time to create as it's hand formed out of .125 mild steel, and you've gotta work that stuff s-l-o-w-l-y. There ain't no hiding a screw up once it's chromed.

Designer Profile: Rikki Battistini

Born in England, Rikki Battistini is currently working as a designer at Arlen Ness, contributing a certain European flair to certain items in the Ness catalog. A former partner in the Battistini design and fabrication shop, Rikki is the man behind the Battistini hand grips, pegs, and even wheels and pulleys.

Rikki says the hard part of designing is to develop something new. "With so many designs out there it's hard to come up with something that is different. I have always loved the look of early, board track bikes, the British racers, and the cool Italian motorcycle products. My thoughts were to bring the H-D stuff more up to date and get a more racy feel."

"Battistinis was the largest distributor of Arlen Ness products and it seemed the natural choice for me to use Arlen to bring my ideas to life, as the logo shows designed by Battistini and manufactured by Arlen Ness."

Less is more, and in this case very unique. The ventilated designs bring a certain early-Bonneville feel to the custom bike world.

"The grips and pegs came first followed by wheels, pulleys and rotors. The see-through design allowed me to develop a whole range of products which are machined from aluminum and have a lighter look and feel. The range has continued, I have designed floorboards and saddlebag latches for the tourers, bikes which often go untouched."

"Most of my ideas come from bike building, when you are trying to develop the bike's lines an area springs up that needs "work." Then an idea will begin. Once the ideas start to flow it's easy to keep them going."

"This year I have started experimenting with finishes and color and this brings a whole new market to life."

Rikki Battistini, the man who started out bringing American designs and ideas to the European market, is currently working on-staff with the best known American customizer, Arlen Ness.

Designer Profile: Cyril Huze

If you had to describe Cyril Huze in one word, the word would have to be passion. For Cyril, if a design isn't right, and the customer doesn't appreciate it, he won't build the bike. It might sound like a cliché, but for Cyril it isn't just about the money. He says that "he will never design and build a bad motorcycle because somebody could buy it...".

Theme bikes have gotten a bad rap of late, perhaps from too many quick and dirty Monday-night TV machines. That doesn't mean all theme bikes are bad, as witnessed by some of the creations to come out of Cyril's Boca Raton facility. Whether it's a Blues Brothers bike or a Stray Kat machine, Cyril's bikes simply work. They get the point across without being garish, without hitting you over the head with the "theme."

With help from his wife Brigitte, Cyril Huze is a man building bikes that are very custom and very unique (at a time when not all custom bikes are). After more than fifteen years building bikes, Cyril has also developed his own line of very "Cyril" parts. Parts that are just as unique and soul-full as his motorcycles. If enthusiasm is one trait that nearly all bikers share, then Cyril Huze is one hell of a Biker.

Cyril Huze gave up a very successful career in advertising to pursue a certain passion - for custom V-Twin motorcycles.

The Stray Kat machine is a good example of a Cyril Huze bike: clean, simple and effective as both as sculpture and running motorcycle.

The finished skirt. Not too heavy, and one more opportunity to mix chrome and color.

I turned the axle spacers on my Smithy.

The idea is to have them flow off the wheels and cover the face of the seals.

Insurance

Note: When we insured the 250 Softail seen farther along in the book, we were able to get full-coverage insurance from Barb at Great Northern Insurance Brokers (see Sources). Barb placed the bike with Foremost Insurance, but explained that, "the company I put someone with depends on their situation and their bike." When asked what people can do to minimize the cost of insuring a custom bike, Barb offered the following advice: "Keep your record clean, don't have unmarried co-owners of the motorcycle, and pay your bills on time because your credit score is part of the way the company decides how much to charge. People can make the process easier for the agent by bringing in the MSOs for the frame and engine, the title or application for title, some good photographs and an appraisal of the bike." Though Barb is only licensed in Minnesota, she can often refer out-of-state callers to a motorcycle-friendly agency in their own state.

Get 'er Done!

Speaking of getting it done, you gotta set a schedule. We all get busy with family and work. It is way too easy to take a week off, and have that week stretch into a month or two. Eventually the new bike morphs into a "basket case" for sale on eBay.

When I built the blue bike, seen farther along in the book, I kept a notebook. I made a note of each job I finished with the date. More important, the notebook is a good way to note the things that I hadn't done, so I didn't forget to do something, like tighten a bolt later. The notebook became a record of all the operations performed, those still to be done, and any missing parts. For me it turned into a big to-do list. Maybe you're more organized than I am and don't need a notebook, but I think we all need something that will ensure we finish the project, and do it as efficiently as possible.

People say the sky is falling. That rising prices and hassles from the EPA are making it hard to build your own bike. I say bullshit. There are more high quality parts available now than at any other time. You can do it cheap with a donor bike and a new frame, or spend a King's ransom on all the latest, sexiest parts. The point is, it can be done.

So just do it. Make a realistic plan, put it in motion, and don't let the doomsayers talk you out of building your dream bike.

We got the mooneyes oil tank brackets from our friend Kevin Baas.

Here we're making the seat base. If someone were to ask me to create this again I'd probably use two air-springs.

The Goodyear air-spring seat idea came from Indian Larry, but it's got major DOUGZ engineering in it.

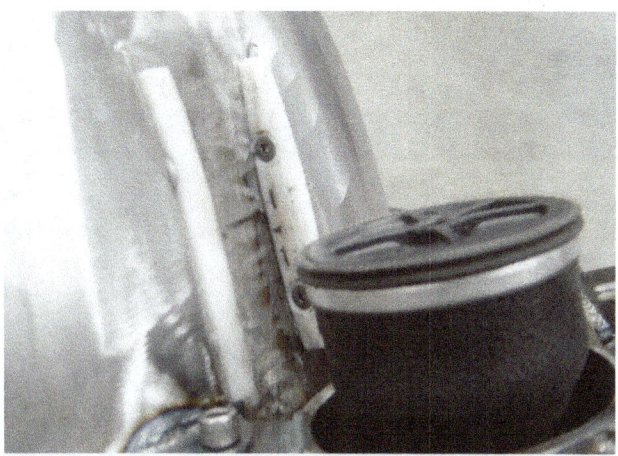

We used one spring, but added the delrin slides at the back that capture a 'tongue' welded into the backside of the seat pan. This way the seat can't twist.

The seat hinge pivots on beveled delrin bushings I turned on the Smithy.

Base colors are a mix of sterling silver and charcoal silver on the highest parts, fading to Charcoal Silver then straight black towards bottom. I shot a gold flake over that, and finally overlaid everything with Brandywine Kandy. All the colors are H of K.

Chapter Three

Frames

Pick a Frame that Matches the Plan

THE FOUNDATION

We've said it before, the choice of a frame is one of the most important decisions you will make. The frame will determine how your bike looks and handles. As mentioned in Chapter Two, you need to know how you're going to use the bike, and what kinds of compromises you're willing to make before you put down that hard-earned cash for this major piece of that new motorcycle. Remember that for everything you gain, you likewise give something up. The hard-tail look and great lines of a soft-tail style chassis come with lim-

Frames come in every style imaginable, from Bobber hardtails designed by Cyril Huze to accept an Evo/five-speed drivetrain to the Ultimate soft-tail from Rolling Thunder built to accommodate the "B" version of the Twin Cam engine.

ited suspension travel and the solid mounted engine. A forty degree rake angle gives your bike a really bitchin' profile but you have to figure out a way to get the trail figure into a reasonable range (see the rake and trail illustration farther along). You need to know what you want. You also need to know what you're willing to give up to get it - you're going to have to live with your decisions for a long time.

THE STARTING POINT

There are three basic types of frames: hardtail, soft-tail (with the shocks hidden under the chassis) or a twin-shock frame (sometimes called an FXR or Dyna frame).

First, a few terms: Rake is the angle of the fork assembly when compared to vertical. Some builders talk about a frame being "raked five degrees." What they mean is that it has five additional degrees of rake. A number of frames are longer in the top tube than a similar stock frame. And some are stretched in the downtube(s). A frame that is "three out and four up" is stretched three inches in the top tube and four inches in the downtube(s). The neck is three inches farther out and four inches higher than a "stock" frame.

HARD-TAIL

The term hardtail frame is pretty self-explanatory. These frames are simpler and often less expensive than a similar soft-tail frame. Hardtails have "the look," the

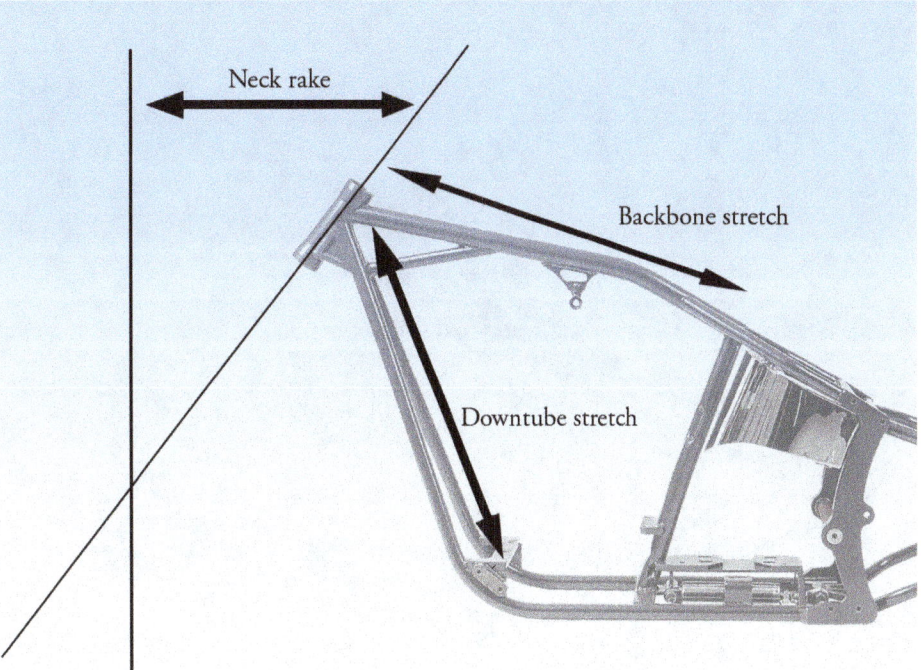

These are the various terms used to describe a modern frame. A chassis that's described as being, "four up, three out, and 38 degrees," is stretched four inches in the downtubes, three inches in the top tube (as compared to a similar factory frame) and has the neck set at 38 degrees.

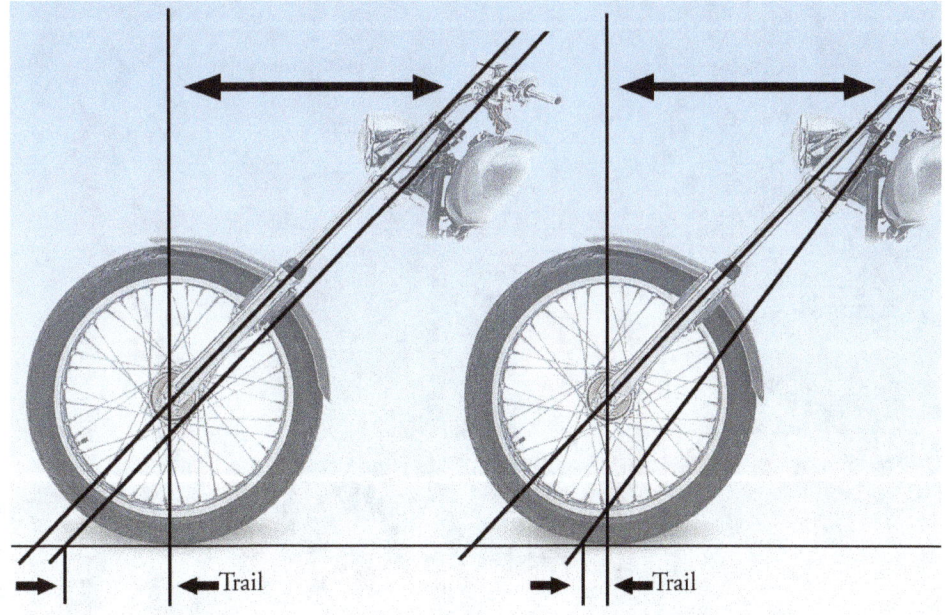

This graphic is meant to illustrate only one point: when you add raked trees to a hydraulic-fork bike, you reduce the trail. Thus, raked trees are often a good idea for choppers or diggers as they often bring the trail from 6 or 8 inches to something closer to 4 or 5, and a very bad idea for bikes with stock frames, as they reduce the trail from 4 or 5 inches to 1 or none.

look of a classic V-Twin. The down side is obvious, though the rough ride can be softened a bit with the suspended seats that seem to be coming back into fashion. There are "wishbone" and straight-leg frames, depending on the shape of the front downtubes. Lately, the trend is to a single downtube. Some frames are short Bobber models and some are as long as a pickup truck.

Soft-tail

Softail is a Harley-Davidson trade mark, because these are aftermarket frames, we generally call them soft-tail designs. Though similar ideas were used by Vincent, (and likely others as well) the first soft-tail as we know it was designed by Bill Davis and called the Sub-Shock frame. Bill built a triangular swingarm, supported by springs under the seat, and grafted the whole thing onto his Shovelhead. Though he suffered through a series of entrepreneurial misfortunes, Bill eventually moved the shock/spring unit under the transmission and sold the design to Willie G. The Softail was an immediate hit in the dealerships. Before long the aftermarket offered very similar designs for anyone building a bike at home.

The soft-tail frame might be called the design that saved Harley-Davidson. It is also the frame of choice for a very high percentage of custom bikes. For all the styling advantages, however, there is a cost. As we've already mentioned, the soft-tail type design allows for only about three inches of suspension

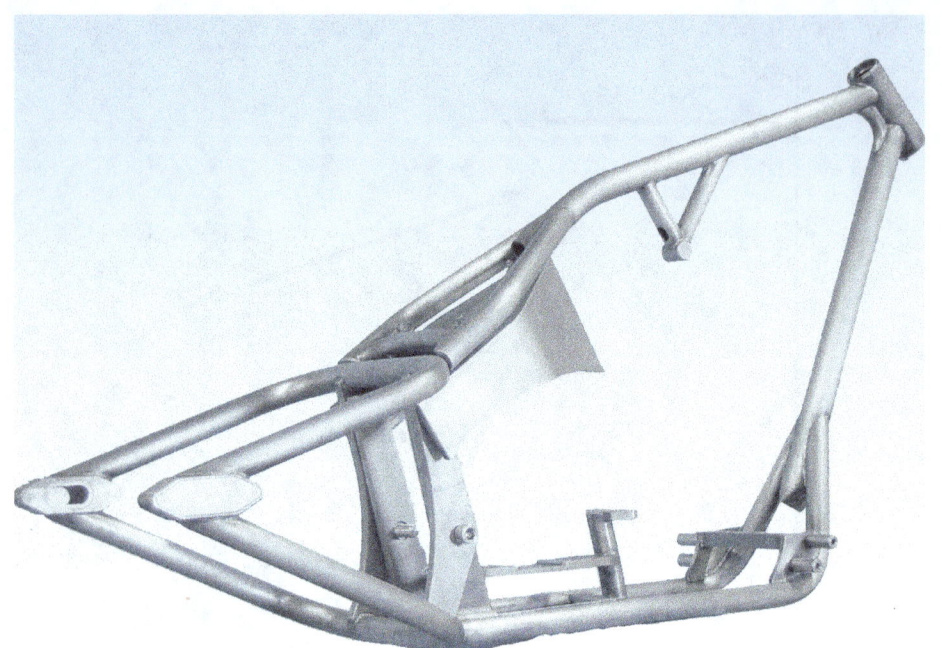

Once known for building only hardtails, Redneck has recently expanded their offerings. According to Vince, "If you want the hardtail look, without any sacrifice in ride, this is your frame. We developed it to look just like our original big-tube Lowlife and Gettinhigh frames. It's hard to tell that this frame has shocks, we even narrowed the center section so the hinge is hidden.

The Y2K frame from Arlen Ness has a number or advantages: like rubber mounting to eliminate bad vibes, very low seat height (the oil tank is under the tranny), and it takes up to a 300 tire, and either an Evo or TC engine.

travel, meaning the ride will never match that of twin-shock bikes with about five inches of travel (lowered bikes have even less travel). Soft-tail type frames mount the engine solid to the frame, meaning the full vibratory ability of that non-counter-balanced V-Twin will be fed to the frame and rider. Finally, a twin-shock frame generally handles, and rides better than the soft-tail design.

Twin shock

The twin-shock frame is a tried and true design with plenty of suspension travel and (generally) good road manners. The twin-shock design makes it easy to adjust the ride height up or down by installing longer or shorter shock absorbers. And though most soft-tail frames mount the motor to the frame in a solid fashion, most twin-shock frames are "rubber-mounted." Thus the vibrations of a V-Twin are isolated from the rider.

The disadvantages of this design include the appearance, these just aren't as sexy as a soft-tail. Before you give up on the idea of using a twin shock consider something like the "Dyna" frame from Arlen Ness, complete with 250 or 300 rear tire and one of the lowest seat heights this side of a drop-seat hardtail.

For anyone who wants something a little more conservative, there are a variety of companies that make OEM style frames patterned after the FX and FXR frames. Chopper Guys, (available through Drag Specialties) Jammer, Paughco and a number of others make a variety of older-style chassis, some only wide enough for a 130 or 150 tire and others set up for 250 and wider rear tires

Baggers

Until recently, there was no way to scratch build a true late-model Bagger using an aftermarket frame. Luckily for anyone who wants to build their own radical Bagger, Rolling Thunder makes an OEM-style Bagger frame in two variations, one of which will take a wider rear tire.

Wide Tires - Left and Right Side Drive – Evo and Twin Cam
Non-Twin-Cam Powered Bikes

In order to run a wide tire in a typical left side drive consideration, the belt or chain must be moved over far enough to clear the tire. A typical Evo powered soft-tail bike uses a separate transmis-

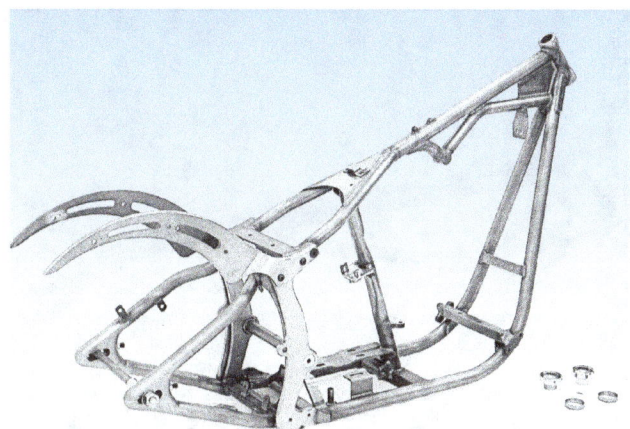

If you don't need a huge rear tire, consider this big-tube soft-tail frame designed for a 180 & Evo. Comes 4 up and 1 out with a 35 degree neck. Kustomwerks

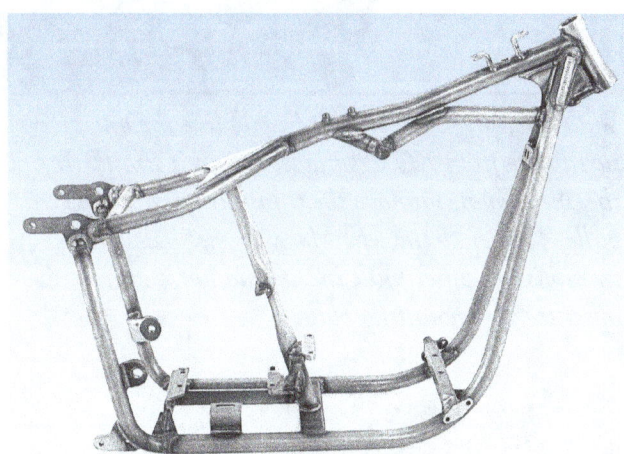

Build a nice early-style FL or FX bike with this swingarm frame designed for pre-TC engines and 4 or 5-speed transmission. Kustomwerks

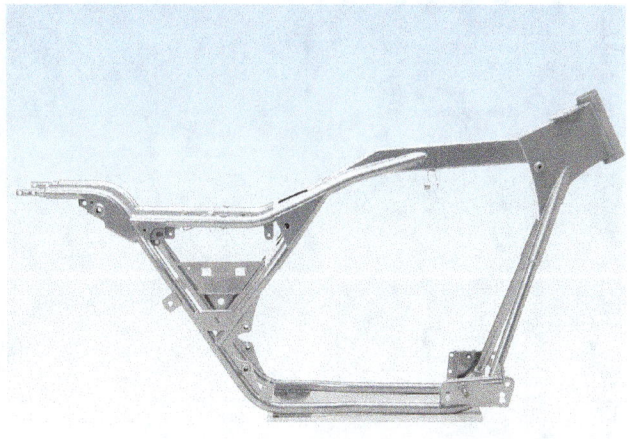

You couldn't scratch build a Bagger, until Rolling Thunder introduced this frame. Available with stock dimensions, or ready for 200 tire.

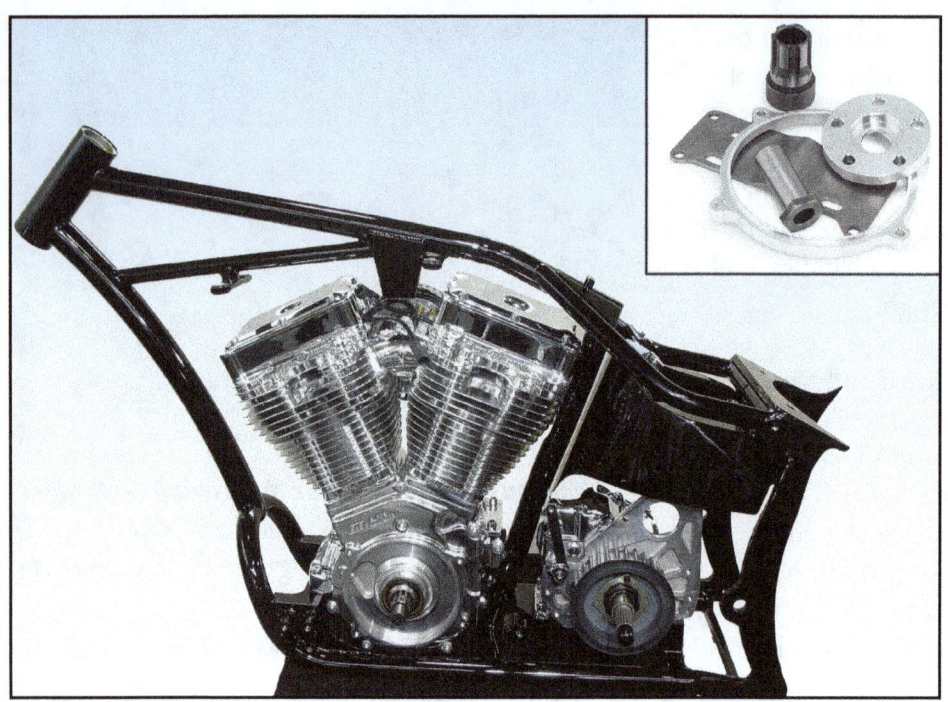

Wide tire, pre-TC, soft-tail frames like the one pictured here from KC Creations, use a kit similar to the one shown, to move the transmission and belt pulley farther to the left. Many frames have some transmission offset built in, and do not require an offset tranny mounting plate.

sion which can be moved outboard, which means adding a spacer between the engine cases and the inner primary, and an extension on the left end of the crankshaft. As tires get really-really wide, some frame manufacturers move the engine over to the left as well. At some point, all these offsets change the bike's balance.

By putting the belt on the right side, however, there is no need to offset the engine, and little or no need to offset the transmission. Some RSD 250 tire frames use a 1/2 inch spacer on the left side, a spacer that disappears when the tire size moves to 300.

Twin-Cam Powered Bikes

With a Twin Cam bike and matching transmission, the two components bolt together so completely as to become a single component.

Because you can't move the transmission alone, companies like Arlen Ness, JIMS, Baker and others offer transmissions with extra long mainshafts, which effectively moves the belt or chain farther to the left to clear the tire. Again, you can only go so far before the offset has an impact on the bike's balance.

What Fits What

To quote my friend Jason, longtime motorcycle nut and parts-person, "The frame will determine the transmission, some rigid frames will take a four or five-speed transmission. In that case the five-speed would be a soft-tail style

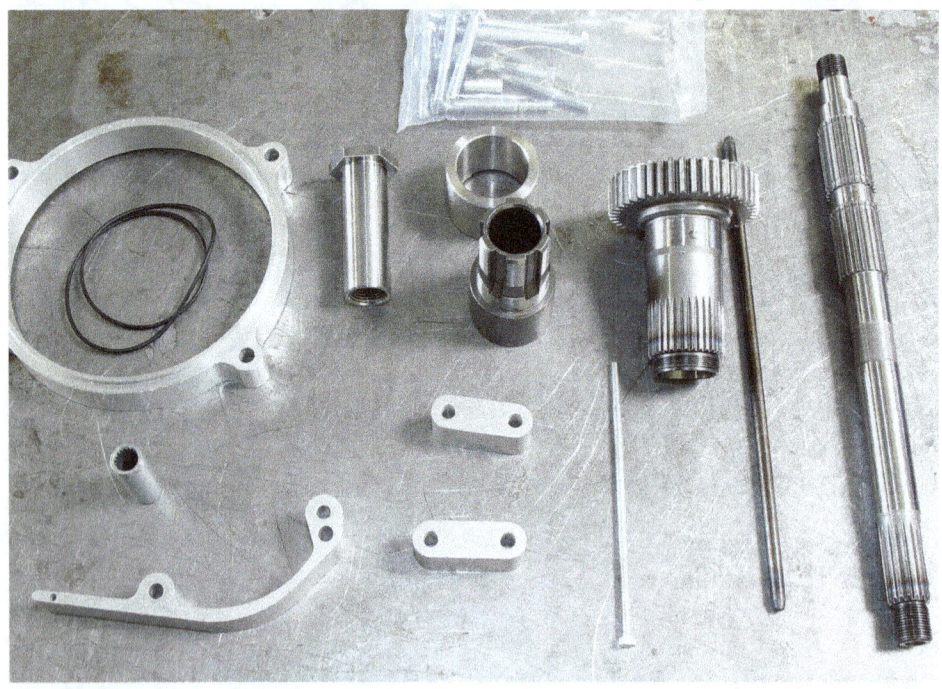

Twin Cam powered bikes running wide tires get the belt out of the way with a longer main shaft, (instead of physically moving the transmission) and the rest of the kit seen here. Ness

five-speed." As mentioned elsewhere, Evos and Twin Cams are taller than Shovel and Panheads. And as V-Twins grow in displacement they also grow externally, not only do they get taller, they get wider at the top as well. The crew at Donnie Smith's shop recently slipped a 145 S&S engine in an FXR for Crazy John, so he could have the ultimate sleeper. Actually, they didn't slip the motor into place, they cut and notched and eliminated the rubber mounts, in order to put the 145 where an 80 lived before. The point is, if you're looking at big cubic inches, be sure the frame is tall enough, and strong enough, to handle the size and power.

When it comes to deciding whether or not a certain frame will accept a 121 Evo engine and five speed transmission, or a 250 rear tire with belt drive, the frame manufacturer is the best source of information.

WHAT TO BUY

If you want a wide-tire bike, look for a frame that's advertised as a 250/300 model. Be sure to ask if you can run that fat rubber and retain the wide belt drive (see the Driveline chapter for more on belts and chains). One of the tougher jobs for bikers working at home is the driveline and rear wheel alignment. If you're buying a kit, ask what it takes to have them line up the rear wheel and cut the spacers, so you don't have to.

This Biker's Choice demo frame shows how the TC "B" engine and transmission connect, and how they mount on "axles" instead of the Evo-style pads.

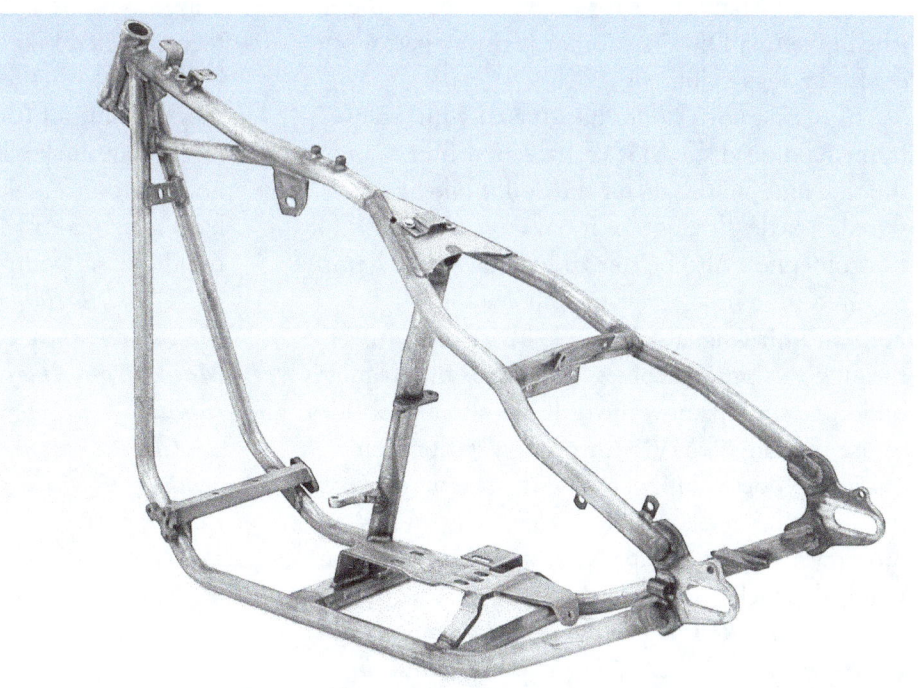

The narrow hardtail frame is designed to accept pre-TC engines with 5-speed transmission, and either belt or chain drive. Comes with a 30 degree neck and no stretch, or a 34 degree neck and 2 inches in the top tube. Kustomwerks.

Legalities & the EPA

MSOs and Titles

When you buy a frame, engine cases, or a complete engine from any legitimate aftermarket supplier you will get a MSO (Manufacturers Statement of Origin). This paperwork is essential if you want to get a title for your new motorcycle. Be sure MSOs are filled out correctly and that any previous transfers are noted. Before providing a title for any home-built or reconstructed bike most states insist that you provide them with the MSO with serial numbers noted for both the engine cases and the frame.

Don't buy parts unless they're legal and come with good paperwork. To break this rule is to risk a hassle with the state when have the bike registered. You also don't want to take a chance on supporting the people who might steal your bike next.

When it comes time for registration, the state will want to see receipts for all the parts you purchased to build the motorcycle. Partly so they know the sales tax is paid and partly so they know they aren't stolen. Professional shops that go through this process on a regular basis suggest you keep a duplicate file of all receipts and a photo record of the project as well. Many states require you to bring the finished bike to a DMV station or highway patrol officer for an inspection.

In the case of a donor bike mated with a new frame, you need the MSO for the new frame, and the title and bill of sale for the donor bike. Each state is a little different, so it pays to call and ask for the guidelines. Also be sure to include all the items required for a motorcycle in your state, i.e. lights, horn and turn-signals. The best advice on getting through this process comes from shops that regularly build bikes, they know the drill. It's also a good idea to use the same DMV or inspection station that a busy shop does, simply because the people who work at that facility are accustomed to dealing with motorcycles and the paperwork involved in a reconstructed vehicle.

We asked Rick Hoffman, longtime motorcycle enthusiast and owner of Logic Motorcycles, for some help with questions surrounding modern VIN numbers and the issues regarding insurance on a home-built bike.

What's the difference between a reconstructed motorcycle, and a true manufactured motorcycle?

A reconstructed bike is built by a an unlicensed builder, an ungoverned builder, with no insurance as a builder. A manufactured motorcycle is built by a licensed manufacturer, from all new parts. It comes with a warranty. At Logic, when we build a bike I act as an agent of the government. I keep all the receipts for all the parts used to build that bike, and if it's stolen and the state comes to me, I can give them all that information. There's a system for the serial numbers, the state or federal government can tell from the VIN number who built the bike. As a licensed builder I have a million dollar liability policy. People ask 'why I don't build my own frames,' it's because the company that builds our frames has their own insurance policy and if there's an accident with one of my bikes, that insurance stands behind my own insurance.

What about getting insurance for the two kinds of bikes?

I do a lot of work with Geico Insurance, and they will insure one of my bikes, for most riders, for only about $350 per year. They won't go near a reconstructed bike though. They don't know who built it and whether or not that person knows what they're doing. If it's a home-built or kit bike, you might have luck with State Farm if you have the house and business with them. Otherwise you might have to settle for riding with liability only and skip the theft and comprehensive. (Also see page 18.)

The situation regarding the EPA is in flux, for the current state of the situation we asked Chris Maida from American Iron Magazine for his input.

Chris, everyone's heard the horror stories about the pending EPA rules and the things CARB is doing in California. Can you tell us what you've heard from shops and readers?

In California CARB is and has been doing random spot checks, like a DUI check. If you don't have the factory original exhaust or a DOT-approved system on the bike, you get a fix-it ticket. Meaning, you have a certain number of days to get the problem fixed. If it's not fixed the bike is no longer legal

Legalities & the EPA

for road use. However, I don't know how common these spot checks are. In New Hampshire, shops that do the state inspections are required to fail a bike that has an engine that has been altered in any way. If the shop does not report the altered bike, the shop is liable for a heavy fine. New Hampshire also tried to institute an electronic check in its yearly inspection. The shop was to plug every bike being inspected into an internet-connected system, which linked the bike directly to a state computer. The system then checked the bike for any error codes, like if the blinkers are disabled or if the fuel or ignition modules had been altered. If the bike failed, the state knew before the shop did and the bike had to be fixed before it could be legally operated on the road again. The state has dropped the program for now because of hardware and software problems.

I want to bring out that the level of enforcement depends on the director and how he/she decides to interpret the rules. The EPA and other federal officials and workers are not the Spanish Inquisition. They are carrying out their federal mandate to clean up the air. However, sometimes a local official gets carried away. A case in point is what happened in Hawaii a few years ago. A state DOT official decided that the law did not recognize aftermarket frames as legal, so every bike with an aftermarket frame was no longer considered legal for road use in Hawaii. Even bikes that were already registered and on the road were considered illegal and were not allowed to be reregistered. Thankfully, one of the state representatives also rode a custom bike and he, with help from some shops, vendors, and owners, were able to change the way the law was written, so aftermarket frames are again legal for road use in Hawaii.

What's happening with the engine certification process?

I just learned that the EPA has issued the Motorcycle Industry Council's requested letter of guidance that sets the guidelines for the much needed engine certification process. I have not seen the text yet, but as I understand it, the letter allows for an engine package to be certified for use in a motorcycle chassis. This will allow bike builders to use the certified engine package in the bikes they build and that these bikes are then EPA-compliant. That is, as long as the engine package is not altered in any way.

Another important point of this letter of guidance is that it does not remove the two exemptions that were written into the EPA Rule thanks to the Motorcycle Riders Foundation. Those two exemptions are the 24 EPA-exempt bikes per manufacturer per year and the EPA-exempt one-bike-per-life for the private individual. In the Rules' preamble, and in comments made by EPA officials, these two hard-won exemptions were at risk once the EPA issued the engine certification letter of guidance. However, as we now understand it, since those two exemptions are part of the Rule/law, they can't be taken out without rewriting the Rule.

How is all of this likely to affect a person who wants to build their own bike at home?

Under the 24 exempt bike rule, a shop that is licensed as a manufacturer (which is a whole other issue) can build up to 24 bikes in a year that are not EPA compliant. These bikes are limited-use vehicles in that they are only to be ridden to and from shows. However, whether or not this is enforced is again up to the local authorities.

For individuals, they are allowed to build one EPA-exempt bike in their lifetime. However, a person can build as many EPA-compliant bikes as they want as long as they use a compliant engine package. Any engine manufacturer that gets its engines certified as compliant to EPA standards will be able to sell engine packages that the home and shop builder can use in their bikes. Individuals and shops can not modify the engine, intake system, exhaust system, or EFI system in anyway to stay compliant. This is also true of the engine in stock Harley-Davidsons. However, the true effect and range of these regulations will be different state by state, depending on how each state chooses to interpret and enforce the law.

Where can people get more information as this situation develops?

The MRF (Motorcycle Riders Foundation) web site is very informative. The address is www.mrf.org. And, of course, we will have updates in American Iron Magazine.

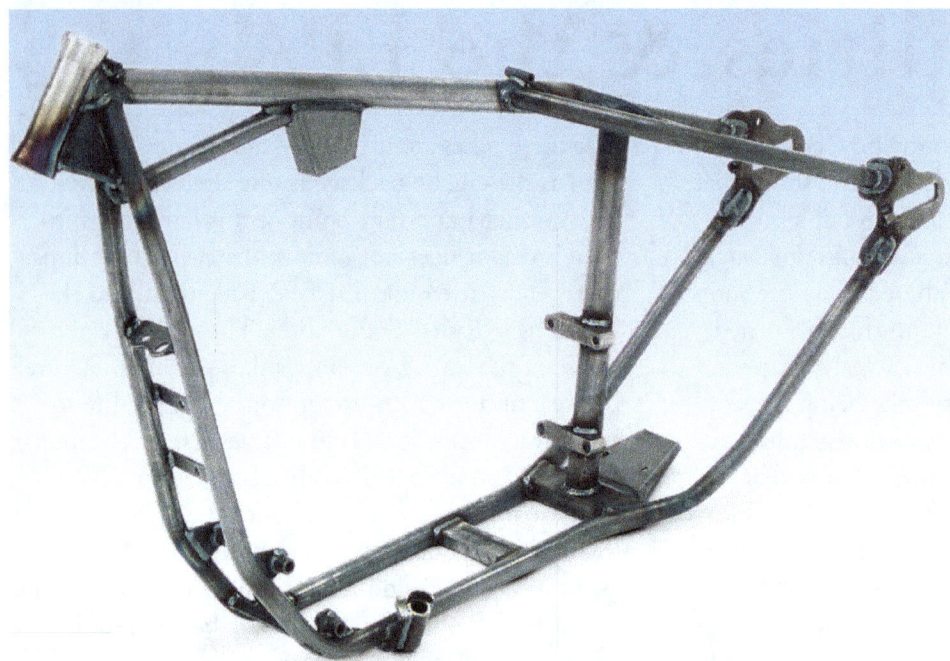

If you have a seldom ridden Sportster in the garage, consider converting it to a hardtail custom with a frame like this from Paughco. Comes with 5 extra degrees in the neck and no additional stretch. Biker's Choice.

Do not assume that all frames are of equal quality. If you ask around at various shops, you're likely to hear plenty of horror stories. Motor mounts that weren't true or fork necks that were so crooked they put the front wheel well off to one side. Most of the frames out there *are* good. The way to find out the difference is to ask professional builders which frames they like to use and why, and do plenty of your own research both on-line and at the various shows. It's up to you to find that perfect high quality frame with the profile you want.

Q&A, Skeeter Todd from Rolling Thunder Frames

Choosing a frame is perhaps the most important decision you will make as part of the bike building project. The frame determines the look, handling, comfort, and in some cases the longevity, of the bike you're building.

For guidance in picking the right frame, we asked Skeeter Todd from Rolling Thunder frames, about the typical questions they get at the booth in Daytona or Sturgis, and how they answer the questions and try to steer people into frames that truly fit their needs.

Skeeter, how do you advise them as to the basic frame type and dimensions?

Most of them have a rear tire size in mind. So

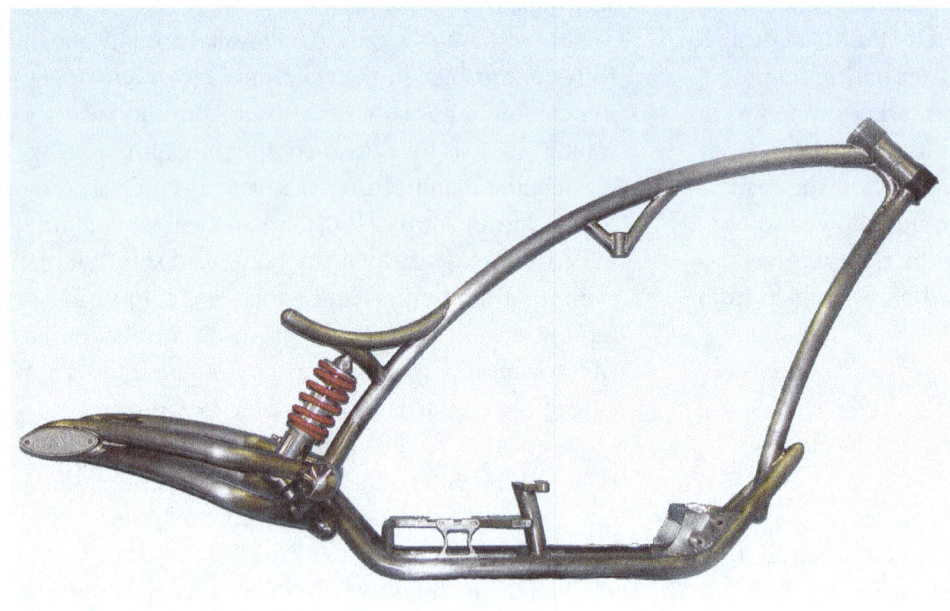

We're not in Kansas anymore. This mono-shock frame from Redneck Engineering would make a good basis for either a Bobber or a custom. Lack of a seat tube provides great freedom in designing an exhaust system.

we ask them whether they plan to use left or right side drive, what are their thoughts on tubing size, what do they want it to look like - stretch and rake, and of course whether it's a soft-tail style frame or a hardtail, or whatever. When guys come to us with a photo of a bike like the one they want to build, that helps immensely.

The tire size determines some of the frame dimensions. For example, when you go to a 250 or larger tire, I like to see them with right side drive, just because you don't have to do the driveline offsets you do with left side drive and a big rear tire. And when the tires get to 330 then there are some small changes we have to make to the back of the frame.

In terms of engines, how do people make the choice between Evo or Twin Cam?

Well, the Evo is a better deal in terms of power per dollar. For about five thousand dollars or somewhat more, you can have a really nice Evo from any one of a number of companies. To get the same amount of power from a Twin Cam you have to buy a motor and then throw a bunch of it away.

Do people have questions about the tubing itself, the size and the quality?

If the bike is a proper chopper, then I try to get them into a frame made with larger diameter tubing, just because it's stronger and does a better job of supporting the neck area. When you put that neck way up and out, it needs to be better supported, with stronger tubing and some gusseting too.

All our frames are made from DOM (drawn over mandrel) mild steel tubing with a .120-inch wall thickness. The thicker wall makes for stronger tubing and also helps to dampen the vibration.

What should people look for when they compare frames, when they go from booth to booth at a show for example?

They should look at the quality of the welds and the structure. How well do the tubes fit at the joints. You do get what you pay for, especially in the case of frames. Whether you buy one of ours or not, a cheap frame is never a bargain.

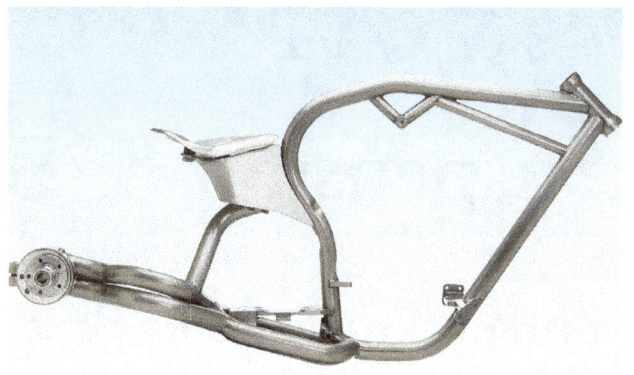

Break away from the pack with this single-sided rigid frame from Rolling Thunder. Accepts up to a 124 inch Evo engine and s-t style tranny.

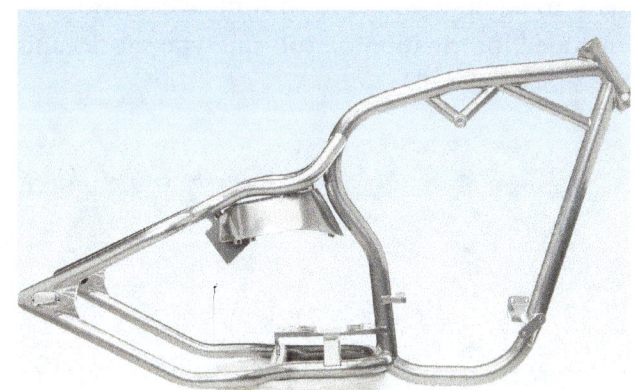

Another hardtail from Rolling Thunder, this one a little less radical. Big-diameter tubing helps provide strength, accepts Evo engine and up to a 330 tire.

Skeeter Todd is a man known to embrace new technology, especially when it makes motorcycles go faster. Here he's seen with a new prototype carbon fiber wheel from Revolution. Lighter wheels mean faster acceleration, or what Skeeter calls, "free horsepower."

Chapter Four

Suspension & Brakes

Forks, Shocks, and Brake Components

Whether the bike you build is a radical chopper or a conservative twin-shock design, you still have to equip it with a front fork. We've also included information on soft-tail type shocks and air-shocks as well.

THE FORK

Currently, your choice for a fork is large and growing. Everything from Springer to hydraulic and even a few leaf-spring Indian re-pop designs.

In terms of fitment, the neck and fork stem bearings are the same on all late model Big

There's a vast array of high quality suspension and brake components on the market. Buy well-known components that make sense for your project. You can even go swap-meet shopping, there's a lot of late model H-D take off parts available for cheap. Just be sure it's legal, and for brakes, stick with the later, four-piston calipers.

Twins, Sportsters and nearly all aftermarket frames. The Timken bearings used in the neck of nearly all V-twins are also a common wheel bearing for many automotive applications. At the auto parts store the bearing and race set is an "A-14," part numbers are: L44610 for the race and L44643 for the bearing. In theory any set of triple trees with stem and bearings should work on any frame. There are, of course, certain exceptions so you need to pay attention to the recommendations of the fork manufacturer.

Before you buy a new fork assembly consider that all the components that make up the front end of the bike must be designed (or modified) to work with all the other parts. A wide-glide fork will require the correct wheel hub and spacers, and the right brackets or spacers to mount the front fender. You need a fork stop, just be

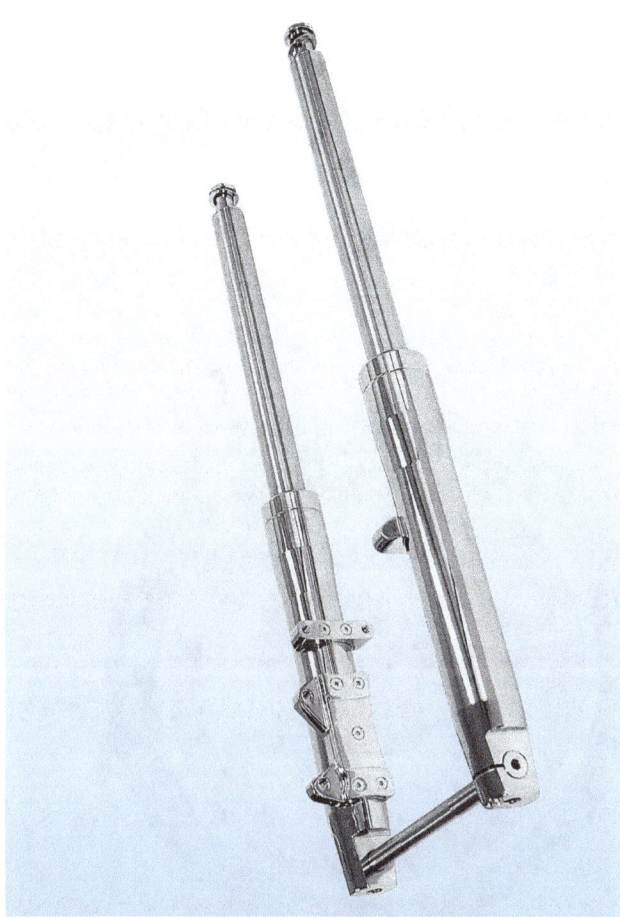

41mm conventional fork assemblies like this are very common and a good value when buying a front end. Most can be ordered with a variety of lower leg styles, set up for single or dual discs. Kustomwerks

sure that any provision for a stop located on the neck matches the provision on the lower triple tree.

If the fork stops are external, just adjust them so the bars can't hit the tank. Leave a little extra clearance so that if the bike tips over in the parking lot, and there's extra force on the bars, they still can't touch the gas tank.

Fork Types

Hydraulic Forks

True to its name, a hydraulic fork is filled with oil, and a set of springs, thus combining the spring and shock in one unit. Hydraulic forks come in wide-glide, narrow-glide, right side up (conventional) and upside down configurations. The terms wide or narrow glide refer to the distance between the two fork tubes. Most factory

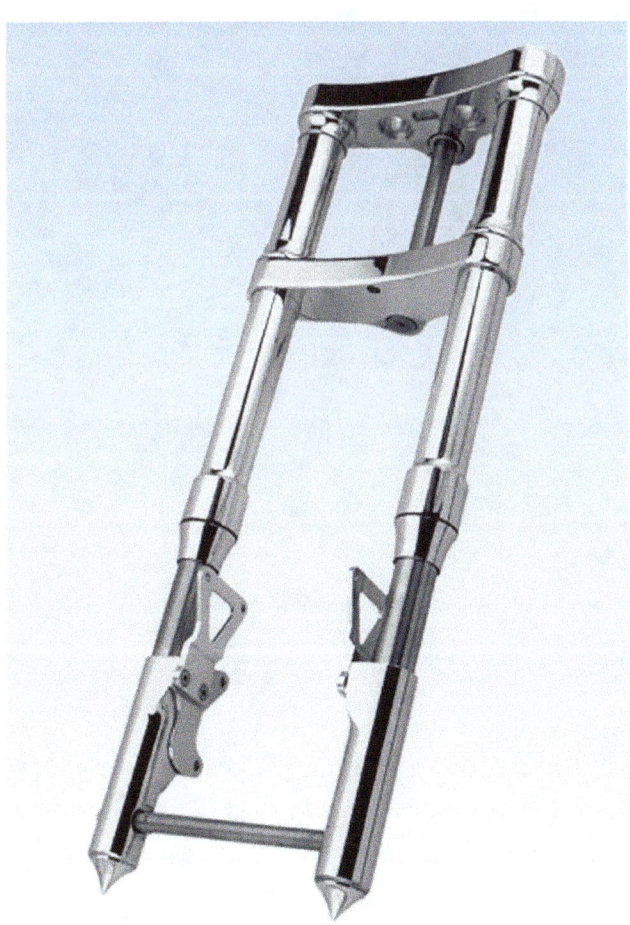

This wide glide inverted front end uses 56mm upper tubes, smooth top trees and a hidden axle. Available in a wide range of lengths. Cyril Huze

Cyril Huze offers this springer, with rounded edges and mounts, in every length from 2 under to 20 over. Available in narrow, mid or wide.

that move up and down with the front wheel. By clamping the larger diameter member to the triple trees this layout puts the strongest member in the triple trees - which reduces flex and makes for a more stable front end. This design also reduces unsprung weight by making the smaller diameter, and lighter, part of the fork the part that moves with the wheel over bumps. The most sophisticated forks are "cartridge style," meaning they have a cartridge (like a small shock absorber) located inside one or both of the tubes.

Until recently, most hydraulic forks used either 39 or 41mm tubes. Bigger is better, and if not better, at least stronger, so the aftermarket now offers tubes as big as 58mm and more. On factory bikes, the 39mm tubes are usually run in a narrow-glide configuration as seen on Sportsters and some Dyna models. The 41mm forks used wide-style forks, for example, measure nearly ten inches center-to-center (exact dimensions vary between the various Harley-Davidson models). Sportsters and many Dynas come with narrow glide forks. In addition the aftermarket offers "mid-glide" forks with tube spacing that's between the narrow and wide dimensions.

Most forks used on street-driven V-twins utilize what we might call conventional fork designs with the smaller diameter part of the fork (the tube) bolted into the triple clamp. The lower leg, the larger diameter part of the assembly with the caliper mounting lugs, slides up and down on the tube. The most modern of the hydraulic forks, the upside down designs, reverse the relative location of the two major components. The larger diameter part of the fork is now bolted to the triple clamps. The tubes become the components

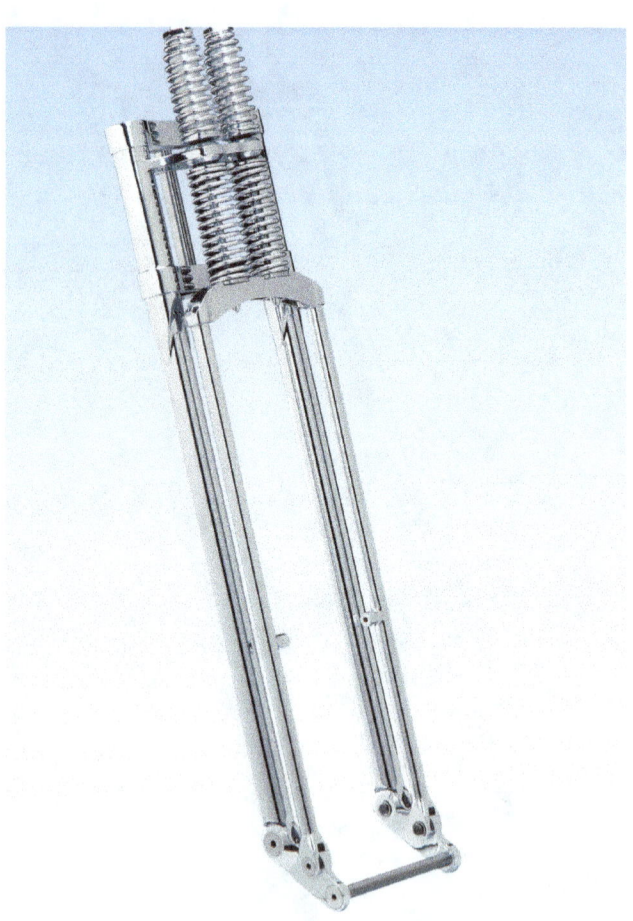

Lovers of springers are lucky, a number of firms now make very high quality fork assemblies in chrome or powder, with high tech features like gas-charged shocks. Many are tailored to your bike. R. Thunder

on most Softail and Dresser models come in three basic versions, FLT, Softail Custom and Heritage (also Fat Boy). The FLT (or Dresser) tubes are the shortest, with Heritage next in length and Softail Custom being the longest of all. Of course longer and shorter tubes are available in most styles from the various aftermarket companies.

In addition to what are essentially OEM designs, many of the catalog companies offer their own fork assemblies with or without triple trees.

A FEW TERMS

One of the advantages of buying a rolling chassis kit is not having to figure out things like the length of the fork tubes. The Drag Specialties catalog both offer charts that help you determine not only trail, but tube length as well. When trying to determine the length of the tubes, remember that the fork will compress roughly an inch once you sit on the machine.

Some frame manufacturers provide a chart, as to which fork length to use with which of their frames.

Terms: A "ten over" front end is one with tubes that are ten inches longer than the stock tubes on a Softail Custom.

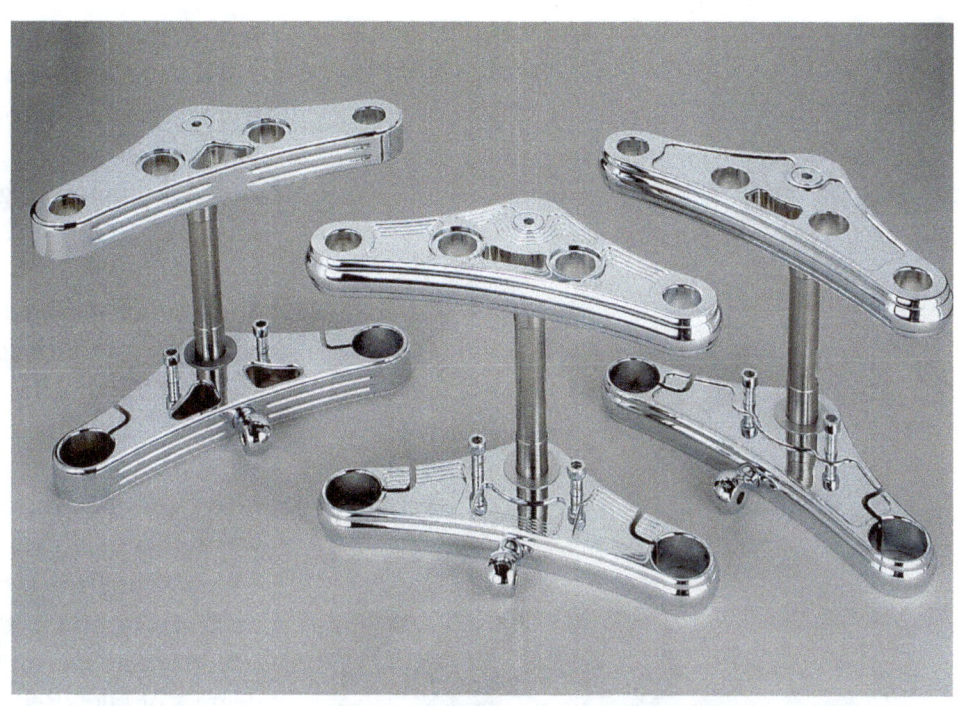

Because the 41mm front end is so popular, a huge variety of triple tree designs are available. This collection from Arlen Ness are cut from billet then chrome plated. Available in various rakes as well.

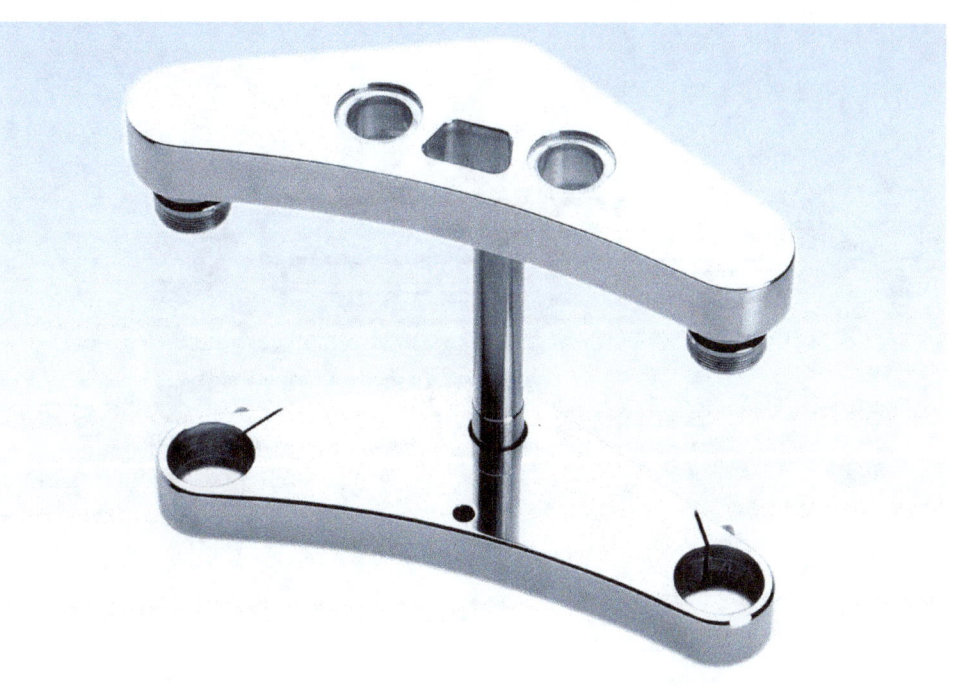

This set of 41mm smooth-top trees is from Cyril Huze, available in rakes of 0, 3, 5 and 7 degrees.

Girder forks have a certain allure all their own. This example, designed by Donnie Smith, uses a sophisticated coil-over for good performance. Jammer

SPRINGER FORKS

Today there are new Springer forks available from a number of companies, including all the big catalog companies, as well as Paughco, Redneck Engineering and Rolling Thunder (and others as well). There's also this other big company in Milwaukee, they make Springer forks too. Speaking of springers, any new Springer should employ a means of controlling the oscillations and harmonics with shocks or some kind of damper.

With a Springer fork the triple trees are often integral to the fork assembly, so there's no easy way to adjust the trail, which is why Rolling Thunder offers two versions of their work, one for frames with less than 33 degrees of rake and one for more radical frames with more than 33 degrees of rake. Redneck will simply manufacture the Springer for your particular frame so both the length and trail are correct.

Many new Springer fork assemblies, like the one from Custom Chrome, use a top tree drilled for conventional risers. A few, like those from Paughco, are available with an earlier-style top tree and accept dog-bone style risers.

Some springers take standard size (factory) axles while others do not. Likewise, some of these retro fork assemblies take stock brakes and sheet metal and some do not. A few allow you to order a caliper at the time you order the fork, so you know the caliper is a good fit.

GIRDER FORKS

While Harley-Davidson used Springer forks, the guys at Indian used the Girder design, which at least some bike builders feel is superior. Because modern Girders use a separate coil-over assembly,

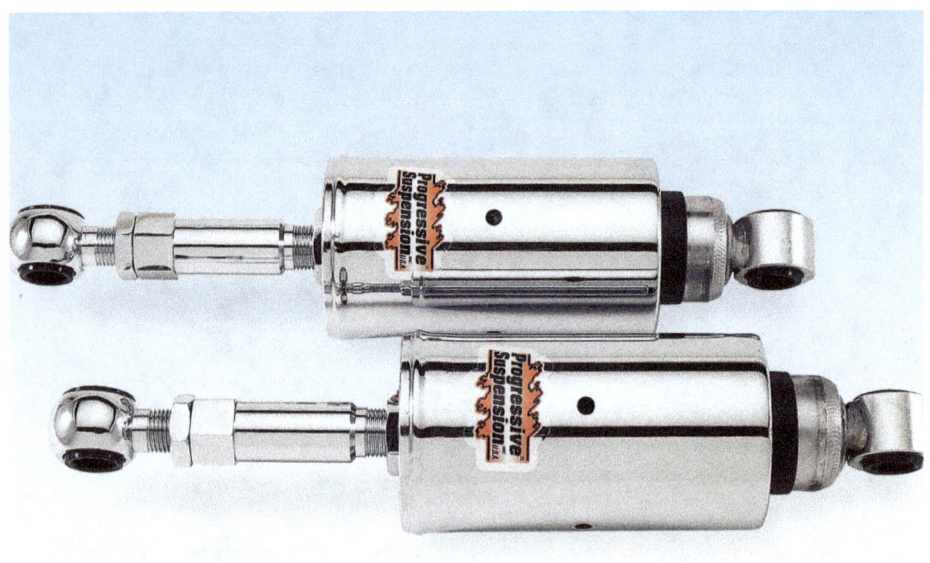

Many Softail shocks come with height adjusters built in, like these from Progressive. Because the soft-tail suspension offers only 3 inches (at best) of travel, it's important to use a high-quality shock. Arlen Ness

it's easy to adjust the spring tension, and even the entire coil-over assembly. Donnie Smith likes the design because they don't "wind up" when you hit the brakes hard." He likes the design well enough to recreate the girders he and brother Happy used to make in the old Chopper days. Today, that fork is available from Custom Chrome as a signature Donnie Smith design.

Soft-tail Shocks
What Fits What

Nearly all aftermarket soft-tail type frames are based on factory geometry. Softails from Milwaukee came with three slightly different rear suspensions. The first change came in 1989 and the next change came in 2000. Even though the shocks for the second generation suspension look similar to those used with the first Softails, the shocks should not be interchanged. Most current aftermarket frames use either the 1989 to 1999, or the 2000 and later, shocks. The two designs are different enough (the earlier shocks use an eye on either end while the late-model shocks use a threaded bolt on the front end) that it would be tough to use, or even buy, the wrong one.

Lowering Kits

Lowering kits for the back of a Softail frame range from add-on threaded "lowering kits" that attach to the standard shocks, to shocks with the adjustment built in, to full-tilt air-adjustable systems from Legends or

The 2000 and later soft-tails use a shock with a threaded "stud" on one end. Again, some of these are height and/or preload adjustable.

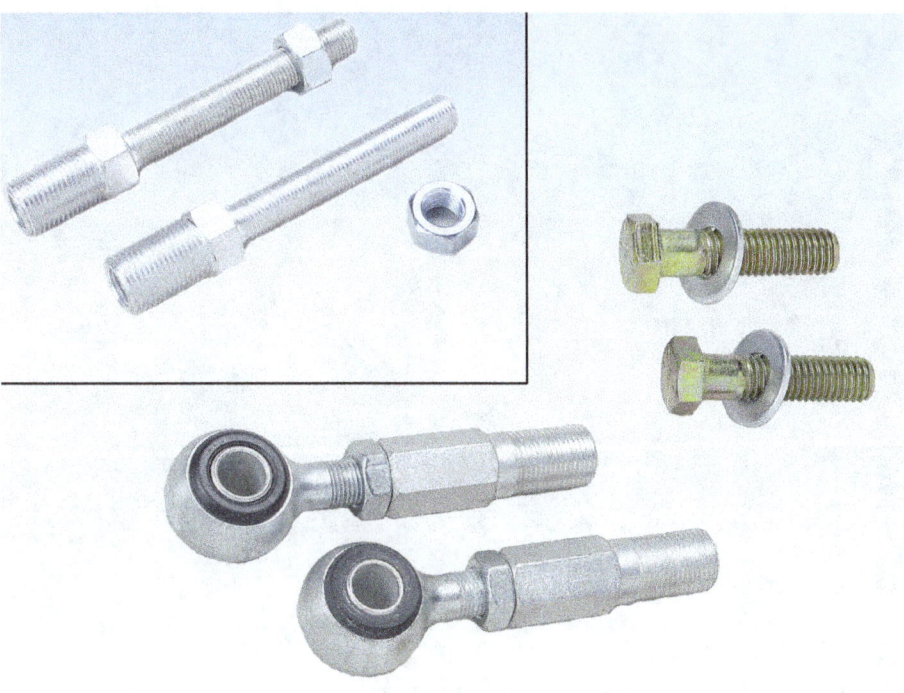

Lowering kits that thread on to existing shock absorbers are available for both early and late style shocks. Essentially, to lower the bike you have to make the shock longer. Arlen Ness

A variety of air-suspension systems are available, including this set up from Independent Cycle. The upside is the ability to vary the ride and height at will. The downside is the cost and extra hardware.

The trend of late is toward a single front brake, which is fine in a case like this where the caliper is a good four-piston design squeezing a rotor of a reasonable diameter (a larger diameter rotor means the caliper has more leverage). Note the non-stainless brake lines.

Progressive. Before buying lowering kits for a new frame, ask the manufacturer what they recommend, some frames have already been "lowered" and others come with height-adjustable shocks.

Air Suspension

The first successful aftermarket air suspension system came from Legends and is based on two air chambers made by Gates, similar in construction to the big air bags used by heavy duty trucks in lieu of true springs. The system features an on-board compressor so the ride and ride height can be adjusted on the go. An air release button lets you drop the air for that really slammed look while cruising slow or while parked at the local watering hole.

The other popular air-suspension system is the Airtail from Progressive Suspension. The Airtail uses one conventional shock (like most motorcycle shocks, this is a shock/spring combination) and one "air shock." The air shock is actually a two-chambered device, one chamber controls the quality of the ride and another controls the ride height.

Progressive feels the two-shock approach offers a number of advantages, including the fact that you are actually riding on a conventional spring/shock, which will hold up the bike no matter how much air is, or isn't, in the system. The standard "shock" does in fact include a high quality shock absorber, something that's missing from some other systems. With this design you don't need an on-board compressor (though one can be purchased as part of the kit) if you just want to add air to either chamber with a hand pump or small compressor.

If you opt for an air ride, be sure that when the system is fully lowered, the fender and under-fender-hardware, can't touch the tire. Because there will be those Murphy's law instances when you pinch an airline or the compressor fails and you have to ride home "on the snubbers."

Air bags actually make a near-perfect spring in the sense that the spring-rate becomes progressively stiffer as the suspension unit is compressed. Downsides include the added complexity of pumps and gauges, and the resulting fact that the whole kit costs considerably more than a standard set of high quality shocks.

Brakes

Brakes are heat machines. When you squeeze the lever the brake pads are forced against the spinning rotor. The bike slows (hopefully) and the byproduct is heat. You've converted

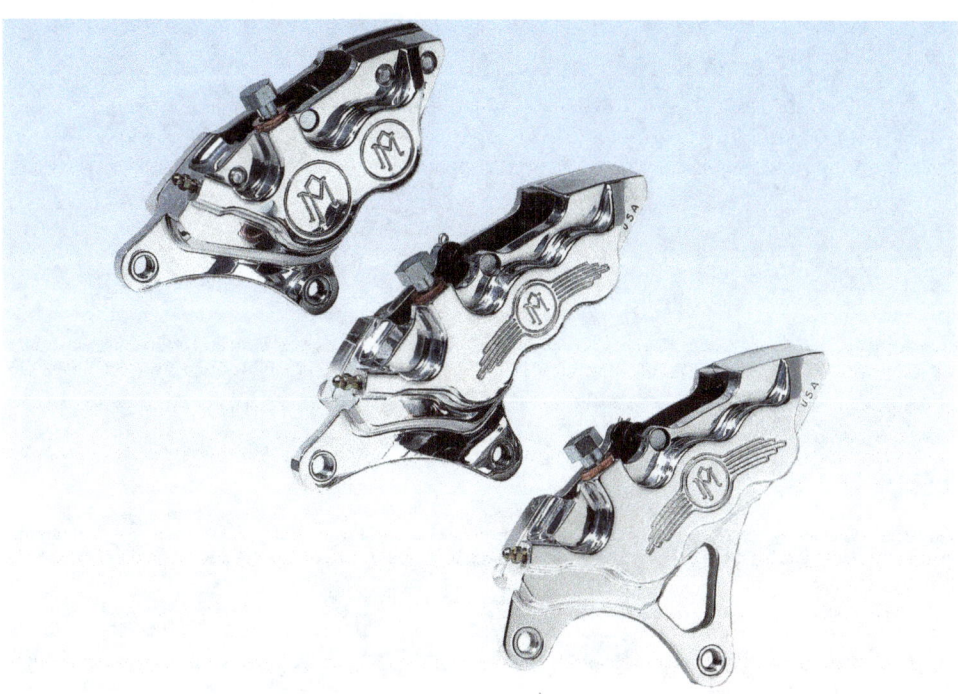

A six-piston caliper does offer more potential stopping power than a four-piston design, but a lot of people install the six-piston units because of the extra sex appeal. The differential bore design (on top) puts a little less pressure on the leading edge of the pad, so the temperature is more even across the pad's surface. PM

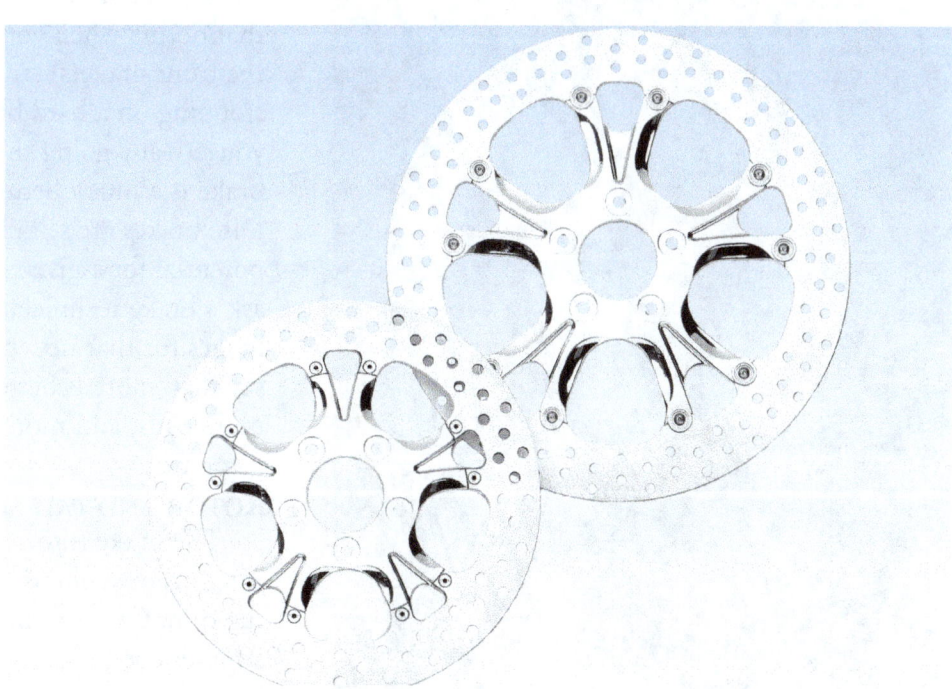

Most rotors are made from stainless, at least the actual rotor surface is stainless. Companies like PM and others offer rotor designs that match the design of the wheels. PM

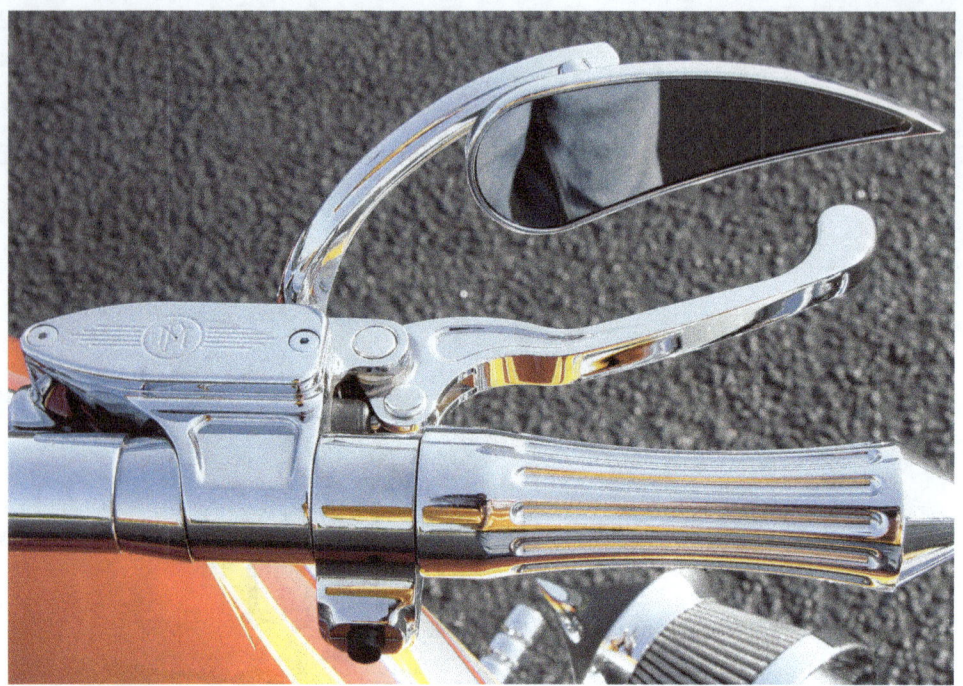

Master cylinders are available in two or three diameters. You should match the piston diameter to the number of pistons and calipers...

...that are connected to the other end of the hydraulic line. In this case the caliper is part of the very slick Phantom front end from American Suspension.

moving (or kinetic) energy to heat energy – you can't create or destroy energy, only convert it from one form to another. More physics: a bike traveling 60 miles per hour has four times (not two) the kinetic energy of the same machine traveling at 30 miles per hour.

Some of the old Bobbers and Choppers were built without a front brake. All part of "chopping" or simplifying the bike. Many riders of the period said that "there's so much of the weight on the back of the bike that it really doesn't matter."

But the times change and real motorcycles (as opposed to those built for posing) need brakes on both ends. Even if the bike is a Chopper with a relatively high percentage of the weight on the back, you still have to consider the weight *transfer* that occurs when you hit the brakes. Meaning the front brake(s) still do well more than half the stopping on a hard brake application. And unless you're really going the extra mile for effect, a disc brake is a much better deal than a drum brake. Disc brakes are self cleaning and offer more brake potential for a given amount of weight. If you ask a brake technician for advice regarding the brakes for that new motorcycle, most will simply say that 'more is better.' More pistons pushing more pads, and more pad area squeezing more rotor area.

Rotor and pad materials

The brake rotors themselves can be manufactured from stainless steel, cast iron, or even ductile iron. Cast and ductile iron have what's called a better coefficient of friction – the material leaves a surface that the pad can easily grab onto. Cast iron rotors are now available from both GMA and Performance Machine with a flashing of chrome nickel to improve the aesthetics.

By far, the most common rotor material is stainless steel. Formed by adding chromium to low-carbon steel, stainless steel rotors are super hard and will virtually never wear out. Though most come with the standard satin finish, many are available with a polished finish.

Brake pads too are manufactured from various materials. Organic pads, including Kevlar, are softer and better suited for use against the softer cast and ductile iron materials. The other major type of pad, sintered iron, is better used in combination with stainless steel rotors. The important thing is to get a good match between the rotor and pad material so you get good braking without damage to the rotor. Questions regarding pad and rotor combinations can be best answered by a good sales person at your favorite scooter shop, or employees of companies like RC Components and PM.

Make music

The diameter of the master cylinder bore should be chosen in concert with the size and number of caliper pistons. Essentially, a smaller diameter master cylinder piston creates more hydraulic pressure but displaces less fluid, than a larger diameter piston (other factors being equal). But before getting too deep into hydraulic ratios we need to add the typical Tim-Remus discussion concerning the laws that govern hydraulics. This boils down to just two facts:

1) Pressure in the brake system is equal over all surfaces of the system.

2) A fluid cannot be compressed to a smaller volume.

Brake fluid

Brake fluid is a very specialized hydraulic fluid, designed to operate in a very dirty environment and withstand very high temperatures without boiling. If the fluid boils it becomes a gas. Gas is compressible, which pretty much defeats the whole idea of hydraulics. Air in the system, either as the result of too much heat or too little bleeding (more on bleeding later) gives you a soft or spongy lever.

There are three common grades of brake fluid: DOT 3, DOT 4 and DOT 5. Dot 3 and 4 are glycol-based fluids and are often used in automobiles. Most custom bike builders don't use them because they absorb water from the environment and they attack most paints.

DOT 5 brake fluid is silicone based, meaning a higher boiling point (500 degrees Fahrenheit, dry), no tendency to absorb water and no reaction when spilled on a painted surface. This fluid costs more and is reputed to be slightly compressible, though street riders never seem to notice any difference in "feel" after switching to silicone fluid.

The times they are a changin'. The world is filled with old Bobbers equipped with some pretty new-wave perimeter brakes. In this case the wheel, rotor and caliper are Cory Ness designs, with a caliper bracket by Gypsy. Parked behind is the long radical ride from Kim Suter.

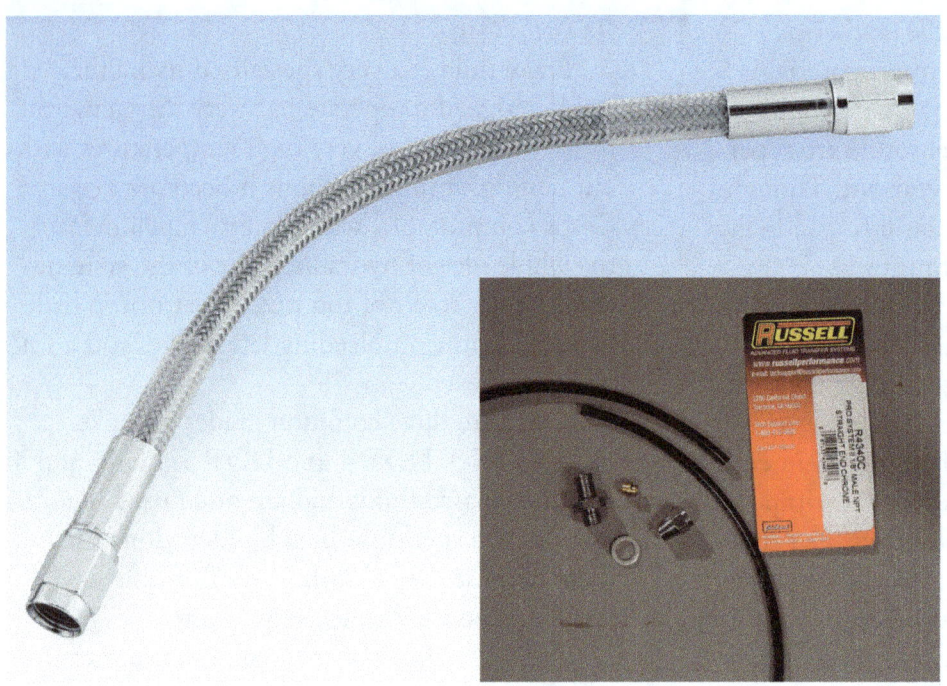

Stainless wrapped brakes lines were always the cool deal. Stronger and neater than the rubber factory-style hoses. Inside the stainless is a tough plastic line and people are running the line alone, without the braided stainless. The example seen in the lower corner is Pro Line from Russell.

New Harley-Davidsons have used silicone-based fluid since the early 1980s and the fluid you will find on the shelf of the dealership or quality aftermarket shop is probably DOT 5, silicone-based fluid. No matter which fluid you decide to use, stick with that fluid. Do not mix the two types.

Because a fluid cannot be compressed, the pressure at the master cylinder outlet is applied fully to the pistons in the calipers. None of that pressure is "used up" compressing the fluid between the master cylinder and the calipers. This also means that the pressure at the master cylinder outlet is the same pressure that is applied to all the surfaces in the brake system.

Final notes

When you install those new calipers on the fork or swingarm, be sure to center the caliper over the rotor (shims are usually provided for this purpose) and use the correct mounting brackets and bolts. The mounting bolts must be very high quality because the full force of a panic stop is transmitted from the caliper to the chassis through the bracket and bolts. Use bolts that came with the caliper kit or those that are recommended by the manufacturer.

Most aftermarket calipers come in a variety of finishes, including satin,

This Perewitz bike follows the current trend of using a drive-side rear brake (from GMA in this case) and putting the front brake on the same side, so the design of the wheel can be truly appreciated when viewed from the other side.

polished and chrome plate. I hate to be a nit picker, but try to buy a chrome caliper if the lower legs and wheel are chrome plated.

Keep all the components matched: the right master cylinder matched to the right calipers to produce the correct pressure and travel at the lever, the right pads matched to the right rotor surface. Keep everything neat and allow no dirt or impurities into the hydraulic part of the system. Remember that brake components do not react well to solvents. If you have to disassemble a master cylinder or caliper, clean the parts with clean brake fluid, not the standard part-cleaning solvents we use for everything else.

The biggest problem most people have with the installation of the brakes comes down to bleeding. They don't get all the air out of the system and the lever or pedal is spongy. There are a variety of brake-bleeding aids and pumps. If you still can't get all the air out, swallow your pride and take it to a good shop and let them do the bleeding. Some-times it's the simple things that give us fits.

Seen at dumbassbiker.com, this brake caliper and mini rotor is designed to be used with a right side drive transmission and eliminate the need for a caliper and rotor on the rear wheel.

No matter what the brand, you want to use DOT 5, silicone based, brake fluid. It won't wreck the paint if you spill a little and it's less prone to absorbing moisture.

Chapter Five

Drivetrain

Power Generation and Transmission

Custom means unique. That no two bikes are the same. Thus, we've tried to catch all the major drivetrain trends and options, from a Knuckle with a six-speed or an Evo with a four-speed.

There are at least five different engine types being used today, and three transmissions. And then there's right side drive to consider. In many cases it isn't that you can't combine a particular engine with a particular transmission in a partic-

The current crop of bike builders is looking for more than just big-inch Evo and Twin Cam motors. This BBO bike by Gypsy is powered by a new Knucklehead from Accurate Engineering. Rogue

ular frame, it's just easier if you don't. As always, it's best if you think ahead before laying down your hard-earned cash.

THE V-TWIN

When it comes to picking an engine, there are so many variations that the subject gets downright confusing. Not so long ago, most builders used Evos with a few opting for Twin Cam engines, and even fewer for pre-Evo Shovel and Panheads. Today, we have everything from 145 inch Evos from S&S, to 74 inch Knuckles and Pans from companies like STD and Flathead Power.

THE HEART AND SOUL OF A MOTORCYCLE

Motorcycles are basic, essential machines. The engine isn't hidden under a hood and then under a series of plastic covers. No, the engine is right out there for everyone to see and hear. To

Though it looks like an old generator-Shovel, the new Shovels from S&S use an alternator left side case, and a modern sprocket shaft so this motor provides a 32 amp charging circuit and bolts up to a modern primary. S&S

state the obvious, the engine makes up at least half the visual mass of a motorcycle. When you design that new motorcycle, you want to get this part right. It would be hard to build a true old-skool Bobber with a new, fully-polished Twin Cam engine. So think about the design of the new bike. More important, think about how this new machine will be used. Whatever you buy, buy something that will work on a day to day basis. Something that will burn pump gasoline and start when you push the button.

NEW VS. OLD

The new or old argument is a current one, given the large number of used engines for sale out there, and the number of people who want to build "genuine" Bobbers and Choppers with real H-D motors.

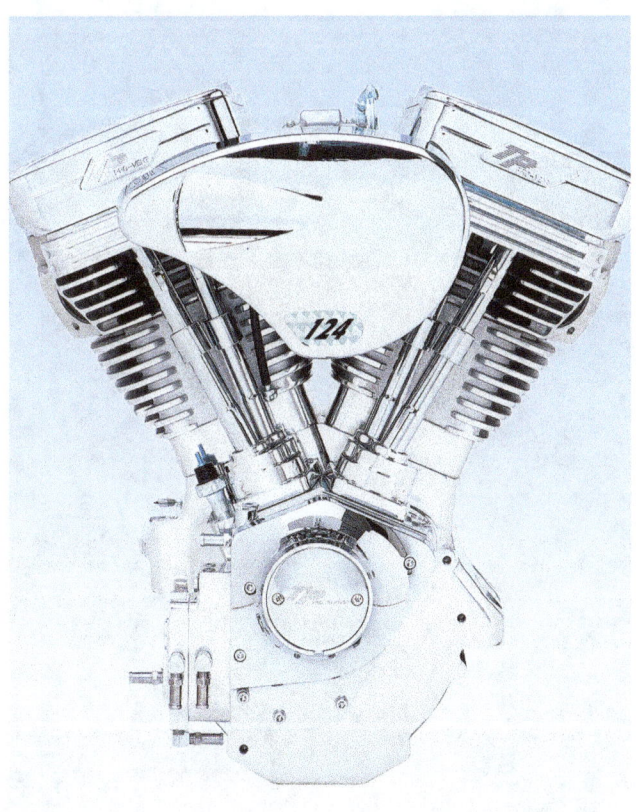

Perhaps the best thing about the growth of bike building is the opportunity it's provided for industrious individuals like Tom Perone, owner of TP Engineering, who started out building engines from other companies' parts. Today they make a full range of motors assembled from 100% TP parts.

Assembled from a combination of S&S, RevTech and STD components, Pandemonium engines displace 88 cubic inches and come with a modern alternator-style left-side case. Jammer

There are additional comments regarding used engines in the Legalities section of Chapter Three, but just remember to buy an engine that comes with clean paper work, and an engine that comes with a Bill of Sale or documentation that will satisfy your state when you go to register the bike. A used hot-rod 80 Evo is a great power-plant and there are plenty of them around, but they're not worth a damn if the state won't let you register the bike when it's all finished.

The same warnings apply to buying original Knuckles and Pans, with a few additional words of caution. Old motors cost more to repair than new ones, and old metal suffers from fatigue. Panheads in particular are known for cracked heads and stripped threads. To quote engine builder Lee Wickstrom, "You can probably buy a new Evo for what it would cost to rebuild a Knuckle or Panhead, but then of course you wouldn't have a Knuckle or a Pan." Lee also warns potential buyers to be careful with the numbers on the old engines, "The number one issue with old engines is a serial number that's been tampered with, it's especially common on Pans and Knuckles, it must have been the thing to do back in the day. In Minnesota it's a Felony to have them in your possession. Don't buy them, or else you have to replace the cases with new ones."

SOME NEW ENGINE OPTIONS
TWIN CAM

What follows is a partial list of options for buying new V-Twin engines, with just a few comments about each possible choice.

Accurate Engineering makes Panheads in displacements up to 120 cubic inches, though Berry Wardlaw says that for good power and reliability, the 103 is a combination that's hard to beat.

For all those riders who want to power their new bike with the latest offering from Milwaukee, complete TC 88 engines are available from your local dealer, in both B and non-B form. Keep in mind the fact that a B motor with its counterbalancers mounts on "axles" and in a style totally different from the A motor. In fact, the A motor can usually be used in an Evo frame, with an adapter, and then mated up to a typical soft-tail-style five-speed tranny.

Many frame manufacturers offer their chassis in different configurations to match the engine of your choice. Rolling Thunder, for example, states that all their frames, "Can be ordered for Twin Cam A or B."

If a 95 inch Twin Cam isn't big enough, the factory offers the engine in a 103 inch version. This is the same B-version engine used in

Everybody talks about power, Zipper's Performance provides dyno sheets for their 131 cubic inch engines (4-1/4X4-5/8 inches) that show a flat torque curve and a peak hp of 165 at the rear wheel.

Screamin' Eagle Fat Boys, now available as a stand-alone powerplant from Harley's New Era program in either silver and chrome or black and chrome. If that's not big enough, the displacement can be boosted to 120 cubic inches or more with kits from companies like Jim's, S&S or Zipper's. And then there's the very popular 124 dual-cam engine from S&S, an engine that Neil Ryan from American Thunder likes to put in Baggers and heavy bikes with rubber mounted engines. "It seems like when you put a big inch engine in a solid mount frame," explains Neil, "it vibrates more, but in a rubber mount frame a big engine always seems to vibrate less, I think because with a big engine you're not pushing it as hard."

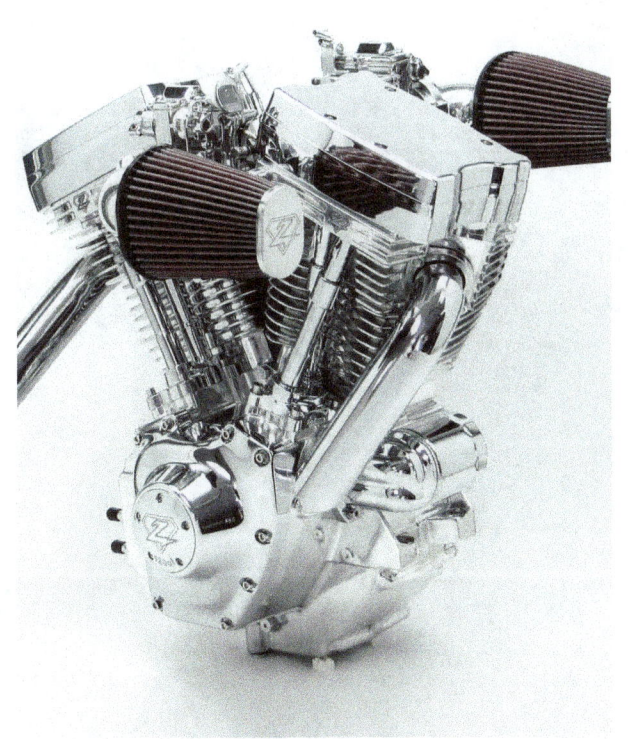

By manufacturing their own billet heads, Zipper's can create twin-carb heads for either TC or Evo engines. Buy them separately or as part of a complete engine. Great hp and even better eye-candy.

Seen at dumbassbiker.com, these new, 80 inch factory Evos are a great value for the budget conscious bike builder.

Evo

Before you call this engine an old timer, consider some of the aftermarket designs from companies like S&S, TP Engineering, Ultima and Zippers. All offer cylinders that measure four inches or more, which can be mated to 4, 4-1/4, or 4-1/2 inch flywheel assemblies. Buying or building an engine with 125 horsepower is no longer a difficult thing to do. S&S offers their killer 145 inch engine, TP Engineering has a 124 cubic inch V-Twin based on a 4-1/8 inch cylinder, Ultima has a 140 inch V-twin and Zipper's offers a 131 cubic inch stump-puller with a bore of 4-1/4 mated to a 4-5/8 inch flywheel assembly – and over 150 ft lbs of torque and 160 horsepower!

If what you're looking for is bang for buck, it's hard to beat an Evo. On the bargain front, you can have a used Evo, often in upgraded hot-rod-80 mode, for a bargain price. As riders upgrade to some of the bigger motors mentioned above, they often leave the original engine sitting on the garage floor. And though Evos are pretty bullet proof, it's always best to listen to any used engine run before the purchase.

New factory Evos are likewise a good deal. Check with your local dealer or look on the 'Net. Custom Chrome offers another good value, the RevTech Evo-style engine in displacements starting at 88 and extending to 110 cubic inches.

Shovelhead

Introduced in the mid-1960s, Shovelheads came as an upgrade to the venerable Panhead. In 1970, however, the Shovel became a much more modern motor with the introduction of the

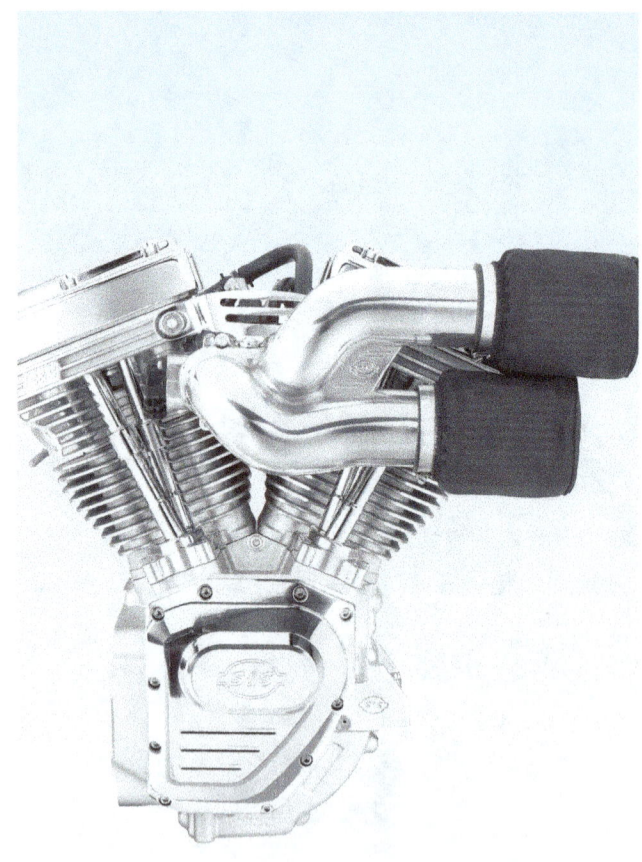

Complete 124 inch Twin Cam engines are available from S&S in either plain aluminum or polished, carbureted or fuel injected. S&S claims nearly 130 hp with a carburetor.

alternator bottom end. Before buying a used Shovel, consider the new examples available from S&S. These may not be genuine made-in-Milwaukee engines, but they come in various displacements up to 103 cubic inches and come with a two-year warranty. Have the best of both worlds by choosing a Shovel with a generator right side case and alternator left side casting. Now you've got the look of the older engine, and the gear whine; with near-Evo longevity, an alternator to power the lights and a left side case and sprocket shaft that will mate up to a modern primary.

The Panhead and early Shovelhead use what is essentially the same generator-style bottom end, so it's possible to add new Panheads from a company like STD, to the new Shovel's cast iron cylinders.

The current king of the hill (for production engines anyway) is this 145 cubic inch brute from S&S. Build yourself a ten-second street bike, just be sure the frame is tall, and strong enough for this big boy.

To repeat what was said in the frame chapter about engine fitment, the engine mounting pads are the same on a Shovelhead or an Evo-style V-twin. A shovelhead will drop into the Evo frame, but the reverse may not be true, as the Evo is taller than a Shovel (note the big-displacement nostalgia motors are taller than their stock brethren).

For old motors that run like a new Twin Cam, we should mention Accurate Engineering. Known perhaps for their Knuckleheads, Accurate makes a full range of pre-Twin Cam engines, including Shovels, Pans and Evos. The Shovel and Panheads include 93 and 103 inch examples, and a special "outlaw" version of the Panhead at 120 inches (4-1/8 inch bore and 4-1/2 inch stroke). Their standard Knucklehead

Though the purists will bitch about the three-hole exhaust flanges and billet distributor, this Pandemonium looks like the real deal. Jammer

47

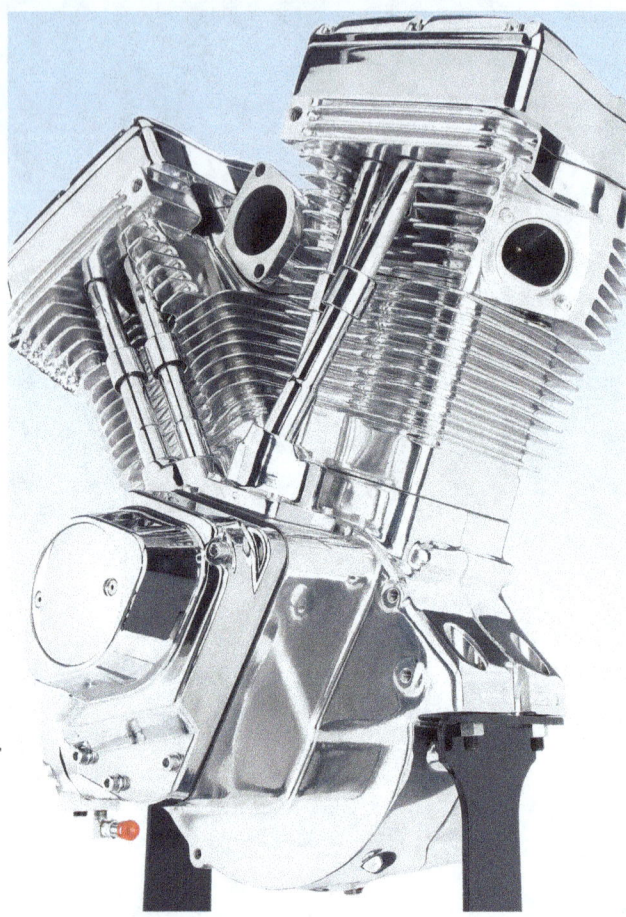

Part of their El Bruto line, the Ultima 127 inch V-Twin uses their own castings and major internal components. With hi-flow heads, the engines are now rated to put out 140 hp and 145 ft. lbs. of torque.

displaces 103 cubic inches, though bigger and smaller examples are available on request. All Accurate engines ship complete with carb and alternator.

As old Harleys and retro customs gain popularity, more and more companies are selling new examples of old technology. J&P Cycles offers a vintage catalog filled with reproduction Knuckleheads, and "modern" Panheads with modern left side/alternator case.

Jammer is not far behind. An old name in the aftermarket industry, they offer a Pandemonium Panhead (also available from Custom Chrome) as well as a variety of Knuckles and Pans assembled from quality components. Both these catalog companies offer a wealth of old-skool parts, from four-speed transmissions to Jockey-style shifter assemblies.

We should mention the fact that even new-old engines may require non-standard exhaust, as many of the exhaust ports use a three-bolt or slip-on connection, neither of which is found on the end of pipes from Samson or Vance and Hines. The generator bulge adds another impediment to the use of typical exhaust systems, and we haven't talked about a kick-start pedal yet. Finally, before buying a truly old engine, be sure you understand what's needed for the primary and which transmission will work most easily with your engine choice.

A SPORTY CUSTOM

Though the book is based on the Big Twin engines, there's no reason you can't build a very cool custom bike based on a Sportster engine. Combine an Ironhead or Evo-style Sportster (or Buell), with a hardtail frame, and some ingenu-

Accurate Engineering is in the business of building Knuckles with the appeal of a 1936 engine and the reliability of a brand new TC. Standard displacement is 103 inches but bigger engines are available.

ity, and you've got the potential to make one very cool motorcycle for minimal bucks. A growing number of companies, from Redneck Engineering to Klock Werks and Rolling Thunder, make frames that accept the Sportster drivetrain.

WHAT'S A DONOR BIKE

Though a little outside the realm of "engines," the whole donor bike concept is one that deserves more attention. A lot of riders have a bike in the garage that's under utilized. Why not strip the parts off that bike and attach them to a new frame. Clever riders will use the forks, controls and possibly the sheet metal and wheels. With used bike prices at an all time low, you could even shop for an inexpensive FXR, Softail, Dyna, Sportster or aftermarket bike and then use that as the basis for the new chopper, custom or whatever. The first choppers were often built from existing motorcycles combined with a new frame and a few well chosen accessories. Look around, in some cases you can buy an aftermarket bike with big-inch Evo, six speed transmission, and tons of chrome accessories for way less than you would pay for those same components if you bought them new.

Maybe your basic black project needs something other than a bright, polished engine. Zipper's makes many of their complete engines available in black powder.

Your custom bike doesn't have to cost $30,000.00. Just buy a hardtail frame from a company like Redneck Engineering, mate it up with a Sporty or Buell donor bike, and you can build a bike for one-third what the other guys are paying. A Buell makes a better donor as it has more power, wider rims/tires and a better fork. If you already own a Buell or Sporty, then it's all that much cheaper.

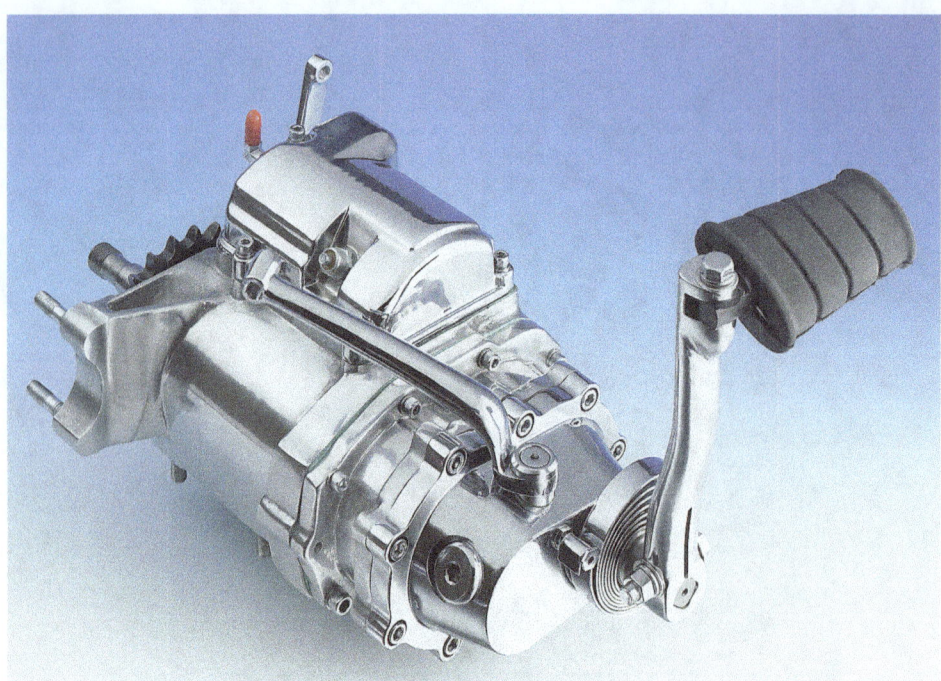

This transmission from Custom Chrome stuffs 5 speeds in a 4-speed case, and provides kick start as well. Works with most '70 - '84 bikes with electric start.

TRANSMISSION CONSIDERATIONS

Most builders are going to use a late-model, soft-tail style five or six-speed transmission. When using earlier style engines however you may want to use the earlier four-speed transmission. There are transmission mounting plates like those from Paughco that allow you to put a soft-tail-style five-speed in a four-speed frame. This option doesn't always work well with wide tires and transmission offsets, however. Some frames, like those from Santee, Paughco and others, will accept four, five or six-speed transmissions, you simply have to use the correct transmission mounting plate.

In most cases, your frame will determine the transmission you're going to use. Though, as always, there are ways to cheat. A number of companies make a five-in-a-four transmission, Baker ever makes a six-in-a-four (with a kicker).

The downside is the fact that some of these transmissions use an early five-speed gearset. This means you will be forced to use the earlier clutch assembly which is not as strong as the typical late-style clutch and hub assembly (see the note below). There is, however, a heavy duty clutch available from Rivera for both the four-speed and early five-speed transmissions.

If you want to make sure your kick start gears don't strip when you kick that 103 inch Pan, install these Klassic Kicker Gears from Baker - cut and heat treated in the US.

Kick Start

As Bobbers and early-style bikes are all the rage, a lot of builders are wanting to put a kick start lever on the end of the transmission. Kick start kits for five-speed transmissions are available from CCI and other suppliers as well, and many of the five-in-a-four transmissions can be ordered with a kicker. Remember that many exhaust systems will interfere with the kicker. Another potential problem is the ignition, most current ignition systems are designed for electric start.

Some people think the current crop of kick-start gears aren't up to day-in, day-out service, and for them there are high-quality kicker gears from Baker Drivetrain.

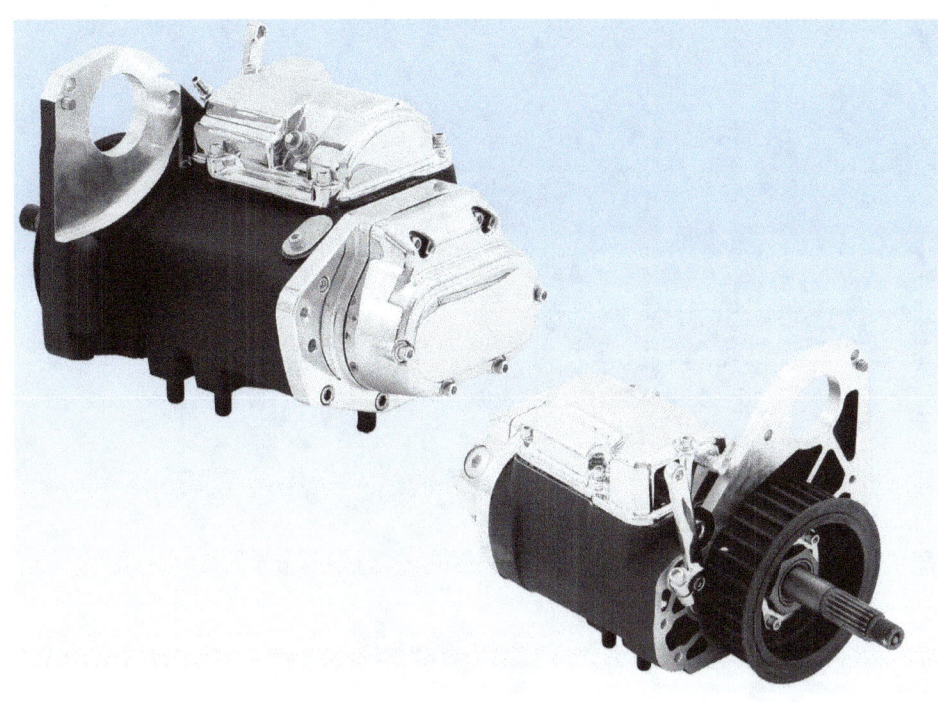

A large number of companies make the basic left-side-drive, soft-tail style five-speed transmission used in many soft-tail and hardtail bikes. Kustomwerks

Five-speed Transmissions

Most aftermarket frames designed for pre-TC engines will accept a typical late-model five-speed transmission. These are available in any catalog that's on the counter at the local parts store.

You can also buy complete transmissions from any Harley-Davidson dealer. Harley-Davidson made a major change in their transmissions in about 1994 when they began the conversion to high contact gears. These are ground in such a way as to reduce noise and increase strength, these gears can't be mixed

Though not as common, five-speed transmissions that fit FXR and FL frames are readily available. This Delkron case is reinforced to withstand high torque loads.

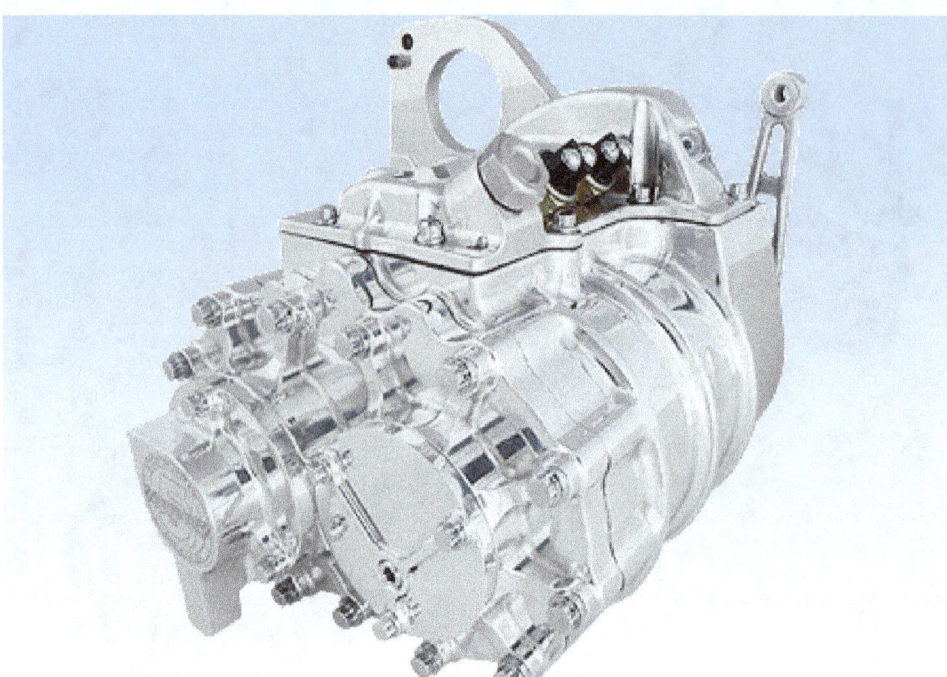

Though they look very different, the Torque Box five and six-speed transmissions from Baker slip into the spot normally occupied by a soft-tail style five speed tranny.

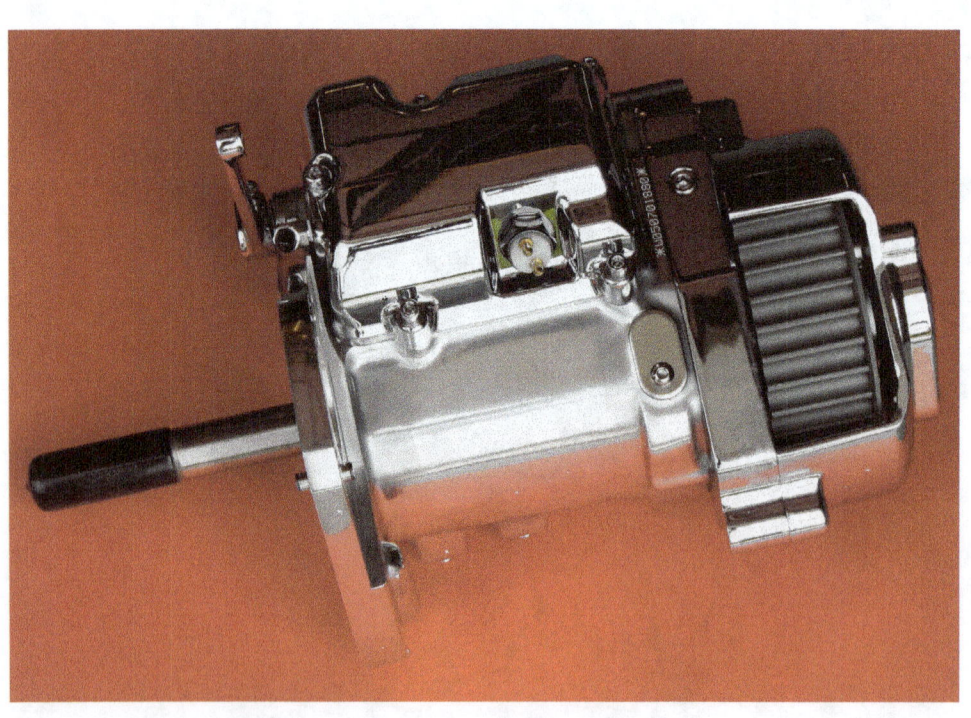

Among the relatively new manufacturers in the aftermarket is Trick-shift, with a full range of left, and right-side-drive, five and six-speed transmission.

with other non HCR gears.

Softail-style five-speed cases are nearly the same from 1986 to 1999, but there are some differences in the starters. Factory transmissions built prior to 1990 used a tapered mainshaft, which requires the appropriate clutch basket (as mentioned, these clutches are typically not as strong as the later clutch assembly). By far, the most common complete five-speed transmissions are listed as 1990 – 1999. The builders' drivetrain kits seen in many of the magazines are all based on this particular five-speed transmission.

Six-speeds

Baker Transmission was the first to introduce a left-side-drive six-speed transmission in 1998. Today there are a number of firms making six-speed transmissions (including Harley-Davidson). The beauty of these transmissions with the extra gear is the fact that the case is the same as a five-speed case. So a primary assembly that works with a late-model five-speed will work just as well with a new six-speed. For the same reason, six-speed gearsets will fit into a standard five-speed case.

The Baker transmission is available with either a .86 or .80 to 1 overdrive ratio, which will drop the RPM at 70 mph by 475 and 680 RPM respectively. The RevTech six-speed transmission comes with a sixth gear ratio of .893 to one.

NEW COGS FROM BAKER

Always known for new products, Baker Drivetrain has introduced the Torquebox five and six-speed transmissions in either left or right side drive models. To quote the Baker web site: "...A small increase in center distance [between the two transmission shafts] yields big increases in torque capacity. All stock Harley transmissions and aftermarket transmissions have a center distance of 2.5 inches. By increasing the center distance 20% to 3.0 inches the Torquebox conservatively increases the torque capacity to 250 ft-lbs, continuous duty!" Not only do these transmissions handle the output of even an S&S 145 on Nitrous, they fit the same spot on the frame normally occupied by a softtail style five-speed.

SPEEDOMETERS

All late model bikes from the factory use electronic speedometers, "driven" by a pickup in the transmission. Obviously you have to decide during the early part of the planning process whether your speedometer will be electronic or mechanical.

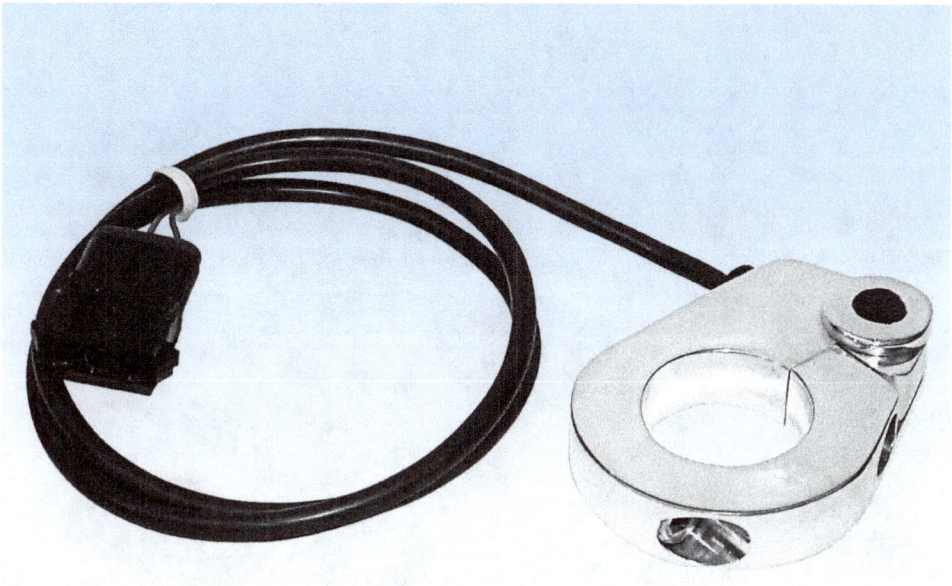

The inductive pickup can be bolted to the swingarm or frame and used to drive a VDO electronic speedo. The pickup can count bolt heads or rivets in the wheel or pulley. Kustomwerks

From Jammer comes this complete early-style four-speed transmission complete with kick start lever. Available in 2 different first-gear ratios.

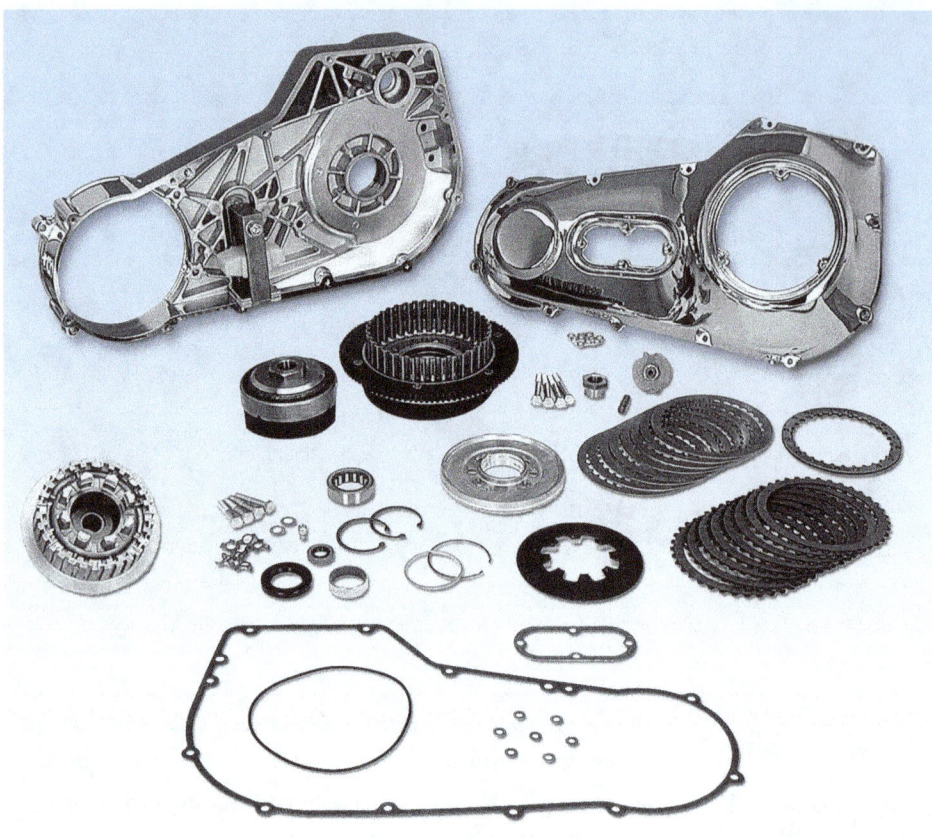

Make the shopping easy, complete chain style primaries for late model drivetrains are available from a variety of sources. Kustomwerks.

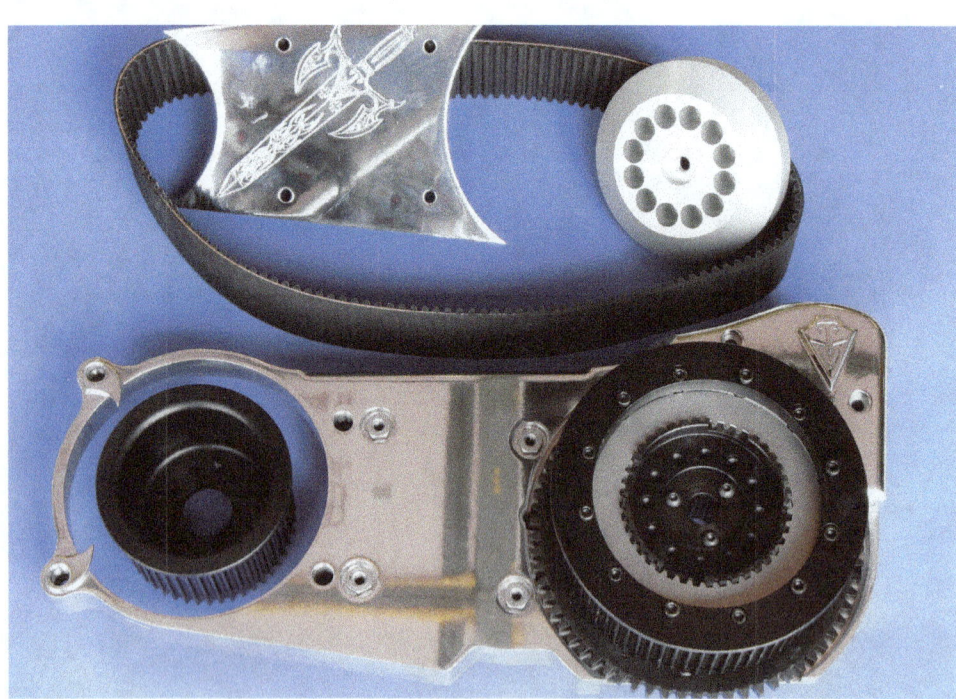

Among the new manufacturers in the aftermarket is Tauer Machine, with their very nice three inch primary assembly. dumbassbiker.com

Assuming, that is, you've decided to use a speedo at all. Nearly all new complete five and six-speed transmissions have the correct gears and the small port to accept the sensor. The factory began the switch to electronic speedometers in 1994, so earlier transmissions, or transmissions listed in the catalog as "1991 to 1994 Softail" might not be equipped to drive an electronic speedometer.

Bert Baker from Baker transmissions reports that all their five and six-speed transmissions, "have the right gearset to trigger the sensor, and the cases are machined to physically accept the sensor.

Electronic speedos eliminate the ugly cable running from the front wheel to the handle bars or up between the tanks. And calibration is never a problem, no matter which front tire you use with which speedo drive assembly. Many of the newest speedometers will accept the signal from a factory sensor as well as their own, and self calibrate without the need for a separate calibration box. Some transmission sensor/speedo combinations do, however, require a recalibration box between the sensor and the speedometer head.

There are two basic styles and three speedo ratios. One-to-one speedometers were used with transmission-driven four-speeds. Two-to-one speedometers were used mostly with FX and FXR bikes equipped with nineteen inch front wheels and narrow-glide forks, 2240:1 was used with Softails with twenty-one inch front wheels and wide glide forks.

If you plan to use a mechanical speedometer, plan to spend time with one of the big catalogs or a good counter person at your local shop. No matter the style, be sure to include enough wires in the front-section of the harness for the speedometer and, possibly, the tachometer.

BELTS, CHAINS, WHIPS (actually just belts and chains)

Not too many years ago, the majority of bikes ran a standard chain primary in an enclosed primary case. Not any more. More and more builders are choosing belts, and some are running early-style chain primaries without any housing at all. To state the obvious, the primary drive connects the engine and transmission. If you pick an Evo motor and soft-tail style, five-speed transmission, this is pretty much a no brainer.

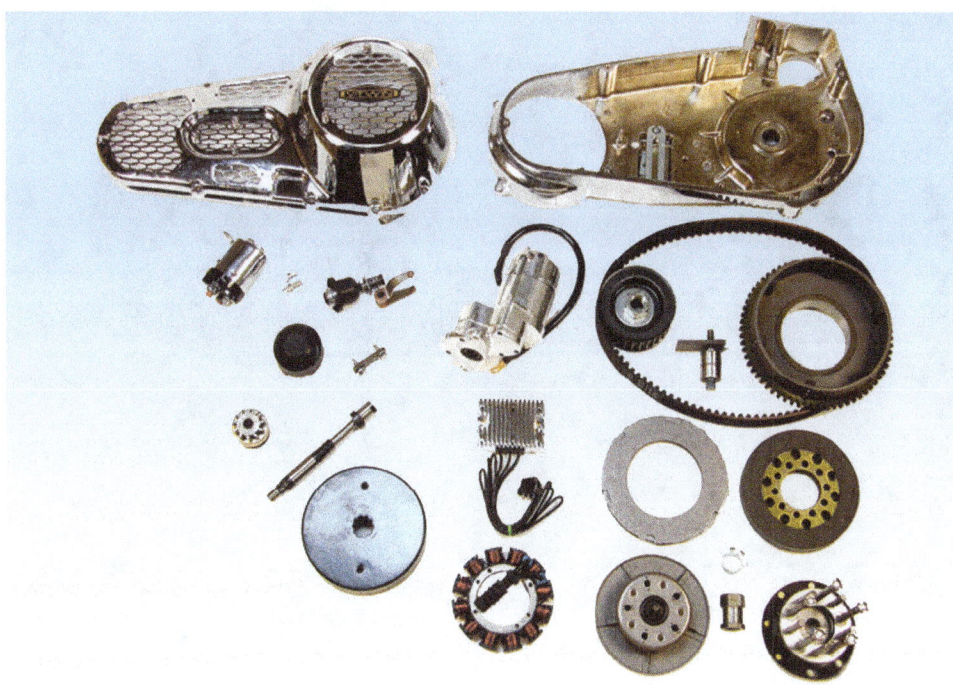

Another complete belt primary, this one an enclosed belt system designed to mate a Pan or Shovel with a 4-speed tranny. Jammer

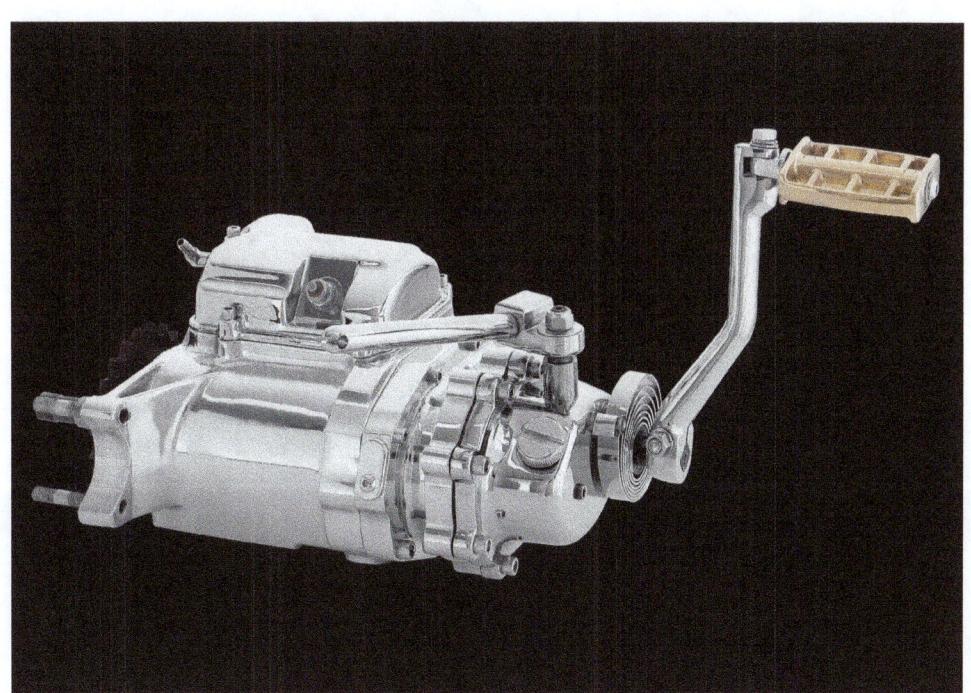

You've heard of the 5 in a 4. Now Baker Drivetrain brings us a 6 in a 4 - with kicker of course.

55

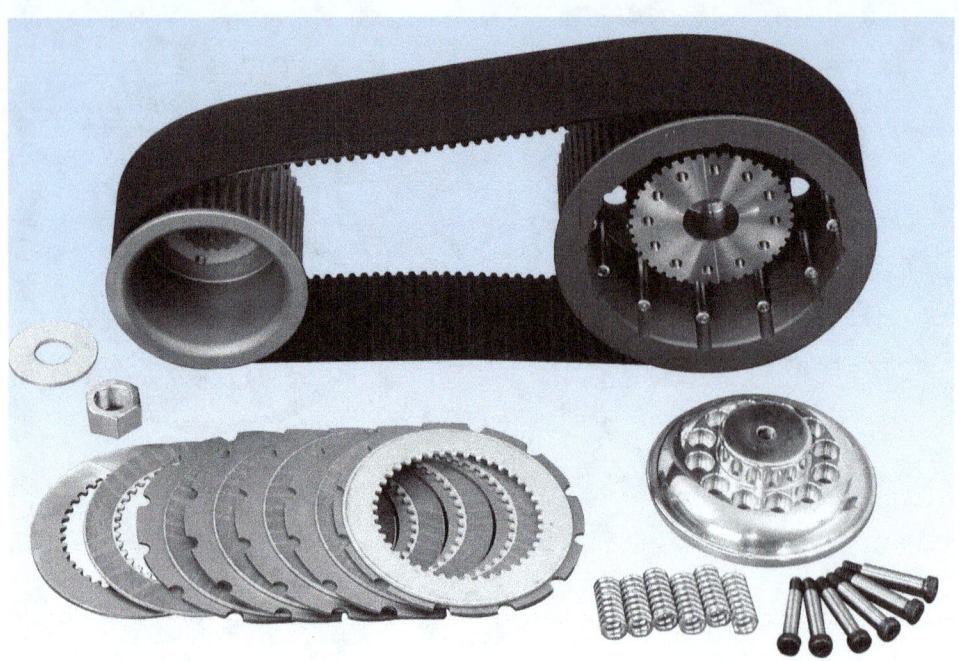

This three-inch BDL belt assembly with clutch, for kick-only applications, fits most Pans, Shovels and Evos. Kustomwerks

Another BDL product, this one an enclosed belt with housings, available for Shovel and Evo applications, including many rubber-mount bikes. Kustomwerks

Though you still have to get the right inner and outer primary covers, with the correct finish, designed for forward controls, along with the compensator sprocket, the chain itself, matching clutch assembly and matching starter motor. This gets considerably easier if you pick a "builders' kit" mentioned earlier.

Among these kits is a complete primary assembly, without a starter, from Biker's Choice for 1989 to 1993 Softails and another for 1994 – 2000 Softails. Custom Chrome and Kustomwerks offer very similar kits, with or without a heavy duty Kevlar clutch. All factory bikes from 1994 on use the same gear-reduction starter, so by using the 1994 and later inner and outer primary you could also use the latest starter motor.

For older pre-Evo engines, primary kits are harder to find and use. The older engines don't necessarily have the same bolt pattern on the left side case or the same sprocket shaft as an Evo. If you're trying to utilize some swap-meet components, it's easier if the engine and transmission are from the same year grouping.

To illuminate this issue we repeat part of an interview with Tom Johnson, employee at S&S

Cycle, from an earlier Wolfgang book.
How does a person get the right primary housing and primary drive for a Shovelhead or earlier engine?

Shaft lengths are the main thing to watch for when mixing and matching driveline components. The basic year groups are 1936 – 1964, 1965 to 1969, and '70 up for the Shovel and Evo engine sprocket shafts. The sprocket shaft and transmission mainshaft have to be compatible lengths.

The 1970 – up Shovel and Evo engines would work with a Harley 5-speed if you had the right clutch, and the frame was set up for the five-speed box. If you had a four-speed frame, you would want to go with one of the "five-speed in a four-speed box" transmissions that are available from different sources. The thing to bear in mind there is that your clutch has to be compatible with the tranny mainshaft and main drive gear. Rear belt drives complicate things too."

"It's tempting to pick up any good deals that you stumble across at a swap meet or whatever and just hope for the best. But, you'll probably run into fewer headaches if you pick a year group for the primary drive and starter and just stick with

Cyril Huze offers a three inch primary belt assembly with external bearing support for both engine and transmission shafts. Stray Kat logos are optional.

Gypsy's BBO bike uses an Accurate-built Knucklehead and a great deal of brass to give the bike a definite period feel. Rogue

Old bikes are all the rage. From the Shadley Brothers comes this side hack based on an Arlen Ness frame and "chair" kit.

Power comes from a Sportster engine that's been detailed to death, including plenty of polishing and the elimination of the lower fins.

it when you're buying parts."

"With primary covers, you have to match the inner primary to your left engine case and the transmission case. The starter assembly and starter drive have to be compatible with the inner primary cover or starter mount, and the ring gear on the clutch shell."

BELTS

If you do decide to ignore Tom's advice, a belt drive is often the easiest way to combine components that weren't typically used together. This can also be a good way to incorporate electric start to a motor/transmission combination that would normally be kick-only. Take a look at the various web sites and see what they offer. Because of the interest in Bobbers and early-style bikes, new belt kits and combinations are coming to market almost daily from well-known companies like BDL and Primo, and newer firms like Tauer Machine. To illustrate the point, Karata recently put together a belt assembly that allowed a builder to combine an 80 inch flathead with a soft-tail style five-speed transmission.

Whether for an Evo or Knuckle, belts come in a variety of widths, some designed to fit inside a conventional inner and outer primary housing, some so wide there aren't any housings big enough to house them. Remember that belts get hot, so if you're putting the primary belt in a primary housing, be sure to provide plenty of ventilation.

FAT TIRES

The bike-building phenomenon seems to be going in two directions at once, at least as far as rear tire widths are concerned. On the one hand, tire companies are making rubber in 300, 330 and 360mm widths (and even a prototype 400mm tire), while on the other, the Bobber and old skool builders are turning the clock back to the days when factory bikes came with a 130 rear tire, or a 5.10X16.

Way back in the 1980s and 1990s when people first starting squeezing 150, 180 and 200 series tires into otherwise stock FXR and Softail frames, the first problem arose when the new, wider tire, ran into the belt. By swapping the belt for a chain these customizers were able to create an additional half-inch of clearance. If that wasn't enough clearance (or if it was an FXR with unitized engine and transmission) they cheated by moving the tire to the right slightly for another quarter or half inch of clearance.

Eventually, it became common, with soft-tail drivetrains, to offset the transmission to the left, and thus make room between the belt and the tire. The first Wide Tire Kits consisted of a spacer used between the left side of the engine and the inside of the inner primary, an offset transmission mounting plate, and a spacer for the compensating sprocket. In this way the engine could stay in the center while only the transmission moved over. Those early kits moved the transmission 1/4 or 1/2 inch. Eventually, builders were moving the transmission as much as an inch to the left.

You can only move all that weight so far to the left though before you affect the balance of the bike. This is not static weight either, but spinning weight with it's own gyroscopic effect. The way to avoid this potential imbalance is to limit the size of the rear tire, some frame builders have begun to offer right side drive.

RIGHT HAND DRIVE

Baker drivetrain was the first to offer a transmission that moved the final drive to the right side which minimizes or eliminates the need for a spacer and the offset transmission. The end result is a more balanced motorcycle.

You can't just put a right side drive, six-speed transmission in that old Softail frame sitting in the garage. The frame itself must be designed to accommodate right side drive.

If you're looking to build a bike with a wide

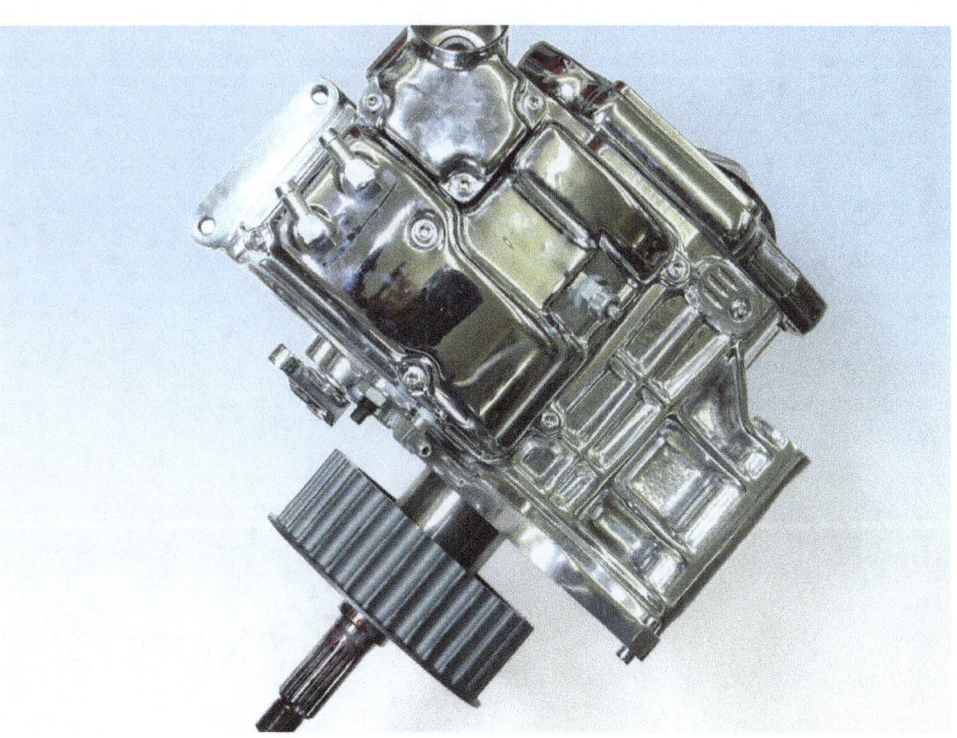

Twin Cam transmissions, with both five and six gears and the extra long mainshaft already installed, are available from Arlen Ness.

Belt drive offers the advantage of no maintenance and no mess, but the real hot rod guys break them on a regular basis. Drive sprockets come in 3 or 4 sizes, with and without an offset, to work with almost any custom application. Bike's Choice

rear tire, you're going to have to figure out how wide is wide. At about 250 mm and wider most aftermarket frames are designed for RSD. Though the cost of RSD transmissions has come down, they still cost more than a left side drive five-speed.

Final Drive Options
Belts and Chains

Up until the introduction of the 2000 models, the Harley-Davidson Big Twins used a 1-1/2 inch belt while the Sportster line used a 1-1/8 inch belt. The larger belt worked well for all but the most twisted rider and stood up to all but the worst abuse without stripping or breaking.

The bigger and more powerful range of engines available now has changed the durability of belt drive. Any hard-riding rider can now break a standard 1-1/2 inch belt. This doesn't mean you can't mix belt drive with big engines. Some riders with big engines have no trouble at all. It depends on how you ride, how much you weigh and the weight of the bike.

Chain Drive

Trouble with belts, and the interest in early-style bikes, means more and more people are running chain drive to the rear wheel. They do require more maintenance than a belt, but

An old idea comes around. Chains are super durable, if a little more maintenance intensive. Drive sprockets come in various sizes, with and without an offset. Biker's Choice

chains do have some definite advantages: they provide more room for fat tires and make it easy to change final drive ratios. You can run an Exile-style sprocket-brake caliper, and some transmissions (and frames) work best with chain drive. Another nice thing about chains is the offset drive sprockets that are available, which makes another easy way to move the chain away from the tire.

Nearly all final drive chains are a "530" size, and the better ones come with O-rings to lock in the factory lube. Some riders use silicone spray, in lieu of conventional chain-lube, which keeps the O-rings soft. You can even buy a chain with nickel-plated side plates for a nice look. Custom Chrome offers a super, heavy-duty 530 chain with colored side plates!

'DE PLAN

Whether you use chain or belt for primary or final drive depends on a whole series of earlier decisions. Is the bike old skool or new, a hot rod or cruiser, a daily driver or a Sunday afternoon bar-hopper? The primary drive, and the final drive, both need to fit the plan and the budget.

RevTech sells 530 chain with nickel plated side plates. You can even find chain with colored side plates!

This tasty chopper turned up at a recent local bike show. Note the chrome frame and Twin Cam powerplant.

Chapter Six

Wiring

Kits and Components

Once you have all of the hard parts picked out and your bike starts looking like a rolling chassis, you will need to start thinking about your wiring. Since there are so many wiring products available on the market today, you really need to do your diligence. You can build your own harness from scratch, buy an after-market harness, or go to your local Harley Davidson dealer and purchase a "factory" replacement harness. We are going to focus primarily on the home-built wiring harness.

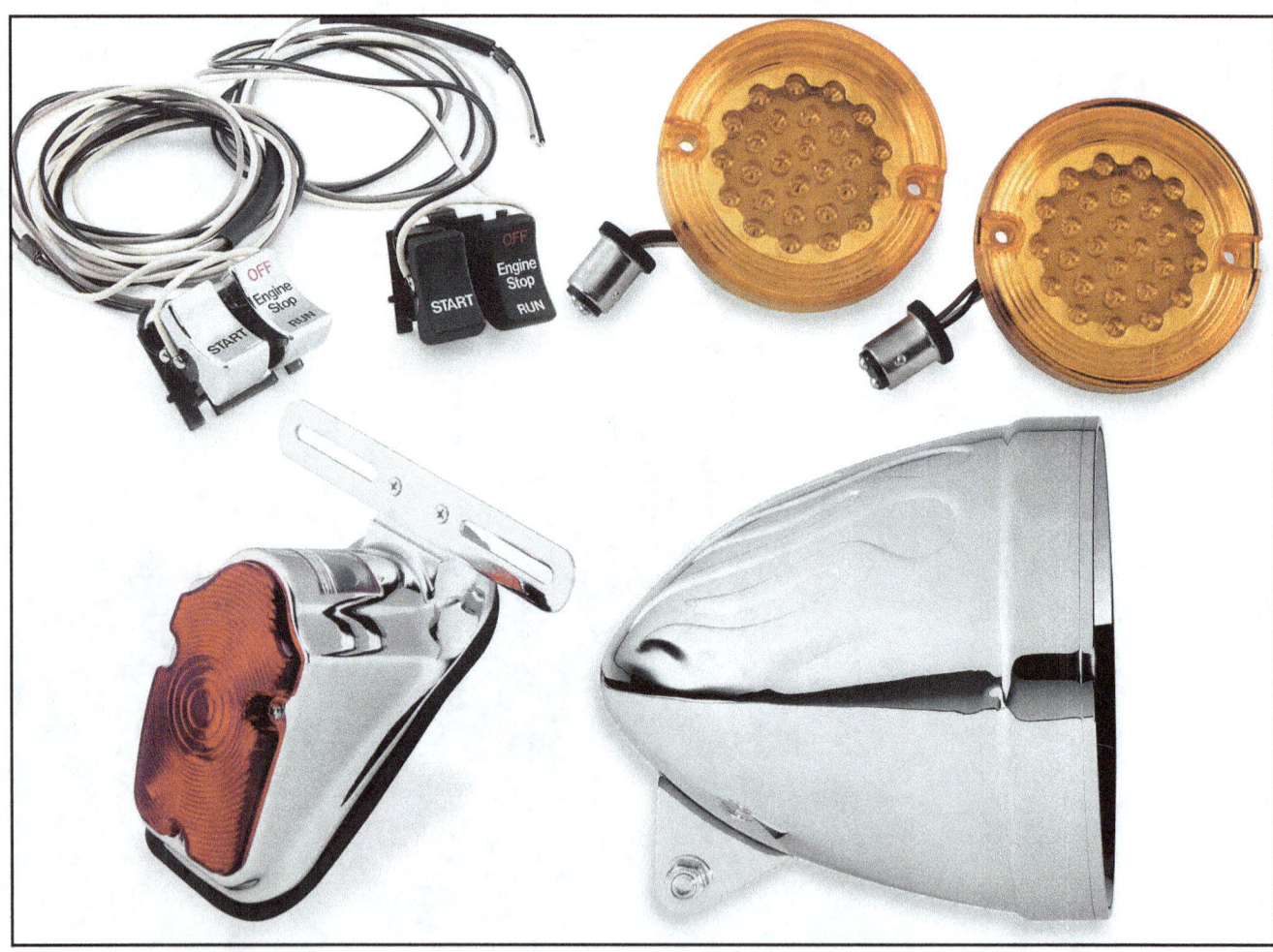

The aftermarket makes nearly every style and type of component imaginable. Most are high quality and most are available at your local shop or on the 'net. If you can't find what you're looking for, you aren't looking very hard.

Research

Before you buy or build your wiring harness there are a couple of things to consider. First and foremost you should think about safety and your state's transportation laws. When you're riding a motorcycle, especially at night, you want to be seen. The brighter the better, and the more you have the better off you'll be. From the legal aspect, most states require turn signals, especially on a custom built motorcycle with a state assigned Vehicle Identification Number, (VIN). So, if you need to have turn signals they must be D.O.T. approved and be strategically placed on the motorcycle. If this is the case, you will need a harness that supports switches and turn signals. Keep in mind if your state also requires a mandated vehicle inspection, all items must operate properly in order for it to pass. Before you get started, you may want to take a ride to your nearest D.O.T. office or look online to find out all of your state's requirements. If you are more the rebellious type and choose not to use turn signals, or your state does not require them, you should think about your safety on the road. It truly is better to be safe than sorry.

Main Harness & Handlebar Switches

Will your bike have stock style handlebar switches or will you go the custom route? It's safe to say that every aftermarket V-Twin catalog offers custom or OEM style switches, with or without housings, available in black or chrome. OEM switches are commonly listed as '95 and earlier, or '96 and up. Although the only real differences are the housings and the connections to the main harness, it is not possible to mix and match these years. With this being said, you should decide on what type of main harness you will use before you purchase switches. Keep in mind that most complete aftermarket harnesses use their own type of connector, or use connectors and a schematic that are similar to a 1995 & earlier Harley-Davidson. Do your homework first! It's much easier to buy the right part first and install it once.

If you make your own harness and you use OEM style handlebar switches, be sure to have the appropriate connectors. For example, 1995 and earlier Harley-Davidson's used AMP connectors throughout the entire bike. Many say that Harley was still working out the "electrical bugs" that haunted them in the 80's but these newer models were much better. The AMP connectors were nice but a bit difficult to work with and they were not watertight. From a technical aspect, it was very difficult to remove pins from the AMP connector. Special tools were made but they often damaged the socket or the pin itself during the removal.

Starting in 1996, Harley changed many of their AMP main harness connections over to Deutsch connectors. These new connectors are very high quality, easy to use and take apart, and

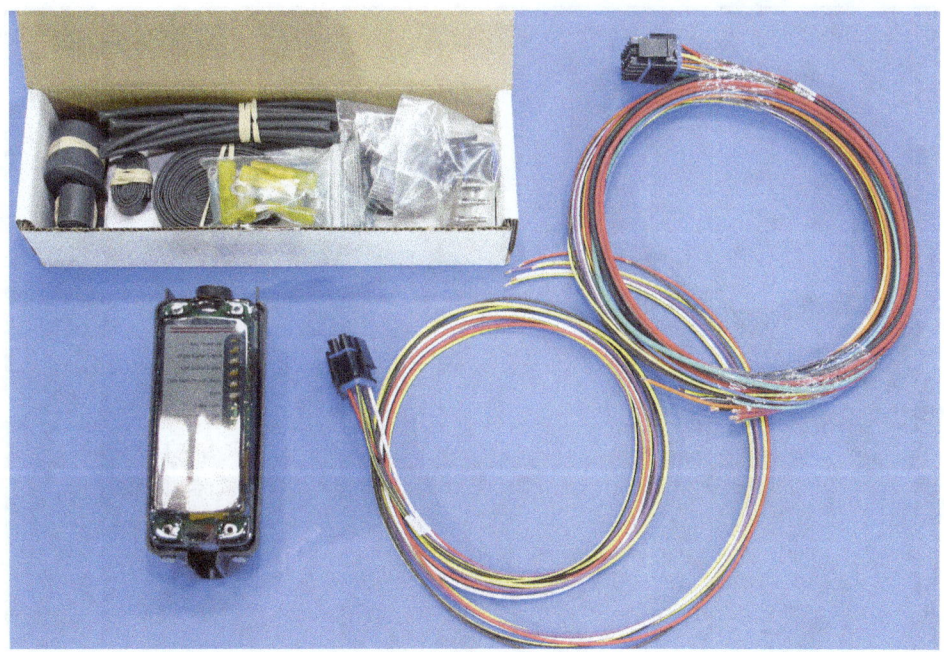

Most harness kits include a fuse panel or junction box, at least 2 harness sections (front and rear) and assorted sections of wrap and connectors. Before installing be sure to lay out the pieces so you understand the kit and components, and determine where all the major electrical components will go. Think first.

63

most importantly, are watertight. They are still being used today for handlebar switches, ignitions, turn signal modules, speedometer and tachometer harnesses, and various other main harness connections. You will also find a different style AMP connector being used on headlights, turn signals and a few other main harness connections. Since most aftermarket catalogs have a variety of OEM electrical parts available you should always be able to find exactly what you need for your build.

Turn Signals

Turn signals are available in several different varieties. You can purchase single or dual filament lights. Most stock motorcycles have dual filament bulbs on the front and single filament turn signals on the rear. LED turn signals, big and small, have become very popular over the last five years. These signals tend to offer more lumens-power or a brighter light making them more visible. It is important to know that not all turn signals are D.O.T. approved. Most states will tell you what the minimum exposed reflector size can be. (This is the limit on how small the actual colored lens can be per D.O.T. requirements.) This will help you to purchase not only what is legal but also what are the brightest and safest turn signals available.

Positioning of turn signals can be a real pain in the ass. You have to pick out a pair that fits, physically and visually. The OEM signals found in flush or bracket-mounted styles are a safe bet but some of the custom models include mirror mounted, built-in signal grips or even handlebar levers with integral signals. Again, be sure that they fit your theme and that they're legal.

Headlights

Choosing the right headlight is much easier than anything else we have discussed so far. There are many styles to choose from but they all pretty much fit the same brackets. Headlight lenses/bulbs are generally found in two different sizes, 5-1/2 and 7 inches. You also have to consider the depth of the housing. You can find small, narrow headlight buckets or long billet versions. Both providing a nice look but you need to pick what's right for your bike. Be sure to install a waterproof connector of some sort close to the headlight bucket for future servicing. It's very easy to overlook the importance of installing connectors. There is nothing worse then having to cut your harness apart to replace a damaged electrical part. Do it right from the beginning and remember that you, or someone else, will eventually have to service what you build. Make it easier on them and yourself!

Battery and Charging Circuit

Now that you have focused on safety, laws and the physically appealing side of your build, it's time to look at making it run, consistently. The key ingre-

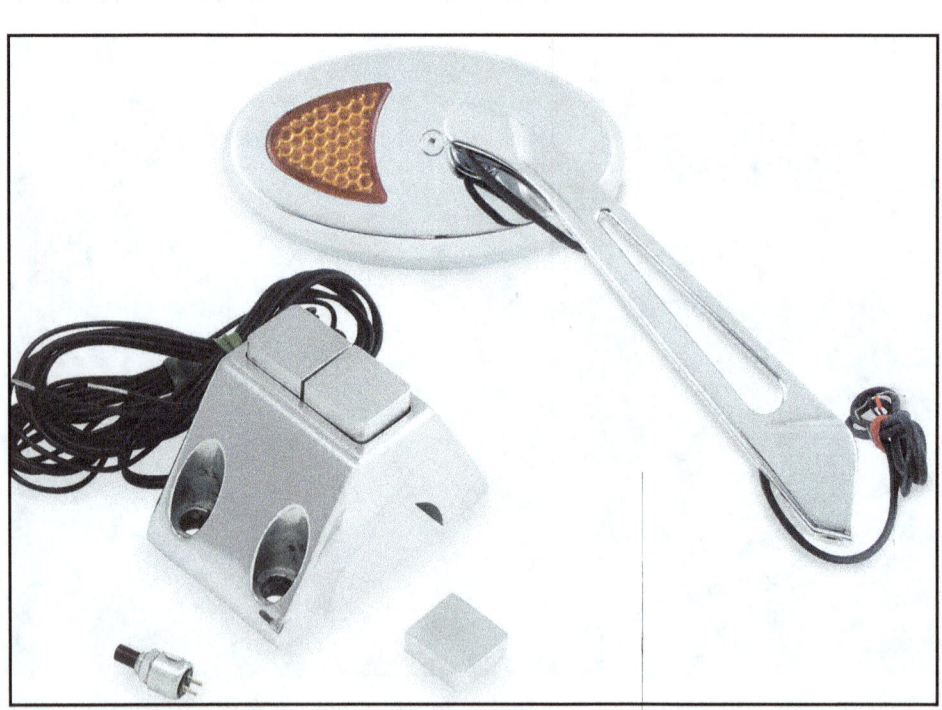

You can have blinkers and make them unobtrusive yet still visible. Note the mirror with integral light, and the slick aftermarket switch assembly. Switches can be purchased with one, two or three buttons. Biker's Choice.

dient for making your bike run is a good battery and charging system. The bigger the battery, the better. A big battery generally has a higher CCA rating or cold cranking amps. This is the amount of power a battery can store in order to turn over your engine. The higher the CCA, the more times you can try to start your bike before the battery goes dead. Not only will a bigger battery help your starter to last longer, the bike will start easier, causing less strain on the rest of your wiring harness.

The average charging system has a charging rate of 28 to 32 amps, and 38 amps for touring models. This rating is the total output of the charging circuit back into your battery, measured in amperage. It is very important to purchase a good stator, rotor and regulator manufactured by a reputable company, complete with a warranty. Remember where the stator is? That's right, it's behind the rotor, which is behind the compensating sprocket & shaft, that's in your inner primary, which is behind your outer primary. In other words, it's not easy to get to. It will take you a good part of three-hours, start to finish, to replace a stator and rotor. So install a good one from the get-go and you can generally forget about it for several years to come.

MAKING THE CONNECTIONS

Let's say that you decided to make your own main wiring harness and use OEM style turn signals. In order to make the turn signals operate you will need a flasher unit. A Wagner 552 flasher relay is the cheapest method for making a light flash on and off. The downside to the Wagner relay is that it needs a switch to turn it on and off. Unlike '96 and up Harley Davidson's, '95 and earlier models did not have self-canceling turn signals. If you would rather have the self-canceling feature, spend the extra money and purchase a Badlands self-canceling module. These guys are the originals. Badlands has been in business for a long time and their products are some of the best available. The average retail of a Badlands all-in-one module is about $100.00 and it offers quite a bit for the money. Not only will your turn signals cancel after seven-seconds, but these modules also have a built-in load equalizer. This is an important feature if you are running a mixture of incandescent bulbs and LED's, or running LED turn signals by themselves. The load equalizer will adjust the amount of load/amperage compared to the wattage size of the bulb. This will allow different styles of lights to work with one another without conflicts.

Now you have to decide if you're going to have handlebar switches or not. When building a custom bike, you may want to use a trick set of after-market handlebar switches or none at all. It really depends on your level of comfort and the overall look you're trying to achieve. As discussed

The stator bolts to the left side case, then comes the rotor, primary assembly and outer housing. The fasteners that hold the stator in place usually have Loctite already applied. Be sure these are tightened to spec. Stator plug must match the plug on the regulator. Regulator must have a good ground.

above, the easiest way out would be to buy OEM or after-market, replacement stock-style switches.

For this scenario we will use a custom set of after-market handlebar controls with switches. As with every other part, there are several styles and brands to choose from. Some sets have two switches on each side and some have three like a factory Harley-Davidson. You need to decide what will work best for you.

Most two-button configurations will do the trick. For example, a two-button set can have a high/low beam and a left turn signal on the left side, and a start and right turn signal button on the right. With this being said, do not limit yourself to these options. You can very easily drill a small hole in the back of the headlight bucket and install a small 250 amp, 3-pole/2-position toggle switch. This would be used as your high/low beam switch and free up a left side button. Maybe you would like to have a horn? State law may require you to have a horn so an empty high/low button would work out well for the horn. Maybe you would rather install a key with a starter function? This feature would free up a right side handlebar button enabling you to use the empty button as an ignition kill switch. Having a quick and easy method for shutting your bike off can be a very nice feature to have.

Now that you know your options, you decide to use a key start switch and a horn for safety's sake. Your final handlebar switch configuration would be as follows: Turn signal and high/low beam (actually the horn) button on the left and a turn signal and ignition kill switch on the right. That's it. You have all of the needed components to get started wiring your custom motorcycle.

WHERE, WHEN, HOW AND WHY

This is the time you have been waiting for. You rolling chassis is beginning to look more and more like a completed "raw steel" motorcycle. That's right. Before you send anything out for chrome, powder coat, polishing or paint, make sure everything fits and works properly. Do it right the first time! An experienced bike builder would assemble the entire bike and ride it before tearing it apart again to apply the pretty stuff. Remember, you want to ride this bike when it's done, not fix it. This answers the when. Install your wiring before you send anything out.

You're probably looking at all of this electrical stuff looking back at you. Don't sweat it, there are some helpful diagrams for you to look at in this book. Here is the best way to get started wiring your bike, hang the bolt-on stuff first.

· Find a spot to mount your turn signals on the front and rear of the bike.

· Mount your headlight onto your triple trees and put it in the correct riding position.

· Tighten on your handle bar controls with switches.

· Position your speedometer.

· Mount your taillight and license plate bracket.

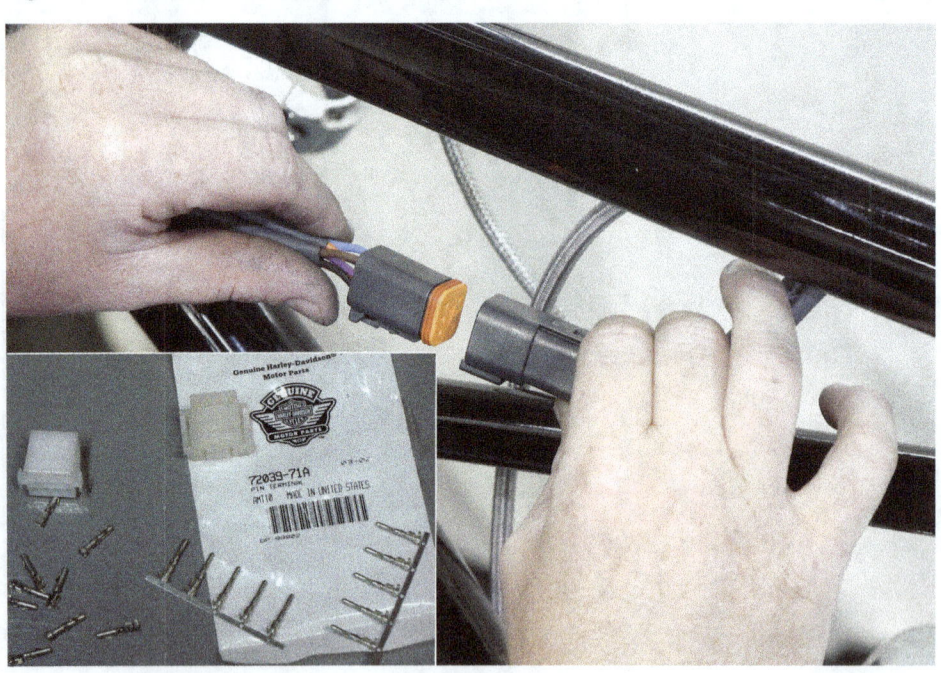

Shown in the upper photo are a male and female Deutsch connector. The lower image shows the pre-Deutsch (AMP), non-waterproof connectors and the pins. Either style can be purchased at most dealerships and aftermarket shops. Radio Shack carries a line of connectors/pins similar to AMP.

· Install your ignition trigger plate in your cam cover.
· Find the final resting place for your ignition coil.
· Guide the stator and rotor over the crankshaft.
· Snug up the screws on the regulator.

This list pretty sums up the major components of a motorcycle's electrical system. Now that all of these items are in place you can begin to plan how you will connect them. Again, don't worry, the diagrams in this book will show you the way. At this time, it is also recommended to finalize the locations of your wiring connections. For example, your handlebar switches, headlight and speedometer could connect to a main harness underneath your fuel tank. Make sure they are not in the way of any mounting hardware where they could be pinched thus causing a major headache down the road. Another idea for front-end connections would be to run the turn signal wiring into the headlight and make the connections inside the bucket or housing. This can look very nice if done correctly. It can also limit the amount and size of connections under the fuel tank. You need to drill two precise holes into the headlight bucket making sure not to blister the chrome.

It is also recommended you cover the wiring with a loom or stainless braiding to protect the delicate wiring harness, not just from the initial fishing of the wires through, but rather from the constant vibration and movement of the motorcycle that can cause a tear in a wire's protective jacketing. Once the pair of turn signal wires are in the headlight, you can attach them along with the two or three-wire headlamp socket into a multi-circuit connector. This would enable you to have one larger wire exiting the headlight bucket towards the back of the motorcycle. In our scenario, we have decided to run the turn signal wires separately and make the connections under the fuel tank. Whichever method you choose, you need to determine what is best for your build and remember to install connectors for easy removal.

Handlebar Wiring

If you are going to run your handlebar switch wires through your handlebars you may want to

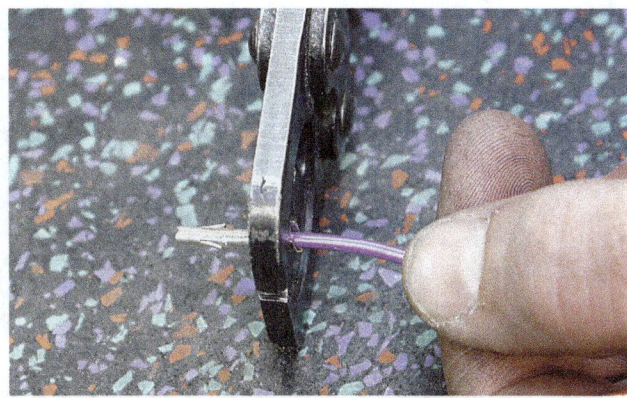

Whether the pins are Deutsch or pre-Deutsch style, they still require a careful double crimp, done with a very high quality crimper (there is a specific Deutsch crimper). After stripping the wire the connector is crimped onto the bare wire.

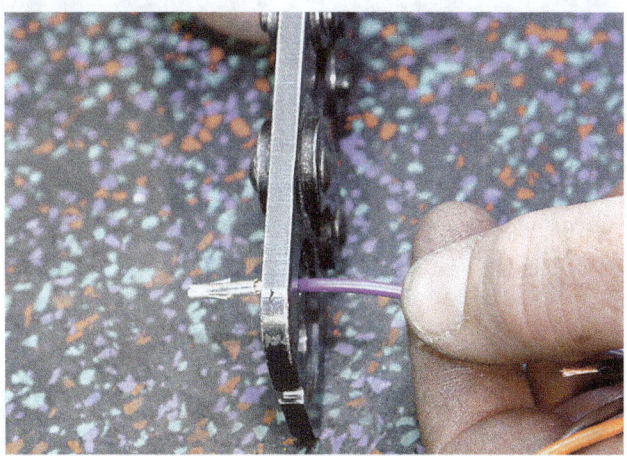

Next, the crimper is repositioned and then the second set of small tangs is crimped onto the insulation.

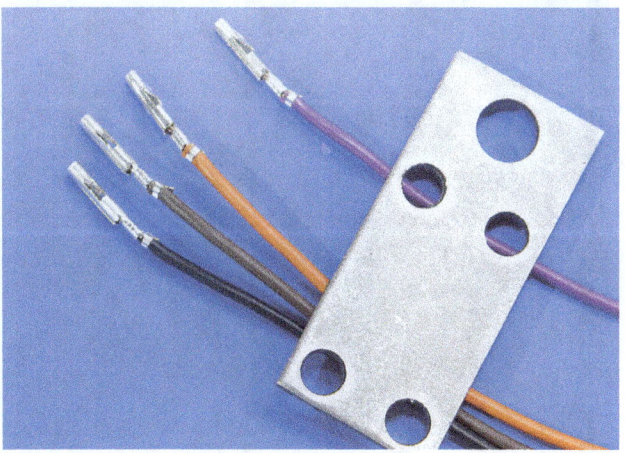

Look closely at how neat these crimps are. You can't do this with a ten-dollar crimper from the auto-parts store.

The module or junction box can often be squeezed in next to the battery, under the seat for easy access. Note the neatness of all the work (done at KC Creations) and how all the harnesses are contained in shrink wrap.

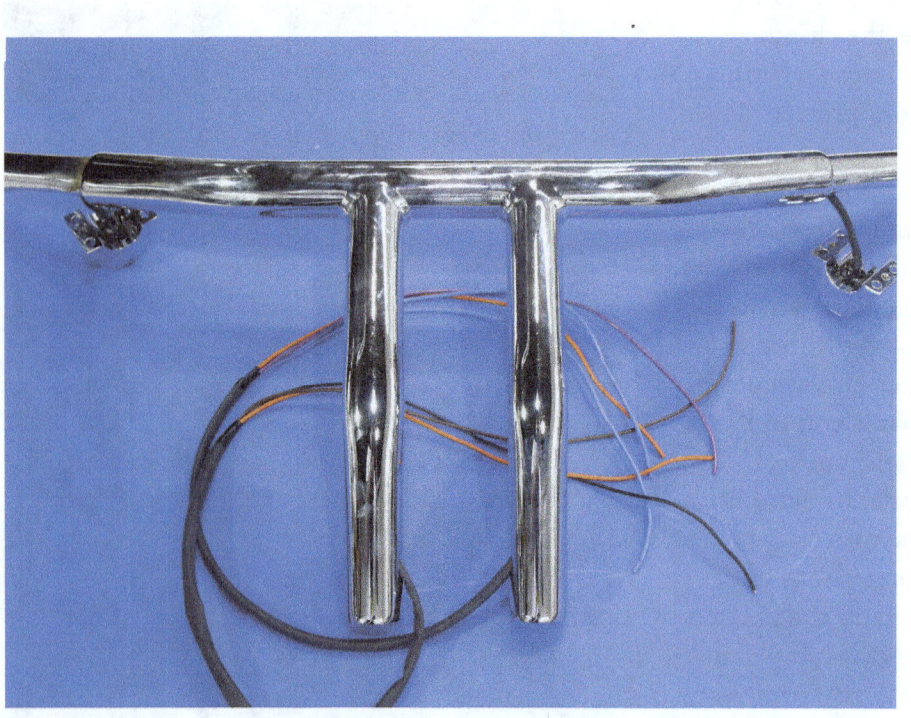

Running the wires through the bars makes for a very neat installation, but it's also a lot of extra work. Some bars come with a pull-wire, otherwise you have to fish a wire or piece of string through for each side.

purchase a pair of handlebars that come with a pull-wire or string already in place. This can save you a ton of time. Once you begin fishing the wires you're bound to hit a snag. Don't pull too hard! You may damage the wire loom or jacketing due to the rough burs of metal or chrome in the handlebars. Take your time. Trying to find an electrical problem in your bars later is no fun.

Some builders like to run headlight and handlebar switch wires through the frame. In order to do so you would need to drill some holes into the backbone of the frame, behind the neck but in front if the fuel tank. Remember to take your time if you choose to run the wires through the frame, to prevent tearing or short circuits.

Your ignition wiring can be run up through the frame tube that is located behind the motor but in front of the transmission. The wires would come up to the seat gusset and a simple hole could be drilled in the back of the frame allowing the wires to exit toward the battery box. Once your wires are here you can make final connections to your main harness and the ignition coil. The battery box is also the most ideal spot to locate a starter relay, fuses and circuit breakers. It is nice and concealed, and offers easy access for testing or repairs. Since some wiring jobs can be very detailed due to complicated electronics, the battery box is the only place to store all of these items.

A nice place to have your ignition switch is to mount it on the motor-mount. The location provides easy access and makes it simple to wire into your main harness. Once the lighting, handlebar switches, ignition system, charging system and starter are installed and wired correctly, you're just about ready to fire your motorcycle for the first time. There are two other small projects that need to be addressed first. You need to install a front (if available) and rear brake switch. Second, a taillight and license plate assembly will need to be mounted. Although a few manufacturers of front master cylinders offer integrated front brake switches, most custom after-market controls don't have them. If this is the case, you can either install a brake tee under your triple-tree with a brake switch, or you can opt to not install a front brake switch at all. Before you make your decision, be sure that you are not required to have a front brake switch in order to pass state inspection. Also, remember that the brake light only lights up when you step on the rear brake.

Brake switches are available in many styles and can also be mounted in several different areas. One of the most common spots for a rear brake switch is on the frame under the transmission. This is a safe yet hidden spot for the necessary component. Now a days,

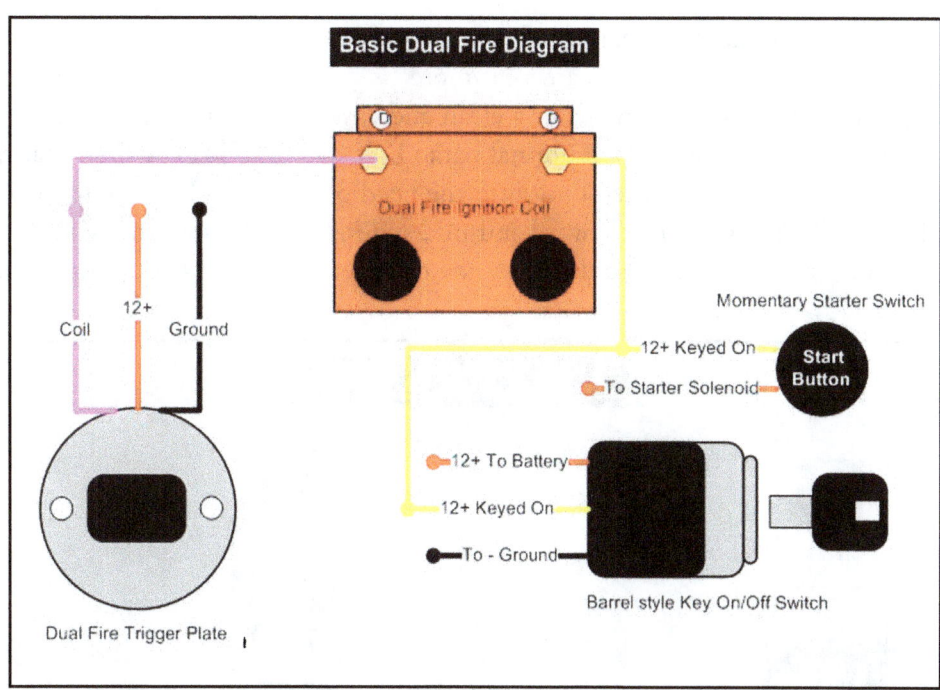

A dual-fire ignition is a pretty simple thing to wire. Unless noted otherwise, all diagrams use 16 gauge wire.

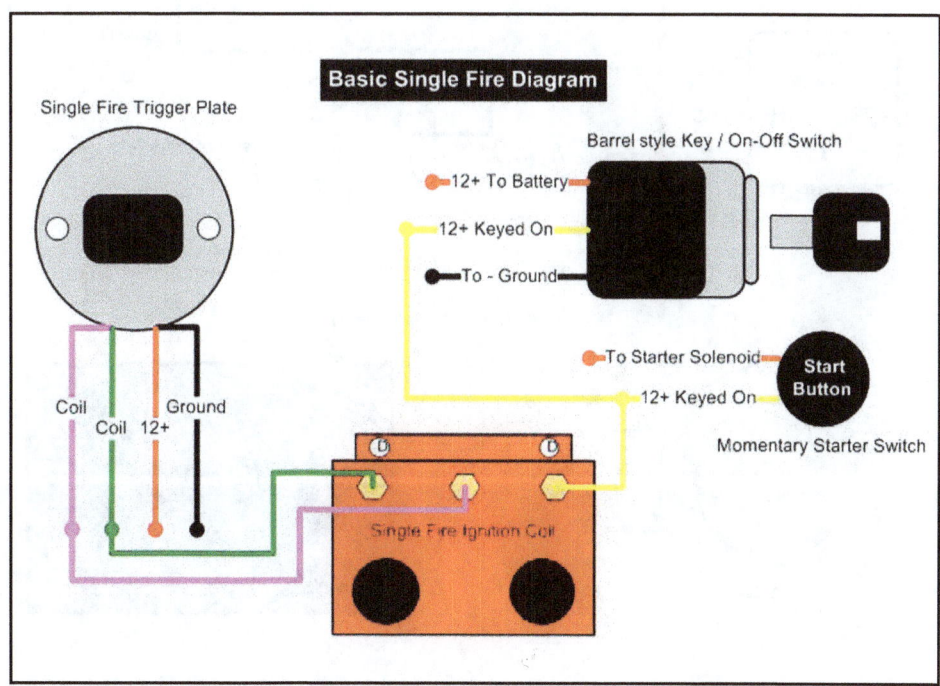

The single-fire ignition is a little more complex to wire, simply because you are wiring two, separate coils.

69

companies are making a banjo-bolt/brake switch combination. These switches are a bit more expensive but can really make for a clean and easy install. It's about the size of a normal banjo bolt but yet has the brake switch built into the head of the bolt. This is great for forward and mid style controls and can save you a whole bunch of time.

Simply supply a keyed twelve-volt power source and the other wire would connect directly to your rear brake light. It's that simple. Be sure to purchase a switch that fits your needs.

It's time to give it try. Before you do, check to be sure that your battery connections are tight. Also look at the battery cable going to your starter. Make sure the stud on the starter has enough clearance from the bottom of the oil tank. Turn the key and check all of your lighting. Are the running lights, high/low beam and brake light all working? If so, twist the key a bit further and see if it starts. If it does not, check the obvious first. Gas, oil, plugs and plug wires? If all seems OK, check the choke. Try it again and hopefully it will turn over. Once running, check all of the lights again. Turn it off after a few minutes and check you main harness and connections. Keep in mind that if you continue to try and start a motorcycle without any luck, your wiring is going to get hot. If your wiring gets hot to the point of meltdown, there is a chance that your battery is too small to turn over your engine, or you have a short circuit somewhere in your harness.

Thanks to Jeff Zielinski, Namz Custom Cycle Products, for all copy and diagrams.

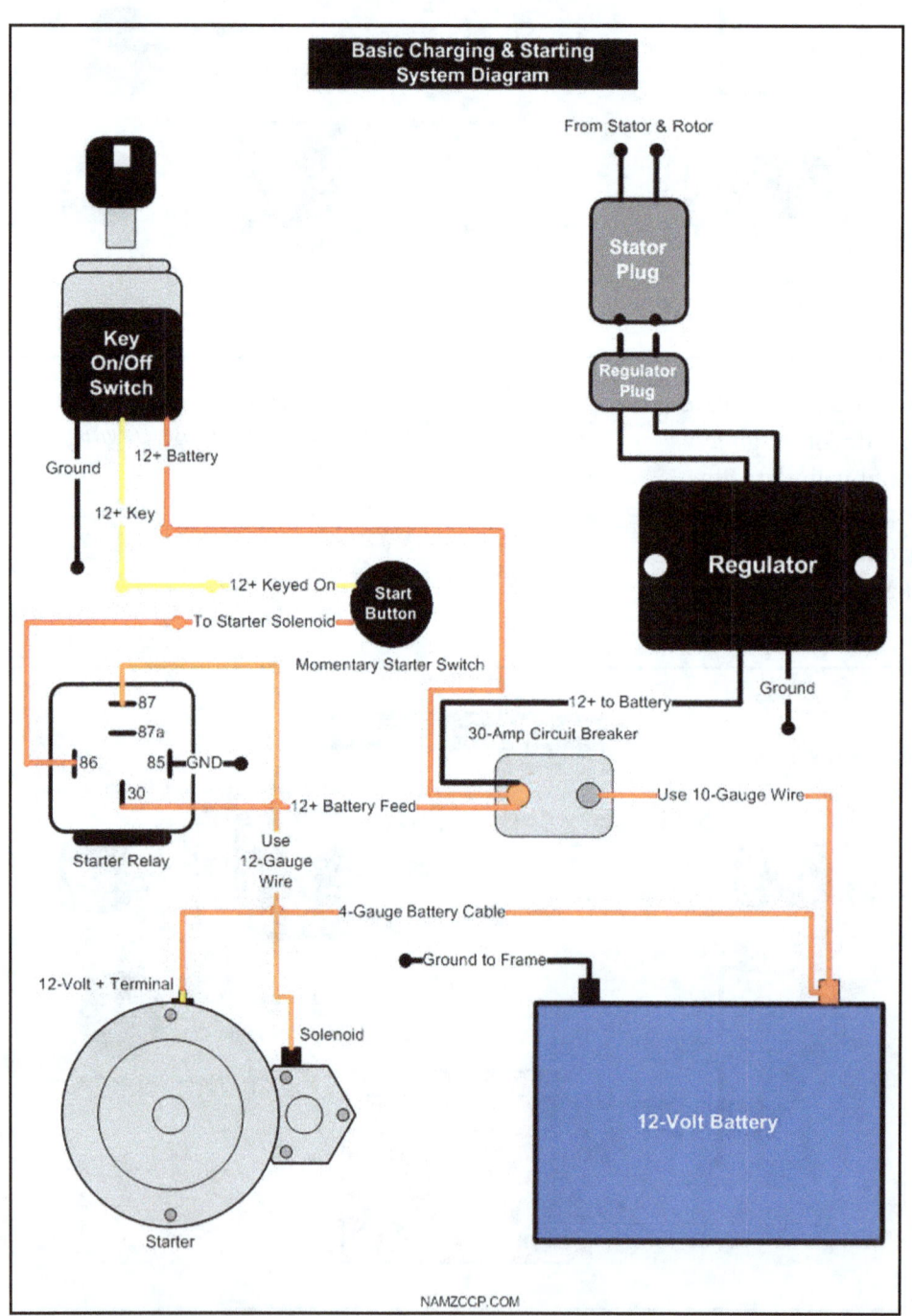

This is the basic starter and charging circuit for nearly all Harleys and V-twins. Unless noted otherwise, all wires are 16 gauge.

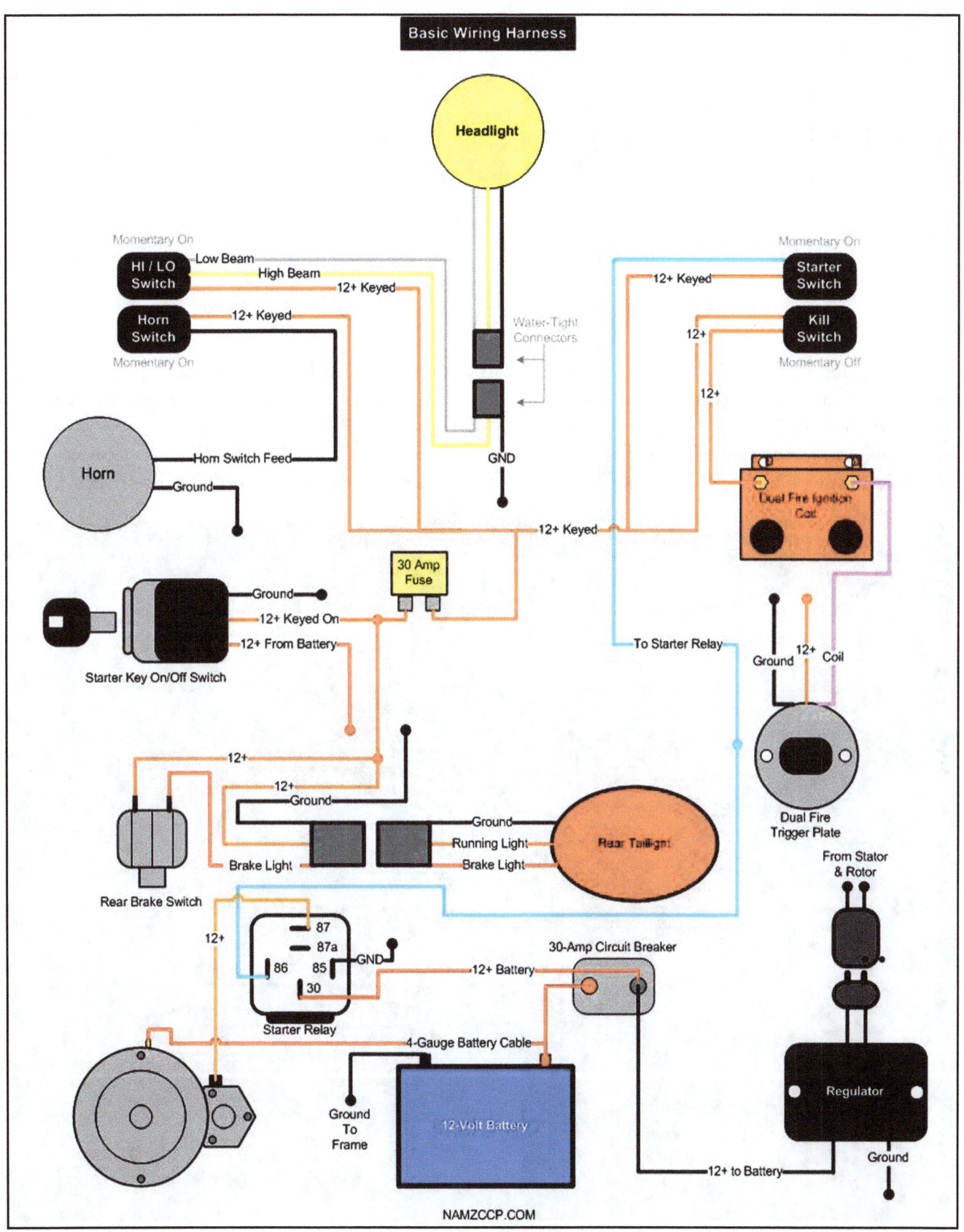

Shown is a good, no-blinkers, wiring schematic. Again, all wires are 16 gauge unless noted otherwise.

Chapter Seven

Did it Myself

The 250 Soft-tail Project

So after ten years of watching other people assemble motorcycles from scratch, and then writing books about it, I decided to put my money where my mouth is and build one myself.

For a starting point I chose a rolling chassis kit from American Thunder in Prior Lake, Minnesota. The heart and soul of the kit is a 250 tire soft-tail frame from Rolling Thunder. Being somewhat conservative I ordered the frame with only two inches of stretch in the top tube, no stretch in the

Subtle and understated (and fast), those were the goals and that's pretty much what I created. Cobalt blue with oriental blue flames are the work of Jon Kosmoski. Engine is a 121 from TP. Tranny is a RSD 6 speed from Baker. Wheels are from PMFR.

down tubes, and a rake angle of thirty-four degrees.

The chrome billet wheels are from PMFR and measure 18 inches in back and 19 in front, wrapped by a 250 Avon and a 110/90 up front. I chose the 110/90 rather than the more common 90/90 simply to put a little more rubber on the road for turning and stopping.

THE MOCK UP

The importance of the mock up can't be over emphasized. In order to speed the process along and get some help with things like drivetrain alignment, and the cutting of axle spacers, I asked Neil Ryan at American Thunder if we could do the mock up in his shop, for an extra charge. Troy (one of the bike-builders at American Thunder) and I spent the better part of two days putting the bike together in the raw, and trying different front fenders and handle bars. We decided (hard to believe) that the bike looked better sitting as low as we could get it, and that even a small change in the position of the front fender makes a huge difference in the way the bike looks.

In order to get it low we used FLH tubes in the 41mm front end, and added a lowering kit as well. In the rear we adjusted the shocks for a low ride height, though we had to come back later and adjust the preload as well. The mock up is essentially a raw assembly, which starts when Troy installs the swingarm

The project starts with this rolling chassis kit from American Thunder. Engine shown is an S&S unit that we used for the mock up. Transmission is a Baker RSD six-speed.

Using a socket as a driver, Troy installs the pivot bearings in either side of the swingarm.

73

Here you see the rubber snubbers that act as suspension stops for the swingarm.

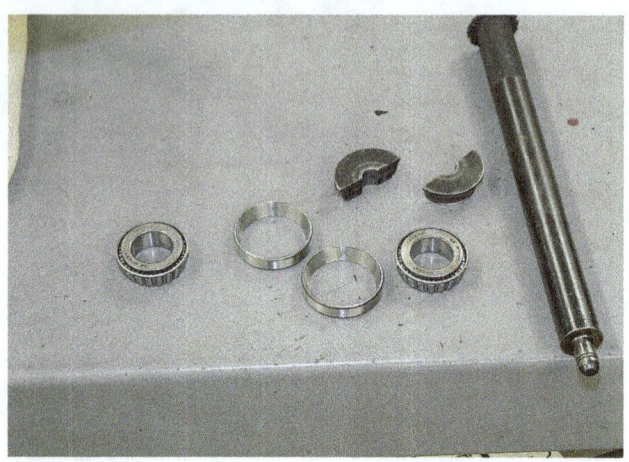

The tapered bearings and outer bearing races are the same for nearly all V-twin motorcycles. The tool shown on the right is used to drive in the races.

The swingarm pivot axle is coated with anti-seize before installation. The two thin washers are installed...

The bearings need to be packed before installation, most shops use a water-proof wheel-bearing grease (the kind you use on your boat trailer).

...on either side between the swingarm and the inside of the frame.

The small ring that Troy installed on the bottom triple tree is part of the fork stop assembly and will interface with the tab on the neck of the frame.

The bearing driver seen earlier is used to install the bearing races.

Not all aftermarket triple trees are the same, this particular set from American Thunder uses a stem that screws into the top tree.

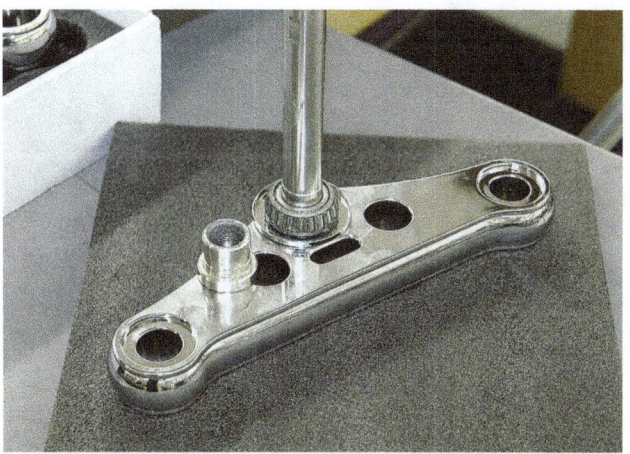

Once screwed together, the stem is locked in place with a set screw, then the dust shield and upper bearing are pushed down into place.

The fastener that holds it all together, and is used to adjust the bearing play, screws in from the bottom of the lower tree, held in place with another set screw.

bearings and then puts the swingarm and axle in the frame.

Next up is the front end. First, Troy lays out all the parts, and installs the fork stop bracket on the lower triple tree. The neck bearings need to be packed of course, and the bearing races are installed in the neck with a hammer and installation tool. Once the bearing races are in place, Troy screws the center stem up into the top triple tree, installs the upper bearing on the stem and then drops the stem into the bike and brings the other bearing and the lower tree up from the bottom. As this is just the mock up sequence Troy simply snugs up the bearing adjustment, leaving the final adjustment for later.

The assembled fork tubes can now be slipped up into the triple trees, but not before Troy fills both sides with 15 weight fork oil. The tubes are held in place with a pinch bolt on the lower tree, and the chrome top bolts on either side. Troy

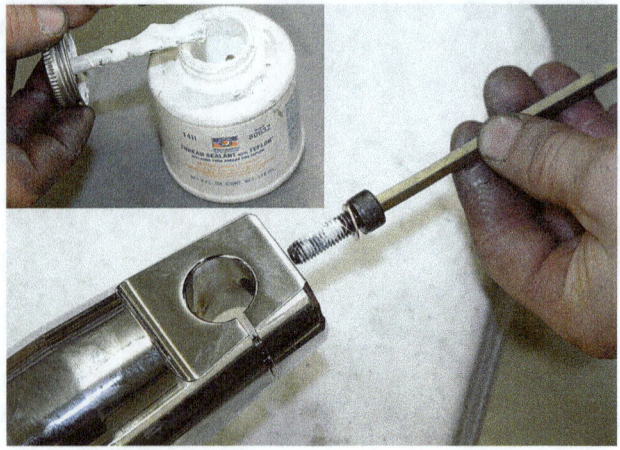

The final step in the assembly of the fork tubes is the installation of the damper-tube bolt, coated first with Teflon-type sealer.

Once the top nut is tightened the pinch bolts in the lower tree can be tightened.

Now each fork tube is filled with the recommended amount of 15 weight fork oil.

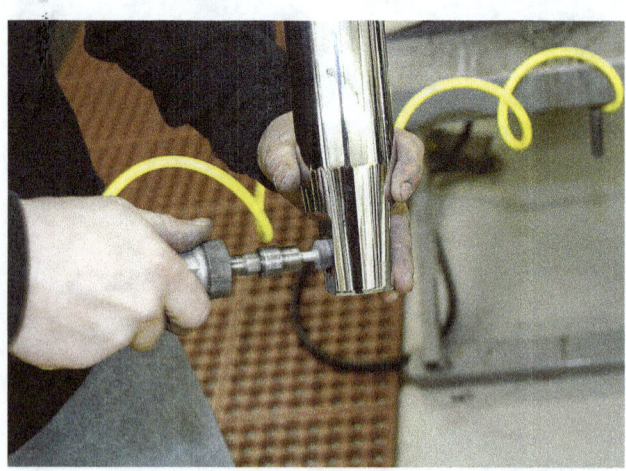

This is one of those situations where a build up of chrome plate had to be eliminated with some careful sanding.

Each tube is slipped up through the lower tree and held in place with the top nut and sealing washer.

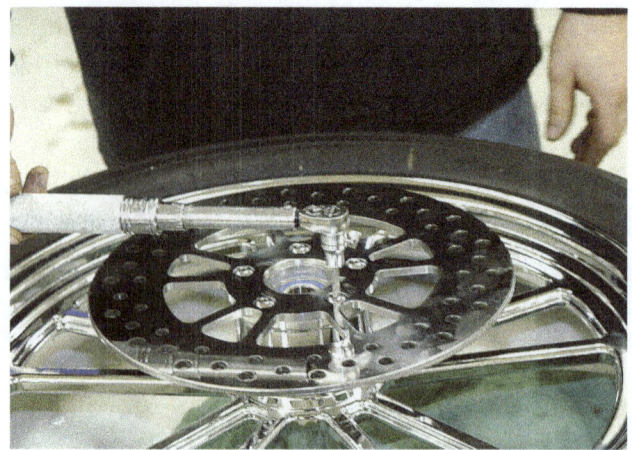

Before installing the front wheel the rotor is installed, and the small Allen bolts are tightened to 16-24 ft. lbs. with Loctite on the threads.

tightens the top bolts before the pinch bolts, so the tubes are fully seated in the top tree before the lower pinch bolts are tightened.

As with a lot of chrome parts, many of the holes and edges on these parts have a build up of chrome, which needs to be eliminated (note the nearby photos). In addition to cleaning up the lower fork legs where the axle comes through, the taped holes in the wheels need to be checked with a tap before installing the rotors and rear pulley. In the case of the rear pulley, Troy makes sure the pulley is spaced out far enough that the belt won't be forced into the tire (note the photo), sometimes a spacer needs to be installed between the hub and pulley to move the pulley out enough to provide clearance.

Now the front wheel is mounted in the fork so Troy can measure for spacers that will position the wheel in the center of the fork. The rear wheel is set in place as well, but measuring for spacers comes a little later.

Aligning first the drivetrain, then the rear wheel is done in a specific sequence and starts after the engine and transmission are set into the frame.

Install Engine/Transmission and Inner Primary

With the engine and tranny sitting loose in the frame, the first step is the installation of the inner primary. In order to ensure that the engine and transmission mounting points on the frame are correctly located, and the two are correctly aligned, it's important to follow a specific sequence. Troy's sequence goes like this (some builders use a variation of this sequence):

1. Get the engine and transmission sitting loose in the frame. Both should sit square on their mounts.

2. Loosely bolt the inner primary to the engine and transmission.

3. Tighten inner-primary to engine bolts first.

4. Tighten inner-primary to tranny bolts.

5. Get down on your hands and knees and see if the engine and transmission seem to be sitting square on the mounting pads. If so, tighten the engine to frame bolts.

6. Now, check for any clearance between the transmission and the mounting points, and if

Once the fork legs are free of extra chrome, Troy can lift the wheel into place and slip the axle through. He still needs to measure for spacers that will leave the wheel centered between the two legs.

Using a straight edge, Troy checks that the pulley is out far enough from the hub so the belt won't rub on the edge of the tire.

With the rotor and pulley in place, the wheel can be rolled into place and the axle slipped through the wheel.

Once the chassis is a roller, the engine...

Most 250 tire RSD frames use a 1/2 inch spacer on the engine's left side. If in doubt about the need for a spacer, ask the frame manufacturer.

...and then the six speed transmission, can be set in place. If possible use the actual engine you intend to use for the mock up process.

As explained, achieving good alignment between the engine and tranny is a multi-step process, you will likely have the inner primary on and off many times.

The bearing race seen on the transmission shaft needs to be removed with a puller before proceeding with the project.

Here you can see two of the shims used under the transmission to create perfect alignment.

everything seems OK, tighten the transmission mounting bolts.

After going through this procedure, you might think you're through mounting the engine and transmission, but really the fun has just begun. To ensure that the engine and transmission are lined up correctly in relation to each other, you need to take off the inner primary and then see if it will slide back on with no hassle. If it won't go back on, the engine and transmission are not aligned. Any attempt to force the parts together will usually break the inner primary.

When Troy encounters a problem like this he shims the transmission until the inner primary will go on and off with no trouble (with the engine tight and the tranny only snug you can check the need for spacer-shims with a feeler gauge slipped in between the transmission and frame at each mount). Any shims you use to get the engine/transmission/inner primary aligned have to be saved when the bike is torn down so you can get it all aligned again during final assembly. It's a good idea to use the real engine and transmission for this mock-up exercise, as a plastic engine or simply another V-Twin than the one you are going to use may not have exactly the same mounting dimensions and this could cause you to go through this whole procedure again during final assembly.

Position rear wheel

Time now to position the rear wheel in the frame and cut the necessary spacers. The first step involves getting the wheel straight in the frame, which Troy does with the simple tool shown in the photos (a more elaborate version of this tool is available from Revenge Cycle).

The heavy plate just behind the battery box is centered in the frame and Troy uses this as an aid in positioning the wheel correctly from side-to-side. Essentially, he positions the wheel so the measurement from the ruler to the edge of the plate is the same on both sides. Warning, find and mark the center of the tire first, the tire's seam is generally not in the center.

With the wheel and tire centered and straight in the frame Troy can measure and cut the axle spacers. A snap-gauge is used to determine the dimension of the spacers, though a good caliper

Made from welding rod, this simple tool helps Troy keep the wheel straight in the frame as he adjusts the belt tension.

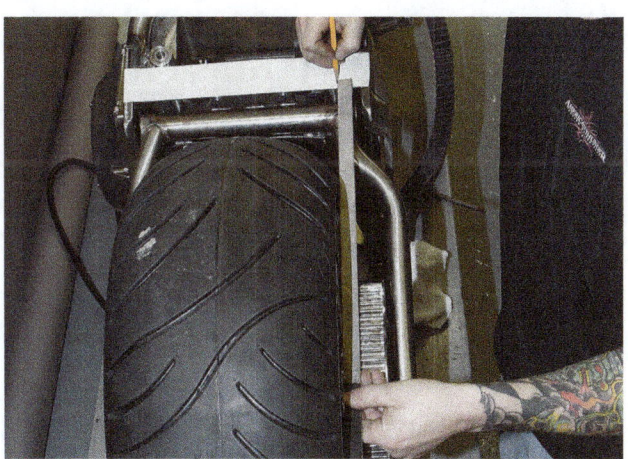

After getting the wheel in what he thinks is the center of the frame, Troy uses the two straight edges as shown...

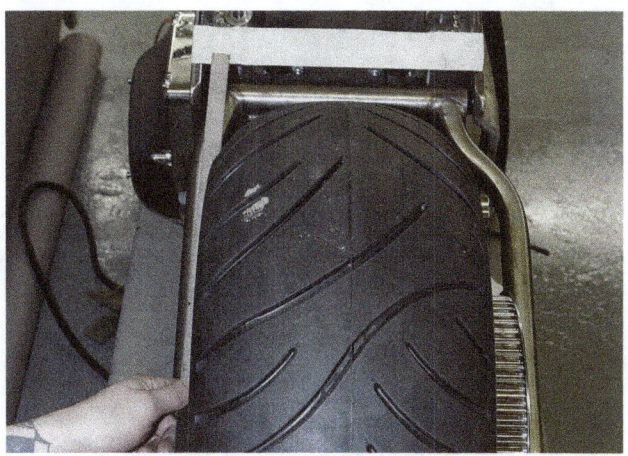

...to mark the edge of the wheel on the crossmember.

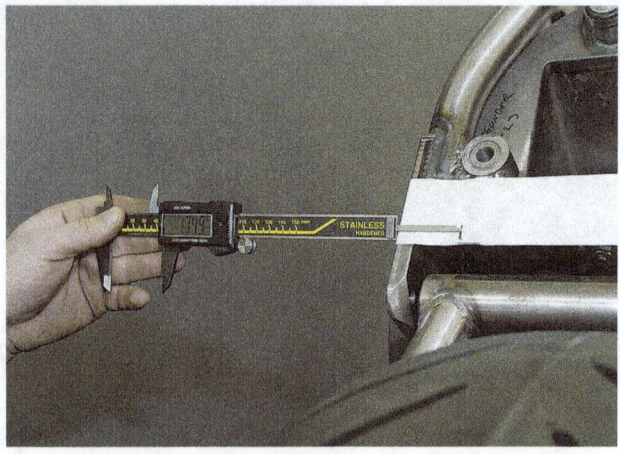

Careful measurement with a caliper allows Troy to get the wheel in exactly the center of the frame (there are no axle spacers in place yet).

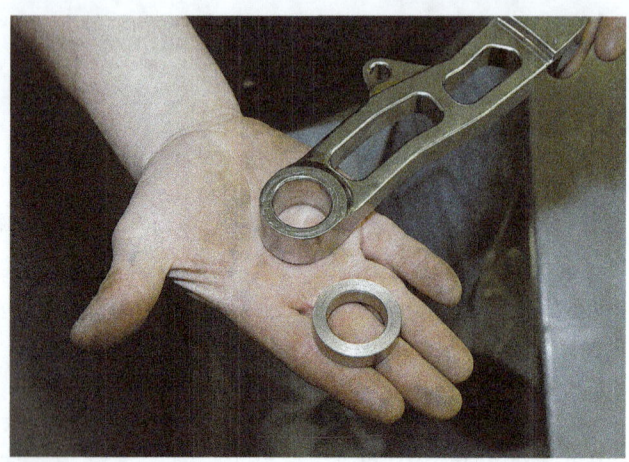

Here you see one of the left side spacers used in conjunction with the caliper carrier to correctly position both the caliper and the wheel.

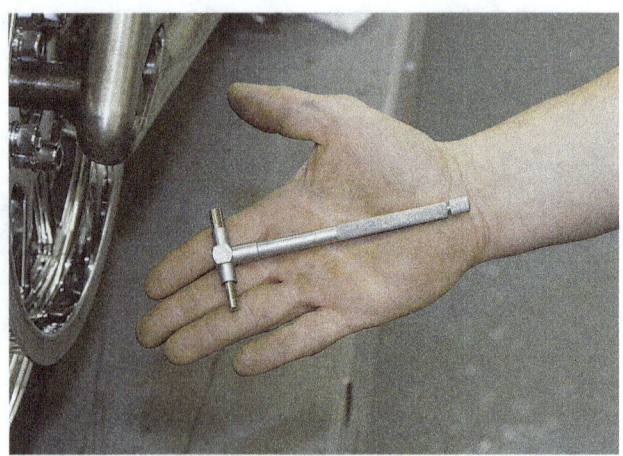

This snap-gauge can be uses as shown...

With spacers in place and tight, you have to ensure the wheel and caliper are in the correct position and that the belt runs true without crowding...

...to determine the dimension of the spacers.

...up against one side or the other when the wheel is spun in a forward direction. You also need to bottom the rear suspension (take the shocks out) and make sure the tire/swingarm doesn't hit the frame/fender.

can often be used here as well. On the left side the brake caliper mount becomes part of the spacing equation as Troy has to determine where the caliper and carrier should be positioned so the caliper is centered over the rotor. Then he needs to determine the dimensions for the spacers that will be used on either side of the carrier.

On the right side, Troy measures for, and cuts, a single relatively large spacer that is installed between the outside of the outer bearing and the inside of the frame.

When all is said and done, the wheel/tire should be in the center of the frame, and you should be able to spin the tire in a forward direction and have the belt stay in the center of the wheel pulley. Though it ain't rocket science, this drivetrain and rear wheel alignment is probably the most frustrating part of the whole assembly (other than wiring perhaps), so plan to take your time and consider asking for help before you start throwing wrenches across the garage.

Visual Mock Up

The idea of the mock up is to make sure everything fits, but things need to fit in a visual as well as a literal sense. The Rolling Thunder kit comes with a Russ Wernimont one-piece tank, and rear fender. I wanted to at least try some different front fenders, and maybe some different bars. The higher bars with integral risers seen in the middle photo didn't feel comfortable when I sat on the bike so we tried the lower set. In the end we used the fender seen in the lower photo, and a set of simple, almost-drag-bars supported by short risers. This is a combination that fits me and, I think, also looks the best. Though more and more bars come with integral risers, the separate risers allow for more fine adjustment of the handlebar angle and position.

Too Much Trail?

In choosing the rake angle for this bike, I tried to pick a compromise figure that wasn't too radical, yet put the front wheel out there far enough to give it that certain "look" or sense of motion. With only 34 degrees of rake I never worried that the bike might end up with a little too much rake. And, no, I didn't take the time to figure the trail out ahead of time with a web calculator like that at

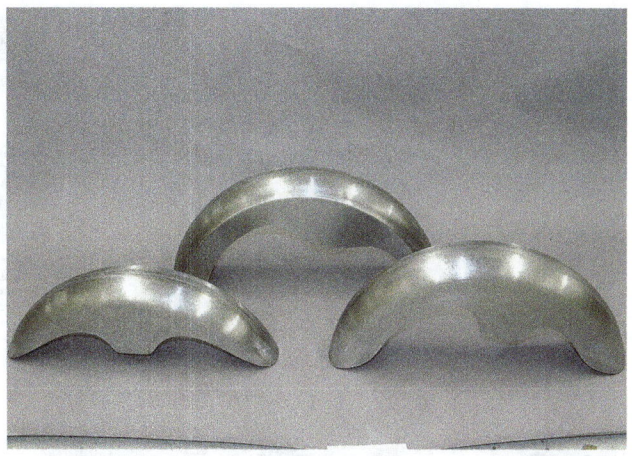

A little time spent with some extra sheet metal pays big dividends in getting exactly the look you're after. We tried a variety of front fenders and handle bars.

For the bars I sat on the bike to see which fit me the best. Though this longer fender doesn't look bad...

...this shorter example seemed a better match for the rear fender. The exact fender position is also very important in getting the bike to sit just right. You have to be able to get back away from the bike to make a good visual assessment.

This simple "trail" tool uses a cross bar that screws up into the stem, with a telescoping rod/pointer.

Troy uses a ruler as the other part of the trail-checking tool kit.

Using a simple tape measure it's easy to check exactly how much trail the bike has.

the Perse website, or the one in the Drag Specialties catalog.

Anyway, using a nifty tool developed by Neil at American Thunder, we checked the rake, as shown nearby, only to find that the bike has six and a half inches of trail, just a little more than the commonly recommended figure of four to six inches. In driving the bike, it's a little heavy to steer in corners, and wants to "flop" when turning at slow speed. My plan is to recalculate and possibly add a set of 3-degree trees (note to readers, be sure to figure trail during mock up).

The last thing Troy did for me was to drill and tap holes in the frame for the small clamps I would need to hold the cables and lines neatly in place.

FOUR MONTHS LATER

It only took Troy about an hour to reduce the rolling chassis into a big pile of parts, which were quickly transferred to my truck and eventually to the shop of well-known painter Jon Kosmoski. At Jon's shop we started by bead blasting all the parts to get them ready for paint. Once all the parts were sanded, primered, painted, masked, painted again, and then cleared and buffed, everything came back to my small shop. Time to put up or shut up.

So like all the people who have done this before me, I started by assembling the frame. Which means installing the swingarm, the neck bearings, and the fork. Then it was time to get wheels on both ends. All of these operations are fairly simple, except for the fact that nearly everything was coated with multiple coats of very high quality, House of Kolor, paint. So you can't just put a bolt in a hole because the inside of the hole is smaller now than it was before. And you may not be able to screw the bolt into the threads because the threads are gummed up with overspray. So before doing anything else I ran a tap through all the threads in the frame and the various painted parts. The inside of all holes had to be scraped free of paint. Rather than leave the steel bare after I scraped off the paint, I went down to the local auto parts store and bought a bottle of touch up paint that roughly matched the paint on the bike. This is what I used to coat the areas where I scraped off the paint, and to touch up the inevitable boo-boos that always occur during an assembly - no matter how careful you are.

Once I had the bike up on its wheels, and the motor and tranny in place, I had to go through the whole drivetrain alignment procedure again, seems

Do as much as you can during the mock up, this includes drilling and tapping holes for the cable clamps.

Once the TP engine and Baker tranny were in place it was necessary to go through the whole alignment/shimming procedure again.

Paint finished, back in my small shop, and partly assembled.

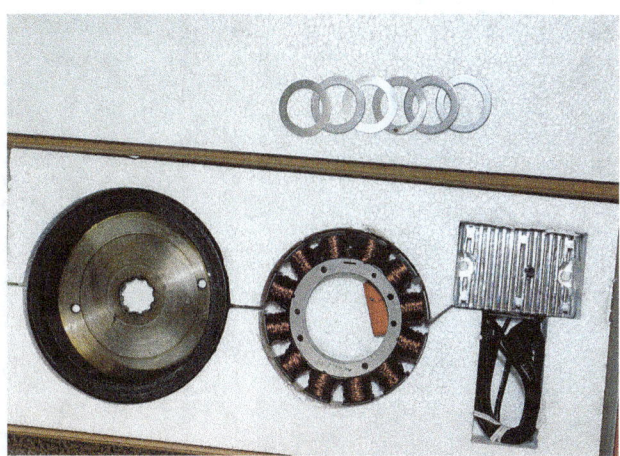

The charging system is the typical 32 amp system consisting of stator, rotor and regulator.

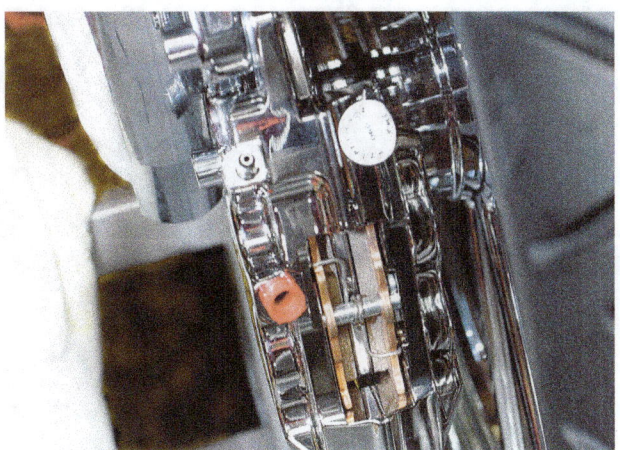

The front caliper is installed so the caliper is centered over the rotor using small hardened shims as necessary between the caliper and the mount.

Four small Allens hold the stator in place, be sure to use red Loctite and a torque wrench, if these come loose it's really a mess to fix.

It's a good idea to keep as much of the frame protected for as long as possible to avoid nicks and chips in the new paint.

The inner primary installed, bolts torqued to 17 - 21 ft. lbs. and the lock tabs bent over as needed.

Once I went through the engine/tranny/inner primary alignment process again, the inner went on for the last time. Be sure shifter lever is in place first.

The primary drive components prior to installation.

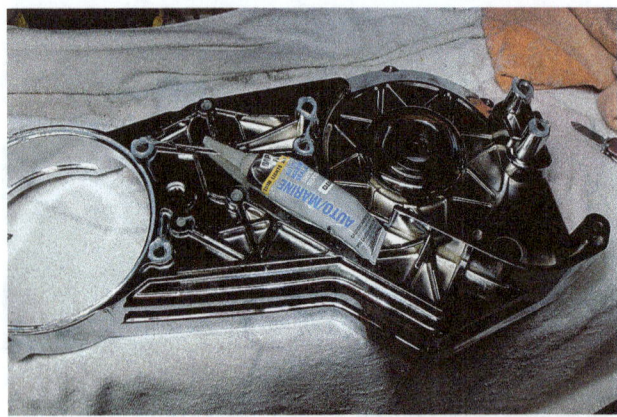

Before the inner is installed for the last time add a little silicone to the back side of the through-holes so the lube can't leak out the back. Also where the inner meets the spacer and the spacer meets the case.

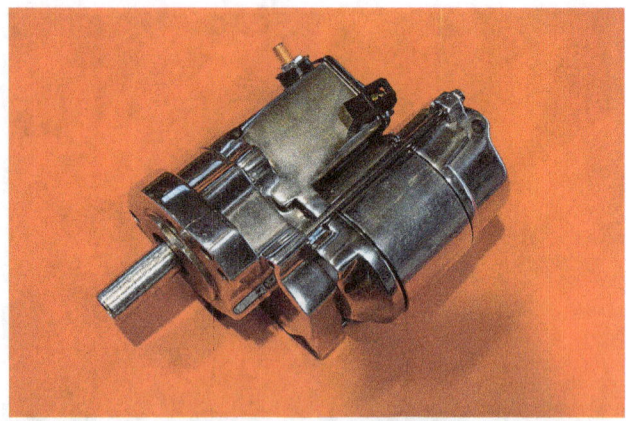

The starter is a 1.6 kw unit from Terry Products. Remember a good battery, and quality cables, are as important as a big starter. Many starters are sourced from metric cars and use metric threads for the stud.

Borrowed from another book - you have to ensure that the primary chain is correctly aligned by checking the chain just behind the compensator sprocket and just ahead of the clutch hub.

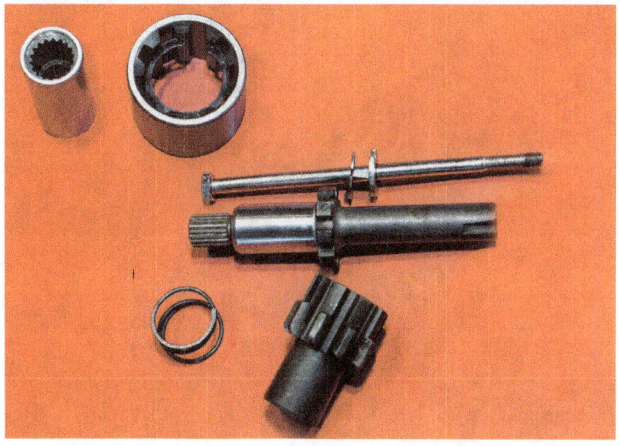

There are two couplers that are part of the starter drive (jackshaft) assembly. The smaller one has a counter bore on one end, which faces the jackshaft, not the starter.

After installing the starter from the other side (with the coupler in place) and then the jackshaft, the spring goes on next...

...followed by the second coupler, which has a shallow and deep side (there is a snap-ring inside). The shallow side intersects with the teeth on the jackshaft.

the shims where misplaced somewhere along the way, and we didn't use the TP motor for the mock up so things probably changed a bit anyway.

First though, I set the engine and tranny in place and marked the outline of the areas where they sit on the mounts, then I pulled both units, and scraped off the paint on the frame mounts at the marked areas so both the engine and transmission would bolt to bare metal. This ensures that the paint won't squeeze out later and leave me with a loose engine, and also provides a good electrical ground. Now it was time to fit up the primary again, which included figuring out the right shims for the transmission mounts so the inner primary would slide on and off without any binding. Then the inner primary could be installed for the last time. Note the details of the primary installation in the nearby photos and captions.

INSTALL THE STARTER

The starter itself installs from the right side, and is held in place with two Allen bolts. Once the starter, with the coupler, is installed I put the rest of the jackshaft assembly in from the primary side. The photos tell this story better than words, just remember to pre-lube all the pieces with a little oil,

Next up is the drive itself...

The shoe assembly was installed first (with red Loctite on the bolts that hold the bracket to the inner primary), then the primary drive goes on as one assembly.

...followed by the long jackshaft bolt, which is torqued to 7-9 ft. lbs. Be sure the tab on the washer closest to the shaft goes in the notch in the shaft.

Remember the clutch-hub nut is left hand thread, tightened to 70-80 ft. lbs. The clutch pushrod, seen here, slides inside the mainshaft and connects to the hydraulic clutch actuator on the other side.

The tang on the end-washer is bent over and acts as a lock to prevent the long fastener from unscrewing.

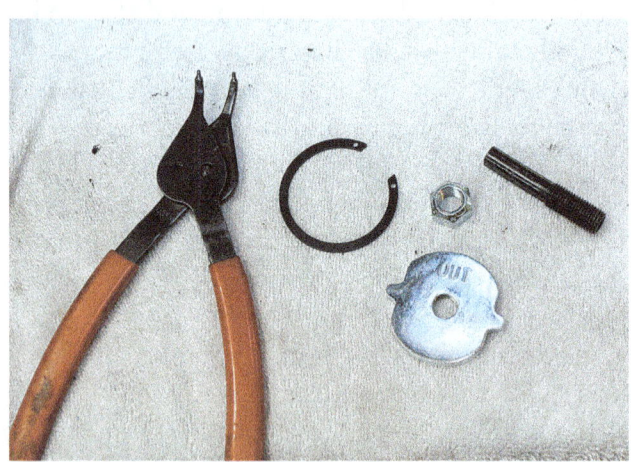

The clutch adjuster stud and plate are held in place with a snap ring as shown.

and that there's two couplers, each has a snap ring in the middle and goes in only one way. The long bolt that holds the jackshaft assembly together has two washers under the head, both need to be positioned per the nearby photos. The next step is the installation of the primary drive assembly, which is slipped up onto the two shafts as an assembly.

The nut on the compensator assembly is generally installed, after applying red Loctite to the threads, with an impact wrench. No one seems to look up the torque specs, they just put this one on as tight as the impact wrench can get it. The nut for the clutch hub is a different story. A left hand thread, this one is installed to 70-80 ft. lbs.

The clutch actuation shaft is installed into the mainshaft, followed by the small adjuster assembly, which can now be adjusted according to the photo and caption.

Once the primary drive is installed, with the chain alignment and tension adjusted correctly, the outer primary can be installed. Note the nearby primary cover assembly sequence. I also need to point out the fact that most aftermarket outer-primaries come pretty raw (some assembly required) while the H-D assembly comes fully assembled, with all the seals and bearing races already in place.

WIRING

You don't want to wait too long to install the wiring harness. If you do, the parts and sheet metal you've installed will just get in the way of installing the harness and components. Ideally, you should figure out where all the major electrical components go during the mock up process, but in my case that didn't happen. I did know I wanted handlebar switches, and the ignition switch to be on the coil bracket on the engine's left side.

The harness kit I purchased is from Wire Plus, and included sub-harnesses for both sides of the handlebars. I couldn't quite get the main module (which includes the circuit breakers and starter relay, but not the flasher for the blinkers) tucked in behind the battery and ended up mounting it behind the transmission. Not an ideal position, but the module is pretty much a sealed unit so I didn't worry so much about having it exposed to the elements.

Here, I'm putting the clutch adjuster plate (or release plate) in place with the snap ring to follow.

To set the initial clutch adjustment, first screw the threaded adjuster in until it just touches the pushrod, then back it out 1/2 turn and lock it (some photos have been borrowed from earlier sequences).

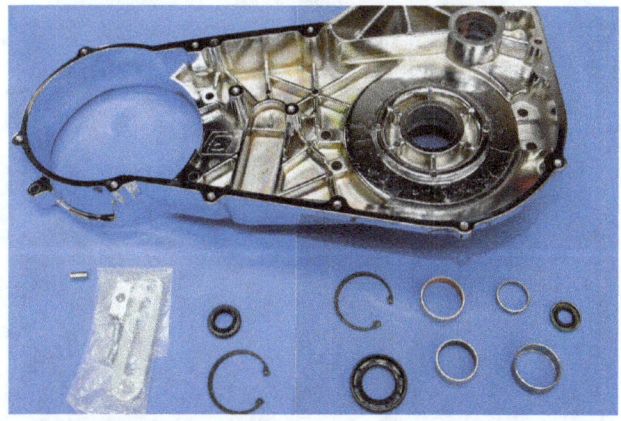

Aftermarket outer primary assemblies require some assembly. Start by washing everything in hot water and soap, check all bores and threads for chrome build-up. If in doubt, ask an experienced tech.

Clutch Assembly

The aftermarket clutch from RevTech seen here eliminates the stock "spring plate" and uses an extra plate and disc in its place.

My aftermarket clutch assembly (an "extra plate" clutch) came as seen on the left. The conversion from assorted parts to an assembled clutch assembly took place at Full Throttle in North St. Paul, Minnesota. So far this clutch works fine with the 121 inch TP Engineering motor, though I probably don't run the bike as hard as some.

You won't be doing this in your home shop, unless you have a press. Not to worry however, any good shop with a press can assemble your clutch for you.

With a little oil on the surfaces the clutch hub is set into the clutch shell.

The press is used to combine the two into one assembly.

Clutch Assembly

A snap ring on the back side guaranteed that the hub and shell remain one assembly.

After all the discs and plates are installed, the diaphragm plate goes in as shown...

Discs are soaked in primary fluid before being dropped into place.

...the press and adapter are used to compress the spring, and the snap ring holds it all together.

The discs and plates alternate. There is no up and down on these discs or plates.

One press, one skilled mechanic, a little patience — bingo, one complete clutch assembly.

Chrome Allens for the outer primary are not all the same length. Use blue Loctite and tighten evenly to 9-10 ft. lbs.

The regulator must have a good ground. Scrape the paint off the frame behind the regulator and use star washers to ensure a good electrical connection.

Our harness kit came with everything we needed except the plugs, pins and shrink wrap. Buy a harness matched to your needs, i.e. with or w/o blinkers, and be sure you know where the major electrical components are going before installing the harness.

Like most current bike builders I wanted the wires hidden, which meant drilling holes in the frame so the main harness could enter the top tube just ahead of the battery, and the sub-harnesses could emerge from the tube just behind the front edge of the gas tanks. A more organized person could have figured all this out during the mock up and drilled the holes in the frame before paint.

I spent a lot of time with the main harness and the wiring diagram, sorting the wires into groups that run to: 1. Left and right handlebar switches. 2. Ignition switch. 3. Headlight (and front blinkers). 4. Taillight and rear blinkers. 5. Miscellaneous wires for the horn and oil sender.

I drilled holes in top tube just behind the front edge of the gas tank (note photos) so I could hide the plastic terminal blocks behind the edge of the tank. I then grouped all the wires that ran to one side of the handlebars for example, and put them in a piece of shrink tube (purchased from the local Donnie Smith Custom Cycles shop) and then ran that group of wires up through the top tube and out the hole behind the neck. I used a piece of light welding rod as my pull wire.

There is only one way to do the wiring, slowly and with patience. It took me a long time to sort the wires, match the wires in the harness with the wires in the handlebars and install the pins and terminal blocks. There is more than one kind of plastic terminal block and matching pin system used (check the Wiring chapter). I used the non-waterproof plugs and pins. When I ran out of components one Sunday, I found very similar components at the local Radio Shack (though the terminal blocks and pins are not identical to the pre-1996 H-D components). No matter which system you use, be sure to buy a good crimping tool. This will ensure that the pins slide into the terminal plugs neatly, and snap correctly into place so they can't back out when you push together the male and female terminal blocks.

In hindsight, I would have used factory style handlebar switches instead of aftermarket switches because: they're cheaper, probably of at least equal quality and the wires are color coded. The little aftermarket switches with their small buttons do look cool but...

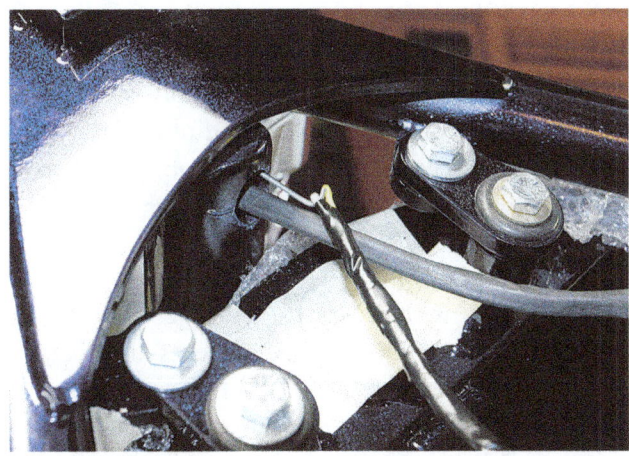

Here you can see the hole I drilled in the back of the top tube, and the pull wire I fished through the top tube from a hole up near the neck.

I used pre-1996 non-waterproof connectors, available at nearly any good V-twin motorcycle shop.

Here's the same group of wires after being pulled up through the top tube.

You have to do a double crimp to get the pins on the wires...

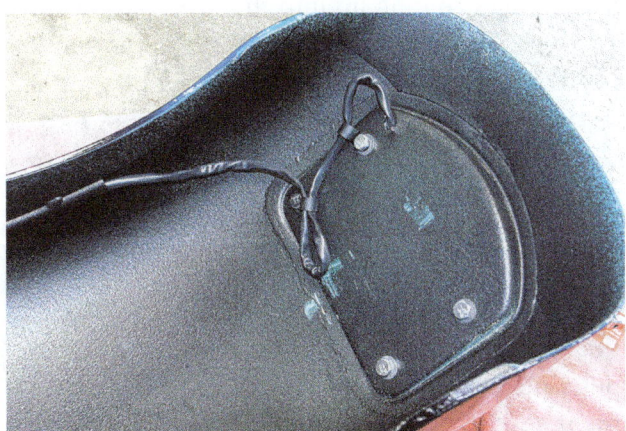

Backside of the Wernimont rear fender. Blinkers are integral with the light, all wires emerge from the back of the light into a harness held in place by clips. The harness plugs into main harness near the battery.

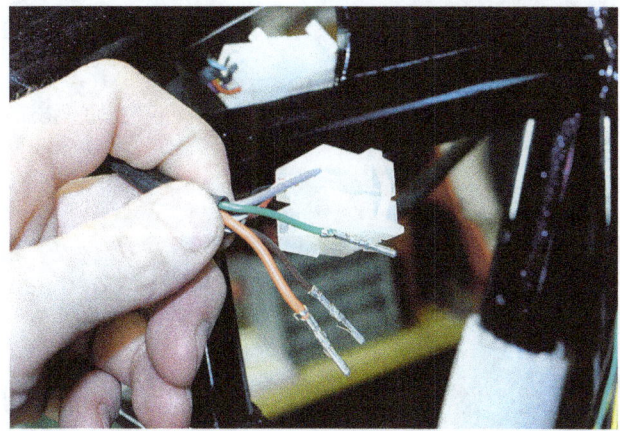

...and then insert the pins in the terminal blocks in the right position so they match up with wires coming from the handle bar switches or the headlight. Be sure each one snaps into place so none can back out.

Here you can see the two halves of the terminal block plugged together. I placed the terminal blocks just behind the front edge of the gas tank.

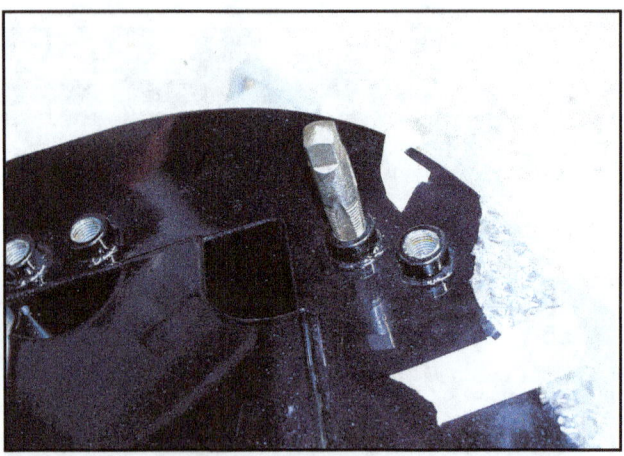

Like all the other painted parts, the oil tank needs to have all the threads chased. The tank also needs to be flushed, some people use denatured alcohol.

I used a Donnie Smith coil bracket and coils. The coils were later sanded smooth and painted to match the bike.

I have three switches on each side of the bars, the pattern is much like a stock bike with start and kill switch on the right switch assembly, as well as high-low and horn on the left, and of course a blinker button either side. I had trouble with the starter button sticking and eventually moved the start "switch" to the spring loaded ignition switch.

Just a couple more electrical comments.

1.) There are two ways to wire the blinker switches, be sure you wire the switches and the lights correctly so they work the first time. 2.) A lot of electrical problems are caused by bad grounds. Make sure the regulator and the ground cable(s) ground to bare steel. 3.) If you've never wired a bike before, don't be afraid to seek help. Some first-time builders take the bike to someone else for wiring.

OIL TANK, LINES, FENDER AND BRAKES.

In the rear, I put the caliper in the apex of the swingarm, because I think it looks really neat that way. The downside is the fact that it's a tight fit and the PM caliper ended up inverted, so to bleed the rear brakes I have to pull the caliper off (not an easy task), put a spacer between the pads and bleed the caliper while holding it so the bleeder is at the top. I hid the brake light switch behind the tranny, but installing the junction there was a pain, next time I'm going to use a banjo-bolt switch on the master cylinder, even if it's not quite as cool.

The front brake caliper was easy to install, and bleeding was a breeze. Basically I filled the reservoir, did multiple short strokes until I no longer had bubbles coming up into the reservoir, then did a series of full strokes, held the lever in the applied position and opened the bleeder. After blasting a froth of brake fluid and air across the shop, I closed the bleeder, released the lever and repeated the process until there was only pure, clean brake fluid leaving the bleeder.

As we keep explaining, the fenders can't be too closes to the tire or they will rub the tire the first time you run it up to 80 or 90 miles per hour. I put a piece of tubing on the tire (as shown), then spent a lot of time making sure I had the fender positioned the way I wanted before drilling holes. Of course, these should have been drilled during mock up. To prevent any peeling paint I drilled

Tucking the caliper into the apex of the swingarm looks good, but it was tough to get it to fit.

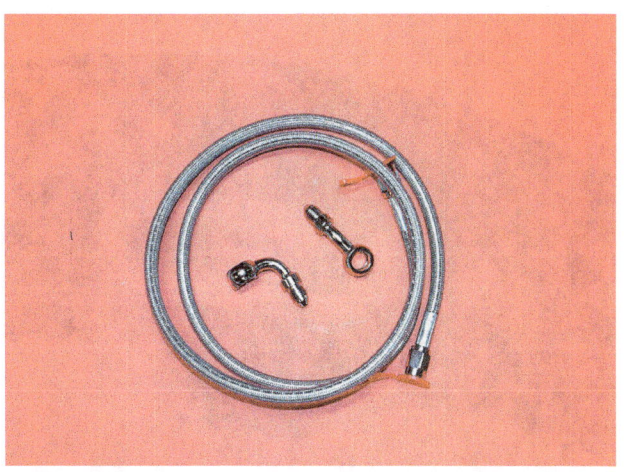

Though the new trend is to the plastic "pro line" I used braided stainless lines and cables.

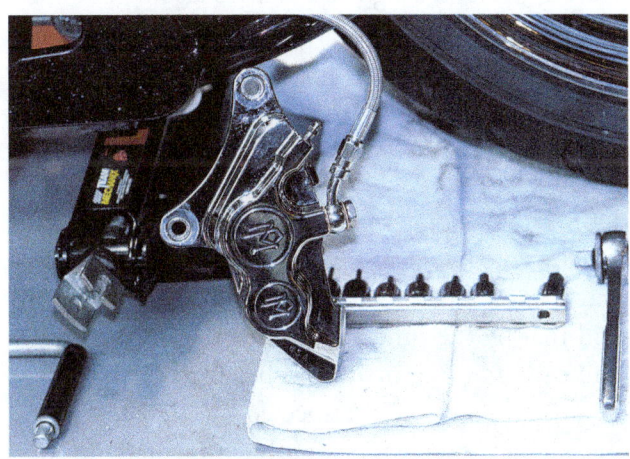

Because the bleeder ended up at the bottom (not the top where the air would be) I had to pull the caliper off and invert it to do the bleeding.

You need at least a quarter inch of clearance between the fender and tire, the hose shown here provides that clearance.

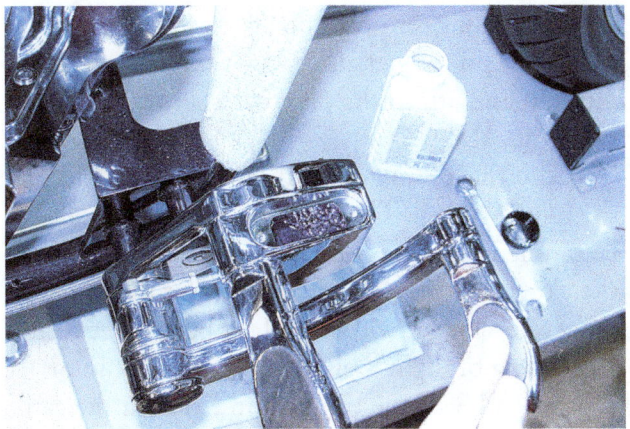

I used a long series of short strokes to bleed the master first. Note the bubbles. Once you get no bubbles you can bleed the line and caliper.

Here the fender is mocked up and the holes are marked for drilling. A small change in position makes a big difference in the look, spend time determining the exact fender location.

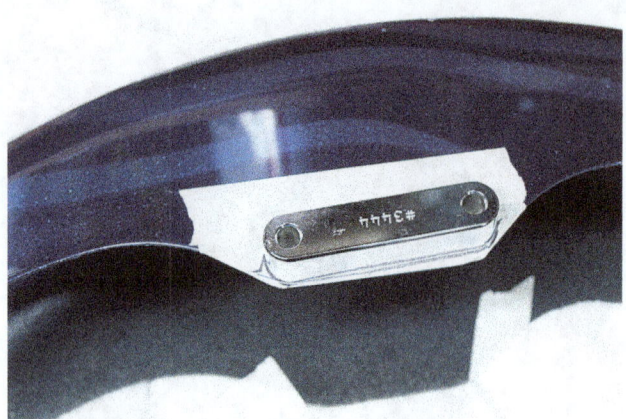

I used the fender spacers as my templates for drilling.

Here you can see the outline of the spacer, and the stepped drill I used for drilling the sheet-metal fenders.

Almost a motorcycle. The front fender is in place, the rear is ready to bolt on. Ready to start except that the coils are out being painted

through multiple layers of masking tape.

Installing the oil tank is a no-brainier, except that the lines have to be run correctly so you don't starve the engine when you first fire it up, and the tank needs to be flushed out because it's probably full of shit from the manufacturing process and the painting. You also need to take time to mount the tank so gaps between tank and frame are even all the way around.

THROTTLE, FINAL DETAILS, FIRST START

Single and double pull cables are available and I chose the single option. Running the cable is pretty simple, though you do have to be sure it can't be kinked, and can't be stretched during a turn or you may inadvertently find yourself accelerating through a tight corner. It's also a good idea to lube the cable with some light lubricant before installation.

By this time I knew the engine turned over, that the lights worked and that all the lubricant levels were full. As a bit of insurance, I invited Don Tima, engine man for Donnie Smith Custom Cycles, to come over for the first test firing. This way I knew I had all the oil lines routed correctly and that by the time we finished the initial timing and carb adjustments would be correct. And because Don is a well respected mechanic, it also meant that if there was a problem on start-up the problem wouldn't be blamed on my installation. To ensure we had oil pressure, I hooked up an old signal light as my "oil light." I attached one lead to the battery and one to the oil sender switch. Then we cranked it over until the light went out - so we knew we had oil pressure. Now we could put the plugs in and attach the plug wires and hit the switch for real.

And the TP motor fired immediately. To hear the motor run the first time is a great rush, one I recommend highly to anyone who hasn't built their own motorcycle. We let the motor run for longer and longer with a cool off period between. Don Tima brought a big fan to keep the motor cool when he set the timing and adjusted the carb.

A few days later I took the bike for the first cautious road test. The shocks were set a little on the stiff side and the rear brake was spongy, but otherwise the bike worked and ran well.

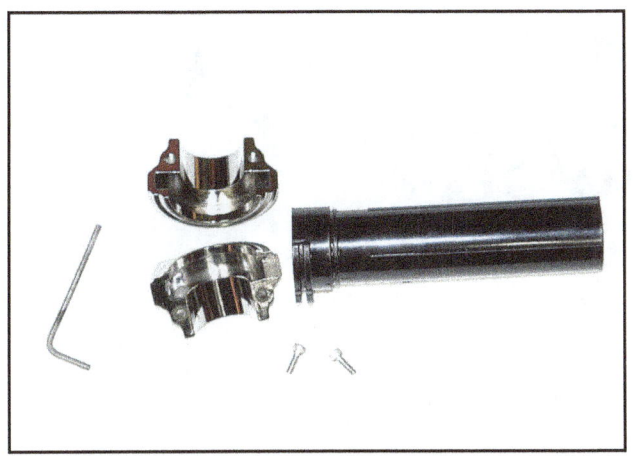

Use a little light lube when assembling the throttle...

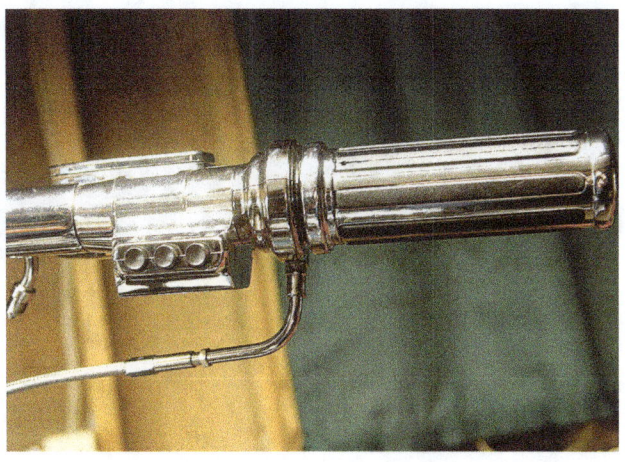

The right side handle bar end. Simple aftermarket grips, PM switch assembly and master cylinder.

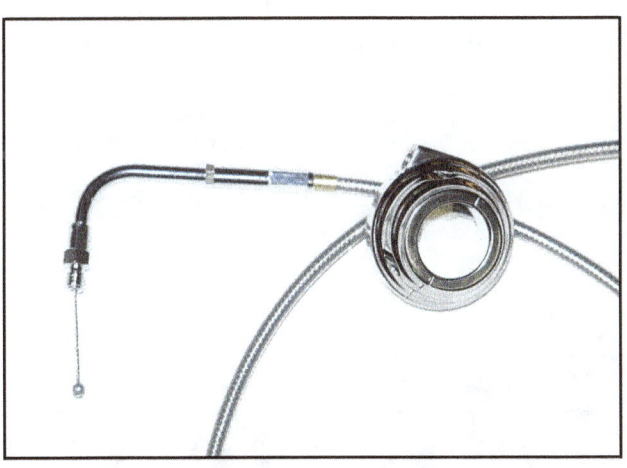

...and use some spray lube on the cable as well. I (obviously) used a single cable system.

Finally outside. The seat, from Kevin at Lemans Seat Company, includes a subtle flamed pattern to match the subtle Jon Kosmoski flamed paint.

Spend some time planning the way you're going to route the throttle cable. It can't be pinched by the tank and it can't be "pulled" when you turn the bars.

The two-into-one pipe is a Kerker, mirrors from Kuryakyn. Finished bike matches my goals: simple, clean and fast. To make room for another project, however, the bike is FOR SALE. See wolfpub.com.

Chapter Eight

Donnie Smith One-off

The Art of Fabrication

When it comes to building beautiful, functional motorcycles, there are very few bike builders with the experience, class and attention to detail displayed by Donnie Smith and crew. Built for Larry Page from Richmond, Virginia, the bike seen here started as a hardtail frame from Frank at Motorcycle Works in Olathe, Kansas. This particular frame is a long one, with 5 inches of stretch and a 42 degree rake angle. The rear section is wide enough to accommodate an Avon 300-35

Long, low and lean, a 300 tire custom with hand-fabricated gas tank from the shop of Donnie Smith.

rear tire and retain the 1-1/2 inch belt drive. The other end of the bike runs a slim 21-90/90, also from, Avon. Both tires mount to PM Contour wheels. The motor is a 124 inch Twin Cam from S&S connected to a Baker right-side-drive transmission. To avoid surprises later, the mock up is done with the real engine and transmission.

Getting Started

Rob Roehl, longtime employee at Donnie's shop and the man responsible for the mock up and fabrication of this bike, starts by building in a new battery box. This frame is designed to have the battery box located above the tranny mount. Rob and Donnie have decided however, to build in a nice neat, hidden battery box behind the mount. Building the box means cutting out the existing supports for the transmission mount, (note the before and after photos). As Rob explains, "with the supports out of the way I can build a battery box, once I have that done I will box-in new supports for the transmission."

To make room for the new battery and tray, Rob cut one tube out of the bottom of the frame, "the tube we left in still provides lots of strength," explains Rob. "And the boxing plates add strength too. On the bikes with a 145 inch engine I won't cut out that other bottom tube, for reasons of strength."

Small threaded tabs are welded to the frame so the battery tray can bolt in from underneath.

Power is provided by a 124 inch Twin Cam engine from S&S. Bolted on behind is a six-speed, right side drive dyna-style transmission from Baker.

Built by Motorcycle Works in Olathe, Kansas, this very strong drop-seat style frame is the foundation for the whole project. The frame, and the sheet metal, determine the profile of the motorcycle. The front end is from Perse, and initially came a little too long for this particular project.

As delivered, the frame comes with the rear tranny mount well supported....

The cover will be part of the whole box, which will bolt in as a complete unit once it's done.

...but Rob cuts out the supports for the mount in order to locate the battery just behind the mount.

Plates shown will be welded in to replace the supports cut out earlier.

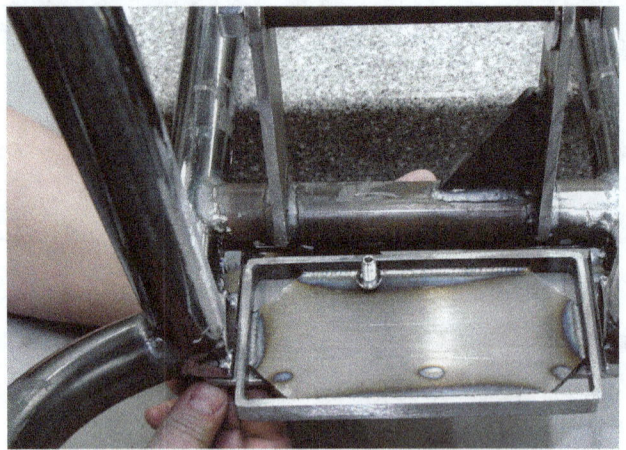

Rob cut out the bottom tube and made the tray. Then he made small tabs, threaded and welded to the bottom of the frame, that the tray bolts to.

Seat pan is finished, formed from 14 gauge cold rolled steel. Rob has already started working on the tunnel for the tank.

Form a Gas Tank from Scratch

Once the battery box is finished, Rob can move on to the biggest single piece of fabrication that will be done on this bike, the creation of the hand built gas tank. "I'm trying something new with this tank," explains Rob. "I made the tunnel first, and I'm going to work without a sketch. I will get the basic shape going and then refine it. The shape is modeled after an old Sportster tank, what they used to call the Elvis tank. The first step is to cut out the top of the tank a little oversize. The tunnel is made from 14 gauge steel, though the rest of the tank is 16 gauge.

As Rob explains, "by doing it this way I can do the mounts before the shell goes on. The bottom seam should be the last thing I do, and because I used an edge roller on the edge of the bottom, it has a lot of strength there, so there should be no movement or warpage when I weld up that seam."

Rob designed the bike so the electronics mount under the seat. "I will run the plug wires up through the frame, and then down to the cylinders. The circuit breakers will mount on the same plate the ignition module mounts to, the

The rear fender started as a blank.

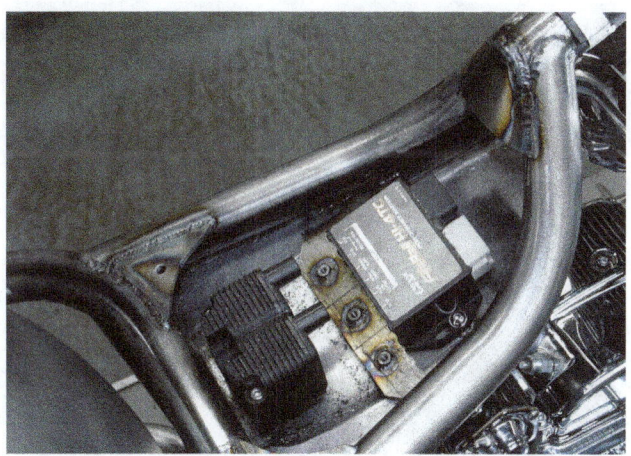

The mock up needs to be as complete as possible, including the location of all major electrical components and how the wires will be routed.

Note how the battery box is boxed in, "the battery drops out the bottom."

Rob made the runnel for the tank first, and will form the top panel to match his idea for the shape, and to match the length of the tunnel.

99

Rob used his bead roller to put a lip in the outer edge of the tank bottom.

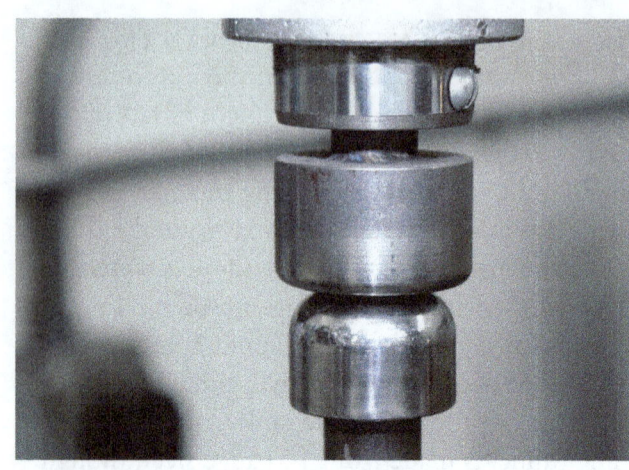

These are the basic stretching dies Rob uses for projects like the tank top (shrinking dies are available as well).

Most of the shaping for the tank top is done with the power hammer.

The English wheel is another stretching operation, one done by squeezing the metal between two wheels (note the photo on the next page).

This is essentially a stretching operation, more crown means more time spent on that area with the power hammer.

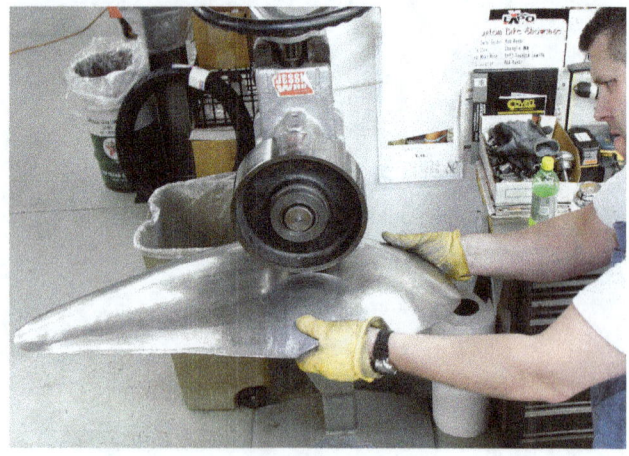

Rob patiently runs the tank top back and forth through the wheels to raise metal through the center of the tank.

wires can run down the frame tubes. Small tubes at the back of the frame support the fender, then I will probably fill in the areas between the fender and the frame (at the front of the rear fender)."

METAL WORK
Shape the Tank Top

After cutting out a piece of 16 gauge cold rolled steel, Rob uses the power hammer to do the initial shaping. "Basically I'm stretching the metal," explains Rob. Next, he moves to the English wheel, "I start with a pretty aggressive wheel on so it's going to raise the crown pretty fast. The wheel will also smooth out the lumps from the power hammer."

Next, he takes the top of the tank and shapes it by hand. Then it's back to the English wheel with a flatter, lower wheel. "I want to get more shape the short way so I change to a less aggressive wheel. The first wheel was so aggressive it almost left grooves in the metal so I'm using the flatter

To raise the metal more the short way, Rob turns the top 90 degrees and begins a series of back and forth motions.

This close up shows the lip Rob put on the edge of the tank bottom, which adds strength to the edge and will prevent warpage when that seam is welded later.

A variety of lower wheels are available, this mildly crowned roller is Rob's choice for much of the early wheel work.

It's important to take frequent breaks to evaluate the shape as it progresses.

Sometimes there's no better tool than a strong back and a pair of willing hands.

Though it's a little hard to see, Rob has the top formed, as well as the tunnel, the two are tack-welded together. Time now to make the side panels...

Rob often uses the slap hammer to roll and edge.

...which start as pieces of light board cut to size...

The leather face on he slap hammer means the tool leaves the metal unmarked.

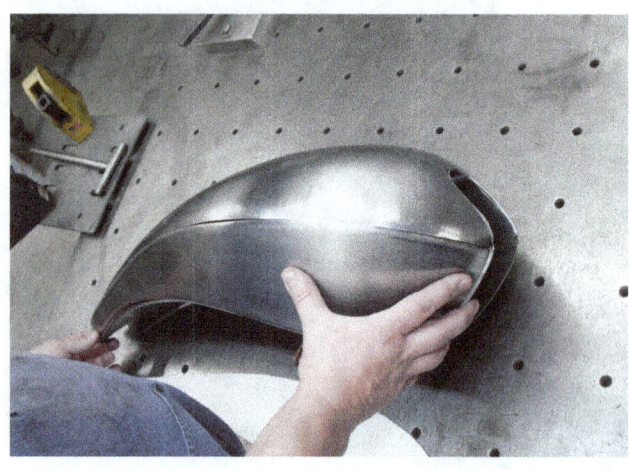

...the panels are then cut out of 16 gauge steel, rolled out over a big piece of pipe for the initial shape and then run through the English wheel.

With the help of a ruler, you can see how the side panel is crowned in both directions.

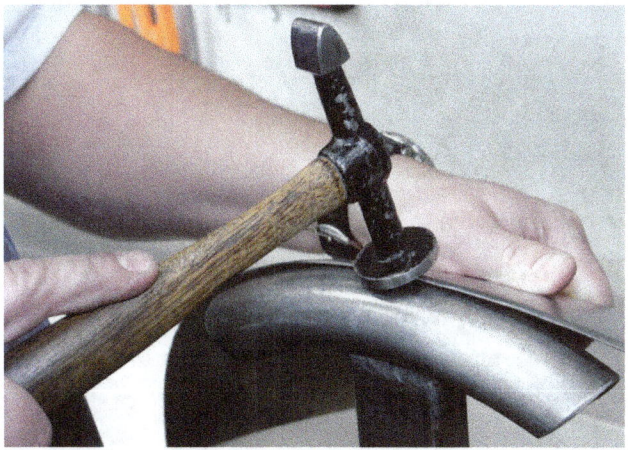

A body hammer and home-made anvil are used to roll the edges of the side panels.

Now Rob starts to add more crown to the side panel by running it...

...through the English wheel.

wheel running the short way to get rid of that and add some shape, pretty soon I will pull it out and evaluate my shape."

"Now I want to create a little more shape at the edges with the slap hammer and the dolly. I'm just trying to add shape, I can deal with the puckers later. The slap hammer is nice because it doesn't dent anything, and with the leather face, it doesn't even mark the metal."

Once Rob is finished rolling out the top, he trims it pretty much to size and tack welds it to the tunnel, which is already fabricated. "I don't finish weld till I'm right at the end," explains Rob, "just a couple of little tacks will hold the top and tunnel together."

TANK SIDE PANELS

For the side panels, Rob takes poster board, makes templates and then cuts the panels out of steel. To do the initial shaping, Rob rolls the panel over a piece of pipe, then does a bit of work with the 'wheel. Not entirely happy with the shape, Rob rolls the edges with a hammer and dolly and then runs the panel through the wheel again.

Before beginning to tack weld the tank together, Rob tapes the side panels in place.

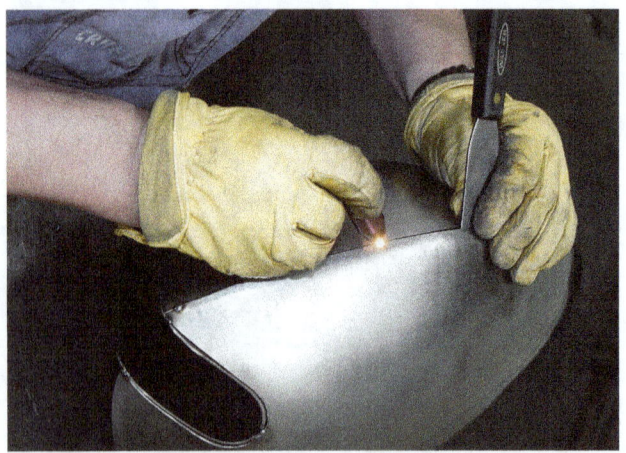

Note the way a putty knife is used to prevent one panel form sliding over or under the other, welder is set at 80 amps DC for the tack welding.

Rob uses just a few tacks to hold the panel in place, then assesses the fit before going any farther.

Before welding the side panel to the top and bottom, Rob needs to trim it to size. "A lot of times I tape a panel to the other parts and then do the trimming, it means I don't have to have so many hands. Once the trimming is done, I'm going to work on the side seam, tack weld it, then drop out the tunnel and work at finishing the seam. The bottom seam will be done last. The hardest part of making the side panels is getting them both the same."

TACK WELDING

"The most important thing to remember during the tacking process is to keep the joints butted together and not overlapped. I can close up the gaps later but if you overlap the joint you never get that out of it. The seam is so strong at that one point that you can't hammer it or shape it."

"At this point the bottom seam looks a little uneven but all that will pull in when I do the welding. Now I'm going to cut the tack welds and drop out the tunnel. Once I separate the top of the tank from the tunnel I can work both sides of the seam with hammer and dolly and slapper."

In one area the seam is low, so Rob rolls the top of the tank over and raises the metal from the back side. "Once I've got the seam pretty even I

Rob does a bit of work on the seam as he moves along with the tack welding.

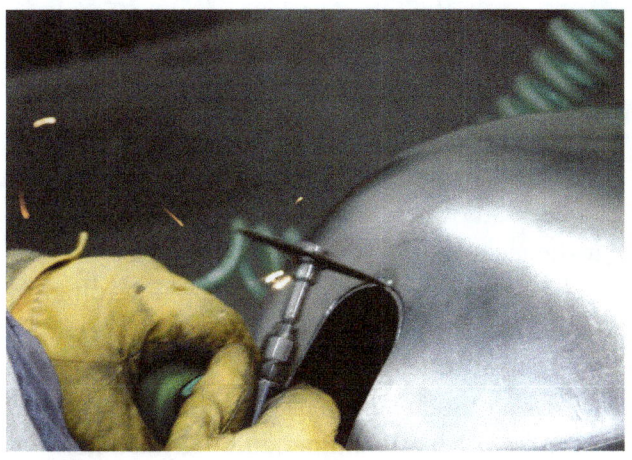

Because the tank top is held in place with just a few tack welds, Rob can cut those...

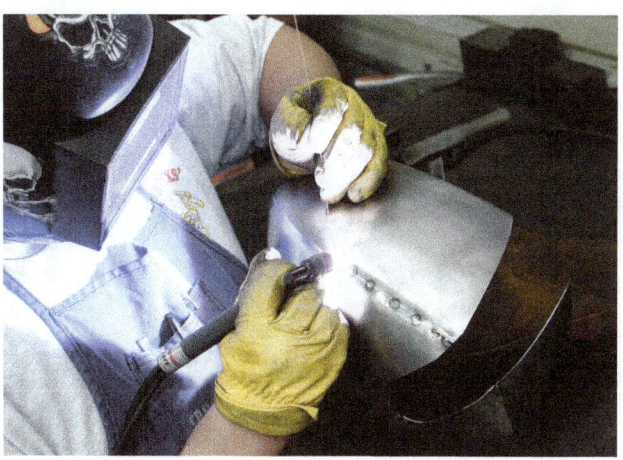

Tack welds are spaced evenly...

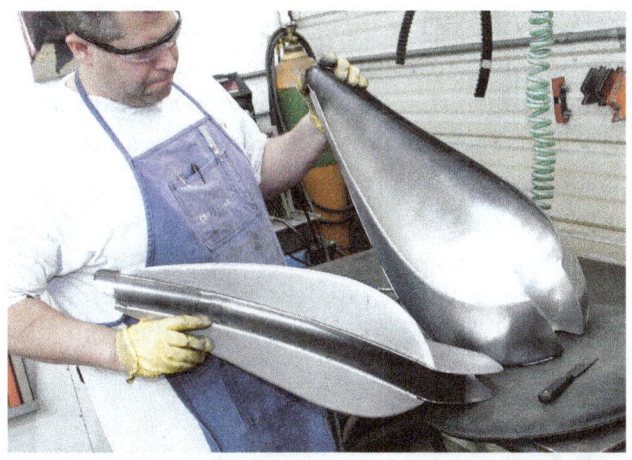

...and separate the two halves of the tank before proceeding farther.

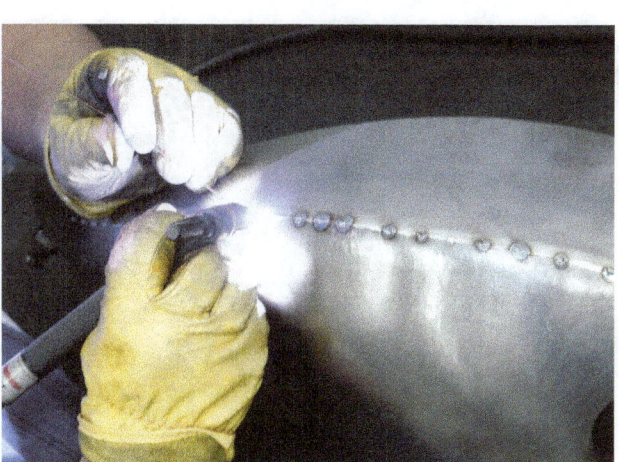

...down the side of the tank.

With no bottom, Rob can easily get at both sides of the seam and ensure that the seam is nice and smooth before finishing the rest of the tacks.

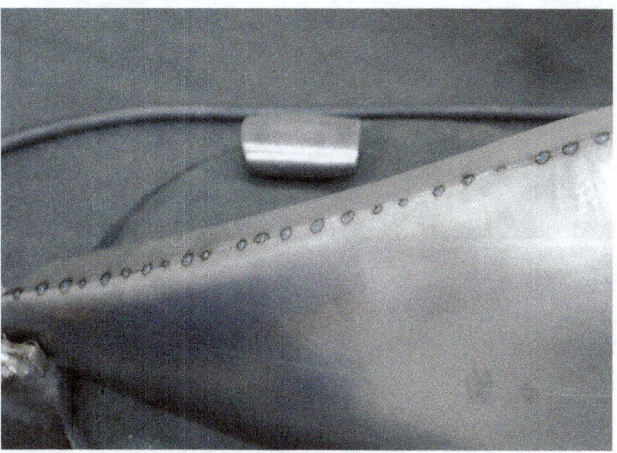

When he's done, Rob has a nice neat seam, with evenly spaced tack welds and no overlapping seams. And he can still get at both sides of the seam.

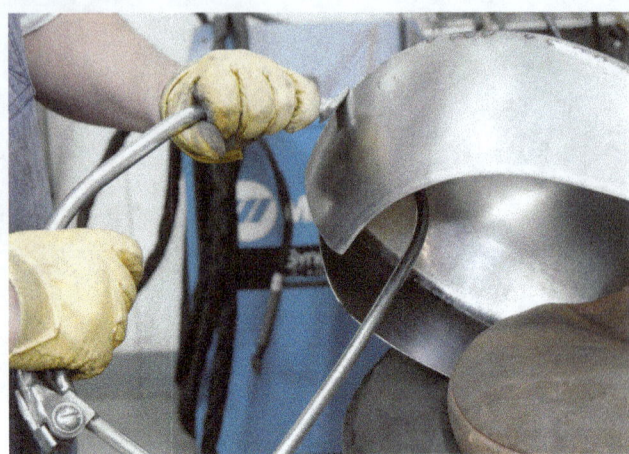

This is the bull's eye pick as described in the text, it's kind of a pick and dolly all in one, good for raising small areas.

The true beauty of Rob's plan is the ease with which he can get at the back side of the seam to correct a low spot before final welding begins.

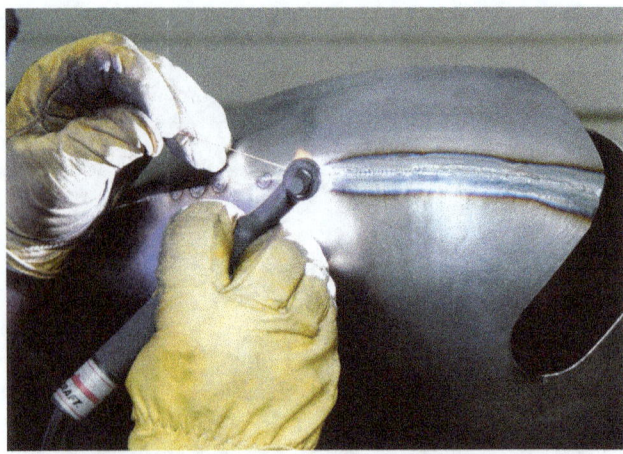

Rob does the final welding with 70 S2 rods, 1/16th inch diameter, "I pick the size of the rod by the gap I have to fill."

can come in and fill in some of my tacks."

There's a little overlap at the front of the seam, Rob tries the bull's eye pick, then a little work with a hammer working over a stationary dolly. "It raised the low part of the seam pretty well. If it had been any worse than this I would have had to cut the tack welds." The seam is looking pretty good now so Rob starts in on the final welding.

"I do an inch and a half of the seam, then stop, look at it, let it cool a little bit, and go back. I don't find much advantage in doing a lot of work on the seam with a hammer and dolly as I go. This seam has a lot of strength because of the shape, and I have it fitting pretty good right from the start, so I can just go over it with a small grinder later.

With the side seam is finished, Rob can weld the bottom, or tunnel, into the tank. As mentioned earlier, this seam is easier to weld without much warpage because both edges have a little shape right where they meet.

THE BOXED STRUCTURE

"I'm going to make this boxed structure under the top tube, which will help to stiffen the frame, and also give me a good place to put the front

In the hands of a craftsman, the tig welder leaves a very neat seam with a small heat-affected-zone.

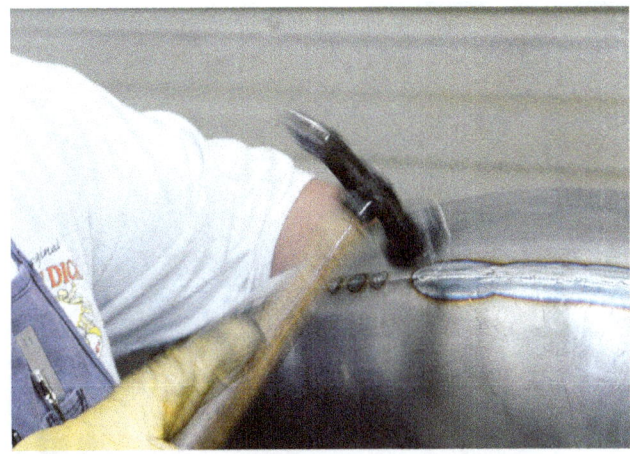

The final welding isn't done all at once, because too much heat would likely cause warpage. Instead, it's done in sections...

Welding in the bottom will be done now - after the side seams are fully finished.

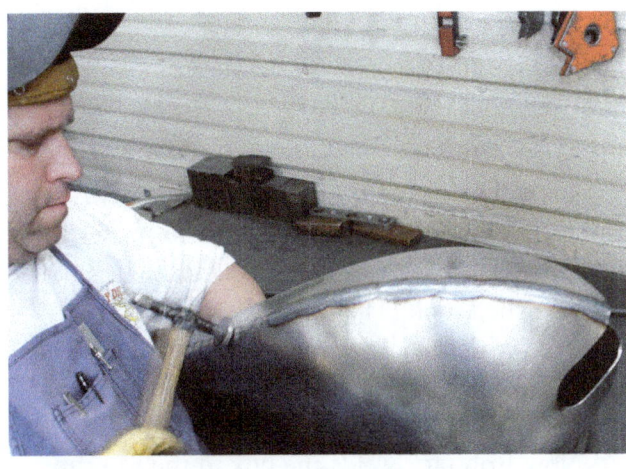

...with time to work the seam, and let it cool, in between welding.

The test fit shows a very nicely curved tank with all the lines converging at the back.

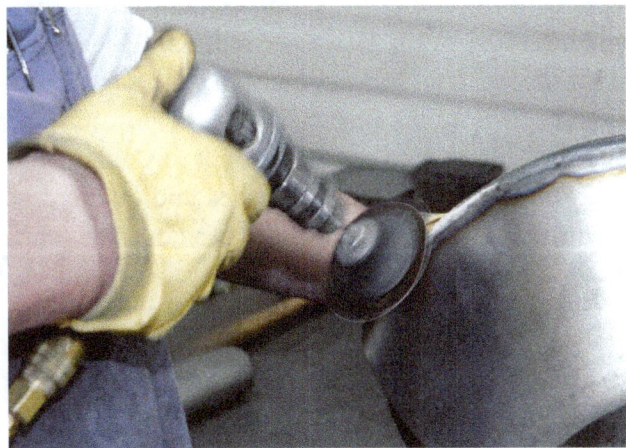

Though a heavier gauge of steel is harder to work, it also means Rob can use a sander on the seam without any danger of over-thinning the metal.

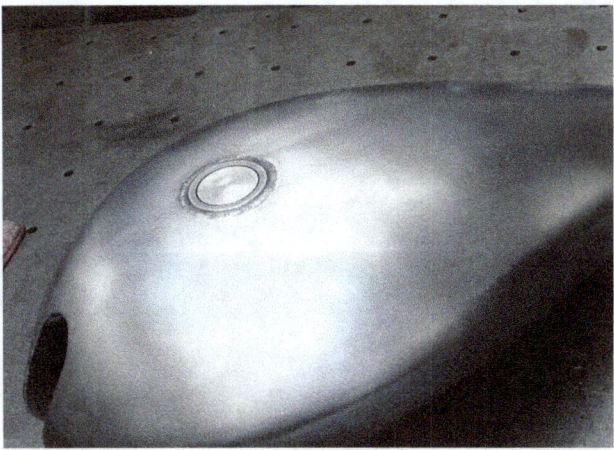

After a little metal-finishing the tank hardly needs any filler.

107

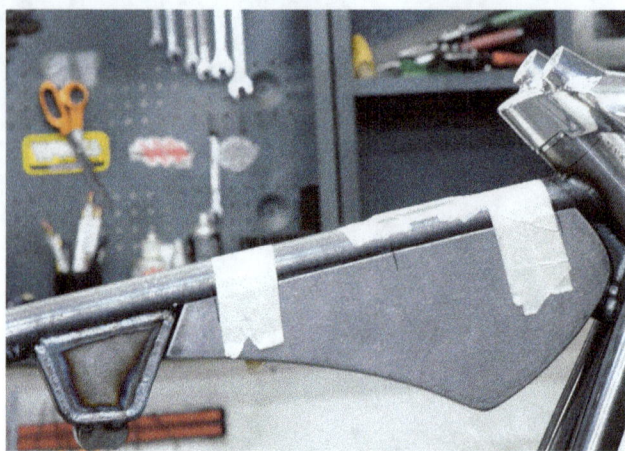

This boxed structure under the top tube will add strength to the frame and also form an external "bottom" to the gas tank.

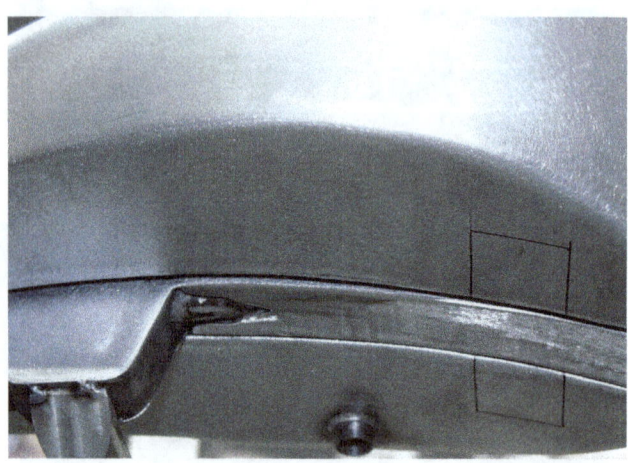

Once he's happy with the fitment of the tank and the boxed structure, Rob marks the location of the front tank mount.

the next task is to carefully cut along the outline of the mount with a cutoff wheel.

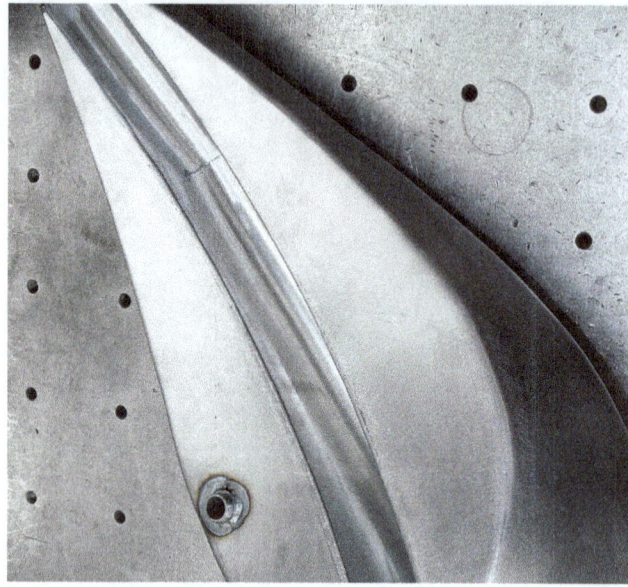

The bottom of the tank is every bit as nice as the top, so nice it's a shame to cut holes for the tank mounts.

mount. In the rear I will use a regular T-mount."

The box is made from 1/8th inch plate. As Rob explains, "The boxed section also makes a very nice 'bottom' for the gas tank and gives it a nice finished look. The fitment of the box and tank are critical. I always spend a good bit of time fine tuning the position of the boxed section and the tank."

Now Rob tack welds the box to the top tube. Small panels still have to be added at the front of the box to close it in. Rob spends a lot of time ensuring that the tank and the inner box line up exactly at the front of the tank before starting the final welding of the boxed section, As is usual, he does the welds in short stitches. After two stitches he uses the slap hammer to adjust the position of the box slightly and then goes back to welding.

The boxed structure is finished and adjusted slightly to match the bottom of the tank, the tank itself is ready for mounts. Note, the rear mount is already cut out, the photos show Rob cutting out the bottom of the tank where the front mount will be installed. After the holes are cut Rob does a test fit then trims the holes with a mini-belt sander. "This is also the optimum time to eliminate all the pieces and grit from the tank," explains Rob.

"I always weld the mounts in as one piece,"

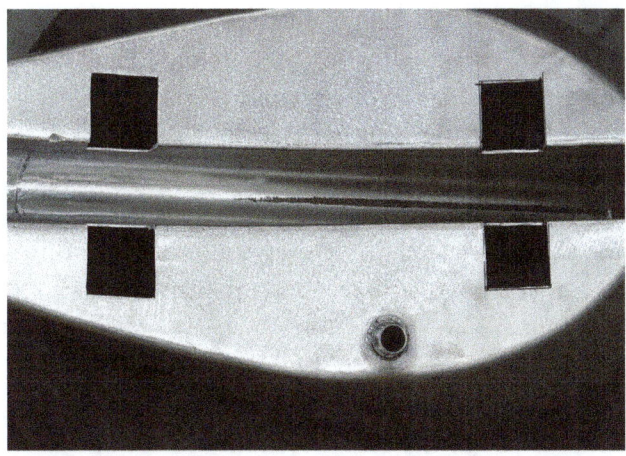

The bottom with the two mounts areas cut out and ready for mounts.

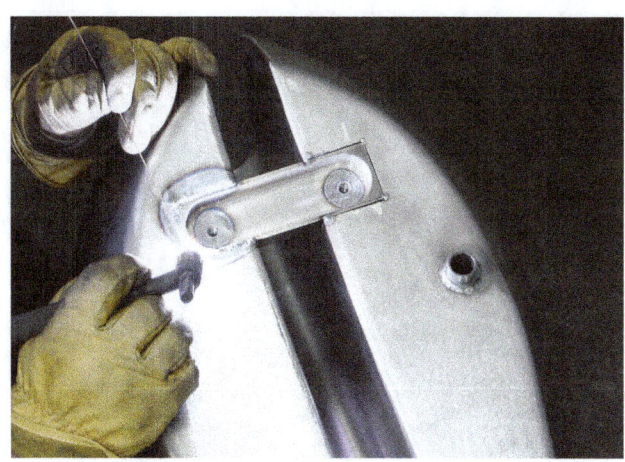

Welding starts with a tack weld at each corner.

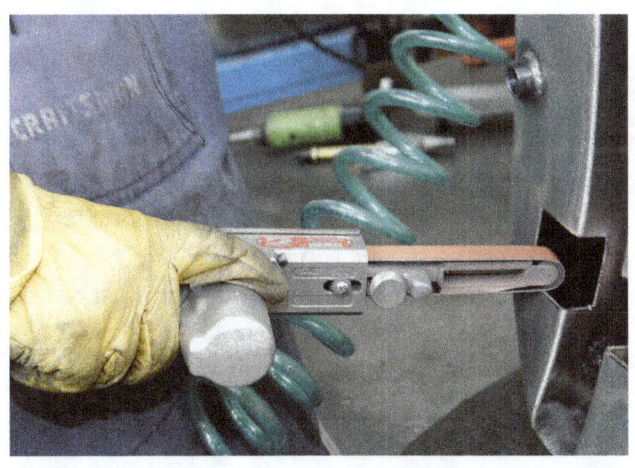

But first Rob trims the holes for a perfect fit with his mini belt sander.

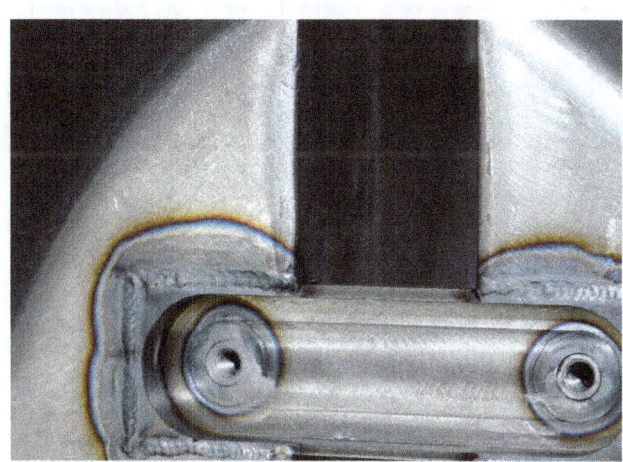

Before the finish welding can be done.

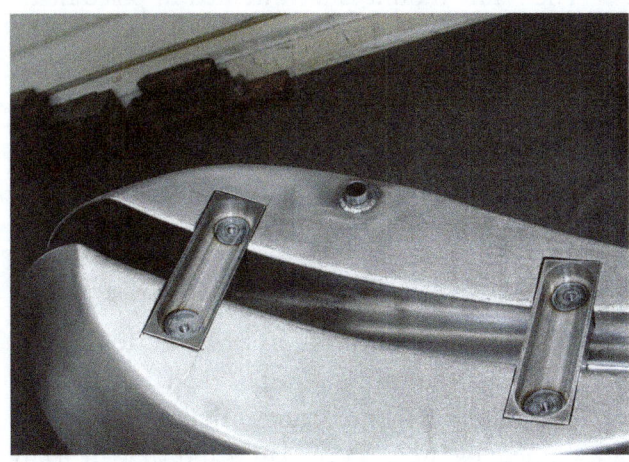

Before welding, note the nice flush fit and the minimal gap between the tank and the mounts.

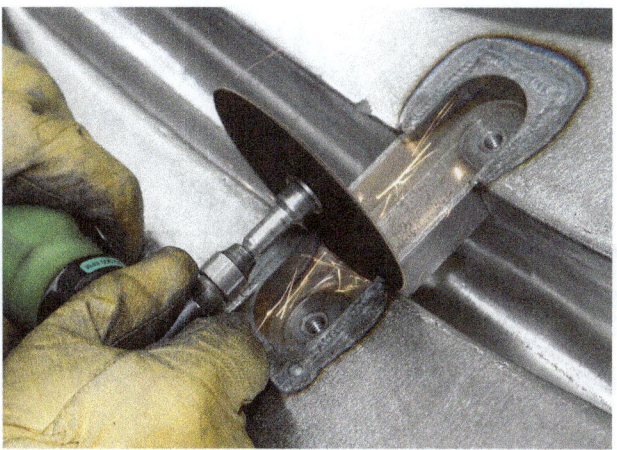

The center piece is cut out after all the welding is finished and the tank has had a chance to cool off.

Both mounts are cut out in the center...

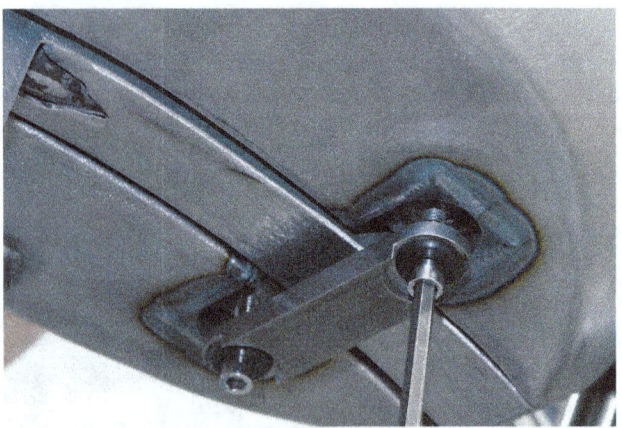

...then the tank is dropped on again, and the frame part of the mount is screwed up into place and marked on the lower box structure.

Now Rob does a cut out for the mount.

explains Rob, "and then cut the center out later. That way the tank doesn't suck in and change dimension when I'm welding. I set the welder at about 125 amps, because these mounts are heavier, and then during the welding I concentrate the power on the heavier piece and feather it out into the sheet metal." The welding is done in sections, Rob works on one corner first, then lets it cool and switches to the opposite corner.

Rob lets the tank cool for a good 15 minutes before cutting out the center sections of the mounts. Once the center sections are cut out, the rough edges need to be trimmed (with the mini-belt grinder again) so they're flush with the sides of the tunnel. (These mount 'kits' are available from Donnie Smith)

It's interesting to note the way Rob uses the big magnets to position the tank so the seams are easy to get at, and the way he uses a small block of steel as a rest for his hand. Note, the rubber pads, these regular softail tank cushions are used on the frame all through the process so the tank floats and isn't resting on the top tube.

With the frame mount screwed into place, Rob marks the boxed structure where it needs to be cut. "I'm just going to notch this with the cut-off wheel to match the thickness of the mount." Now the frame mount is screwed into place with the tank in place also, and two small wooden wedges are pushed into place to hold the tank centered on the boxed structure.

The frame mount is tack welded in place first, then the wedges are removed. Then the bolts are removed. What's left is final welding (the rubber cushions are removed before final welding) and the installation of the rear mount for the tank. "We usually wrap the upper tube with foam, that way it won't set up a buzz when the bike is running.

Hand Fabricated Exhaust Pipes

At the Donnie Smith shop, hand-fabricated exhaust pipes start as a set of port collars, as Rob explains, "Johnny (John Galvin) makes them in-house, he cuts them on the lathe and they fit really nice. I start from the collars with 1-3/4 inch pipe, then I come out from the port an inch and a half

The tank is carefully positioned on the mount as described in the text.

The custom exhausts pipes start as a pair of these machined collars and a piece of 1-3/4 inch mild steel tubing.

Now the tank is lifted off and the mount can be final-welded to the frame (rubber mounts are taken off for the final welding sequence).

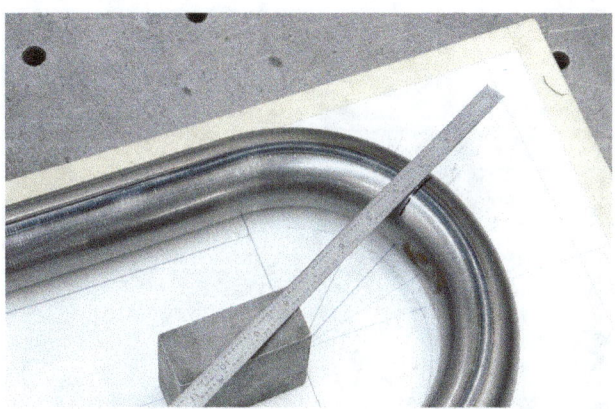

"I made this little cut gauge because when you cut tubing you have to be sure to cut on the centerline. otherwise it won't match the pipe you come up against, the curve isn't round."

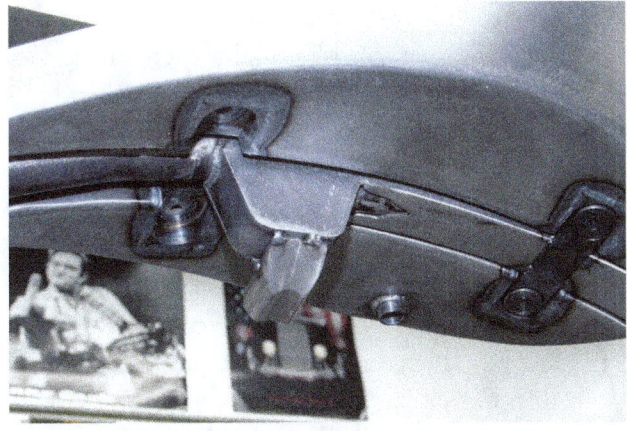

Nearly finished, the flush-mount mounts. "These mounts are pretty heavy, we've never had a problem. The front mount is the most important, that's where all the weight is."

It's important to clean any burrs off the edges of the pipes before welding.

Rob starts with two short header pipes that bend inward to "frame the engine."

Tape lines are used, as shown, to check the line created by the pipes.

Rob tries to make the two pipes the same length, "but it isn't always possible."

before the pipes turn. I always try to frame the motor with the pipes, the actual layout varies from bike to bike in terms of the angle and the spread. I go from 1-3/4 to 2 inches, then to 2-1/4 inches. In terms of power and runability, that design works well for motors from 80 inches all the way to 124, it will work good on this too."

"This is 16 gauge tubing, I mark it as shown and then cut it on the band saw. I used to buy the material from Headers by Ed. Different radiuses are available All are mandrel bent, which is important because the process doesn't crush the pipes. Muffler shops can't do this and keep the pipe round. Another supplier is SPD in California. Don't go to a muffler shop and buy aluminized tubing, because it's hard to weld and hard to chrome. Use good mild steel pipe."

"You have to cut the curves on the centerline, (note the photo on the preceding page). When you cut them like this they stay round, I butt weld them with nothing inside the pipe. Sometimes I figure the layouts by just holding the U-bend up there to see how much angle I need."

"I get the head pipes going in the right direction, then I pick one or the other to be my guide pipe. And then I bend the other one around it. On this bike I'm starting with the rear pipe. Sometimes I pull a tape line to check the angle that I want the pipe to follow. The two pipes come out of the head about 8 inches. I try to get them the same length, but sometimes you can't make them exactly equal."

"The rear pipe has a U-bend at the bottom that I cut, then a piece of straight, then a little wedge that I cut from another piece of U-bend. Then, using magnets to hold it in place, I slip on a piece of 2-1/4 inch pipe. The nice thing about the step-pipes is the fact that you can slip fit them when you're doing the mock up. When I weld them up I only leave a quarter-inch extra on the inside."

"The key is cutting it straight and fitting them well. Ron Covell has an excellent video on working with tubing. (available from Wolfgang Publications). There's really no limit to what you can do if you're patient."

Rob's pipes are commonly staggered, going from 1-3/4 to 2, to 2-1/4 inches in diameter.

Small little collars like that shown are often used to smooth the transition from one size pipe to the next.

The sections slide over one another, which makes the mock up fairly easy.

The front pipe runs down at the same angle as the frame downtubes, before turning toward the back of the bike.

"To make a straight cut, I cut a 2 inch strip out of poster board, (note the photo) then wrap it around the pipe, that way you always get a straight cut, and if you're butt welding these the two pieces have to meet really well. To shrink the end down where it meets a smaller pipe, I use an old piece of fork tube and a body hammer, and I just roll the edge, you can shrink it 1/8th inch or more. I roll the edge until it fits snug on the pipe that I'm sliding it over."

"Then I tack weld them and final weld them with tig. I suppose you can weld with gas or wire-feed but it makes life harder for the polisher. I try to use a center mount for good support. Because our little port-collar is flat and machined our pipes don't move as much as the rolled factory-type pipes do, so we don't have trouble with the pipes

The end of the mock up session. Both pipes are parallel to each other and to the lower leg of the 'swingarm.' "These have nice lines and they're really not that hard to build."

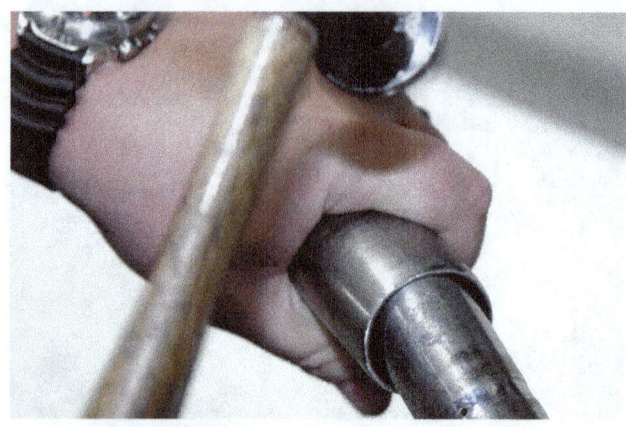

Robs works the edge of a pipe over an old fork tube in order to reduce the ID for a better fit on the smaller pipe it slides over.

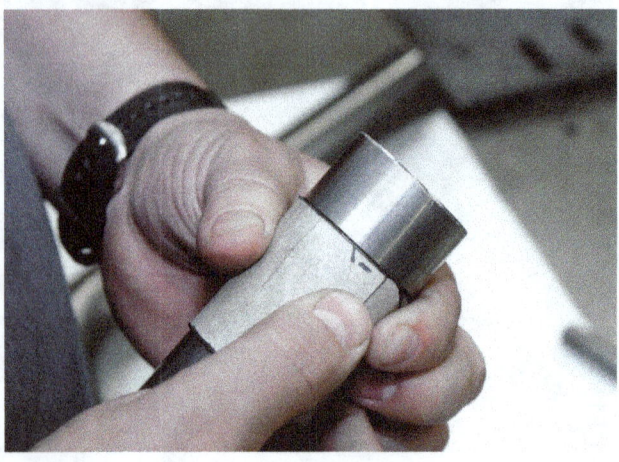

To make a nice straight cut on a piece of straight pipe, Rob wraps it in light board, then marks the edge as shown.

The main support mount comes off a vertical frame tube, ties the two pipes to the frame and to each other.

Neat cuts make for good butt joints which are easier to weld and easier to polish later.

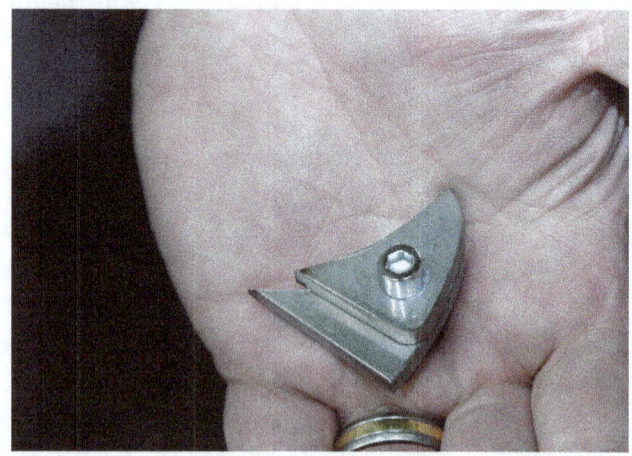

Small tabs can be cut out of mild steel, and welded to a pipe wherever a mount is needed. These two will allow the two pipes to be bolted together.

moving after they're installed. I like to support the front pipe off the cam cover or someplace nearby, but you just can't on this bike. I did make little brackets that tie the two pipes together, and then there's the main support off the frame farther back."

"For a heat shield I cut a piece of bigger pipe, and rip it the long way. Then John makes me a little bung or two, and I screw the shields to the bungs with button head Allens, it's neater and stronger than the way they're usually mounted with hose clamps."

"You have to be real conscious of where the oil lines or cables are going to run. Usually I run the pipes six inches center to center, sometimes I go to four or maybe bigger for more gentle radiuses. The bigger the radius the harder it is to cut nice and straight. But when the bends are too tight it's hard to cut and weld them without creating a corner and then that gets hot. We always make our own pipes, it's part of our signature, the bikes are all hand built."

"These pipes work pretty well, they cover some of the right side drive stuff, and they follow the line at the back of the 'swingarm.'

MOLDING AND FINAL ASSEMBLY

Between the end of the mock-up and the beginning of the final assembly, a number of crucial operations take place. For each of these steps Donnie relies on a network of old and trusted allies.

To eliminate all the visible welds, both on the frame and the custom fabricated sheet metal, Donnie calls on his brother Greg, who does the extensive molding work in his small home shop - after doing commercial body work all day long. Once the surfaces are flat and ready for primer, everything moves to Paint Works, the paint shop where the Kandy Brandywine from House of Kolor is applied. For the tasteful application of gold leaf and graphics Donnie relies on another local legend, Lenni Schwartz from Krazy Kolors.

Oddly enough, once the paint is finished and the bike gets to Greg Gaspard's hoist in Donnie's shop for final assembly, the first thing on the agenda is the elimination of much of that carefully

The finished mock up. Even if you aren't doing a lot of fabrication, the mock up must be complete to minimize trouble later during the actual assembly.

Left side shows the belt drive and the Donnie Smith designed ignition switch housing.

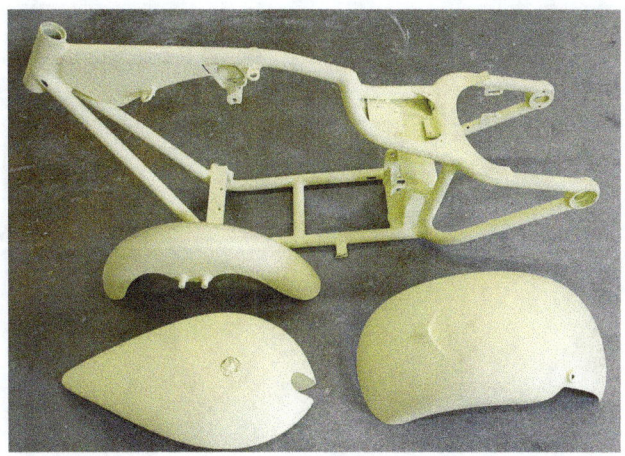

Before final assembly, the whole thing must be blown apart, molded, primed and made ready for paint.

Once back in Donnie's shop, Greg starts on the final assembly. first on the list is wiring and preparation of the frame.

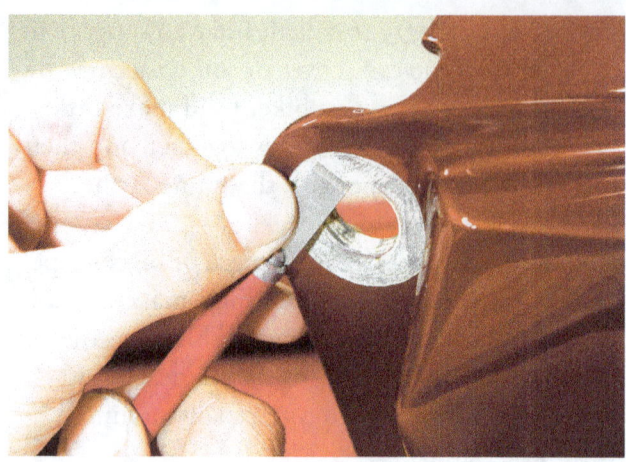

...he then uses another flat blade to peel away the paint.

Mounting the electrical components is easier as everything was mounted during the mock-up stage. All the wires, even plug wires, route through the frame.

If a components slides, like this caliper bracket, the whole area needs to be stripped of paint and then painted with a single coat of touch-up paint.

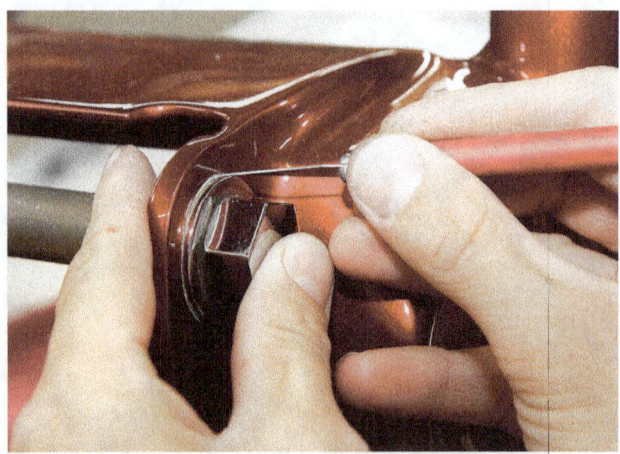

Here you can see Greg cut the outline of the paint with the point of a razor knife...

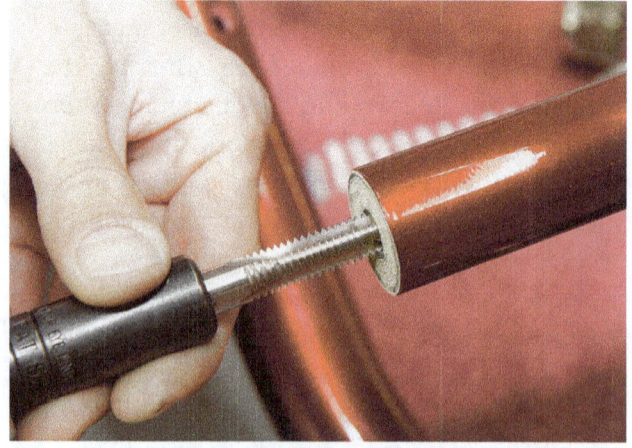

Before attaching anything to the frame, all the threaded holes must be cleaned with a set of taps as shown.

applied paint. As explained elsewhere, the paint on a custom bike is easily .025 inches thick, and in order to ensure the parts don't loosen later after the paint squeezes out, and to get a good electrical ground, you have to cut out around all the areas where things are bolted to the frame. As Greg explains, "First I mark it out, then I cut through the paint and sometimes the filler underneath. Then I scrape that area clean with a razor knife." Greg uses a variety of razor-knife styles to get at all the nooks and crannies on the frame. "Once I have the paint peeled off, I always paint the raw areas with touch up paint so it doesn't show a white line at the edge and so the area doesn't rust."

WIRING

The wiring harness for all Donnie Smith bikes is crafted by hand. Greg, who does all the wiring on this bike, pointed out just a few of the little things he does to prevent trouble later. "The wiring for the headlight comes through the frame (like all the wiring) and then into the headlight bucket. I left the hole in the back of the headlight shell a little too big so the wires can move in the bucket as the fork is turned. And I will cut them so they aren't any longer than necessary, I like to have the wires lay down really really nice and neat."

"I will probably have 120 hours putting this bike together," explains Greg. "How well it goes together depends on how well it was mocked up. If the bike was fully mocked up with the actual engine and the actual belt drive we won't have any trouble getting things to fit when it comes to the final assembly."

"It really helps to know where the wiring is going and where things like the ignition module are going to be mounted. On an Evo you only have three wires for the ignition, but on a TC you're got like 18, which makes it much harder to hide the ignition harness."

"A lot of times we polish the little things, little pieces of hardware, during the assembly. It really adds a nice level of detail to the bike."

At this point, the bike is nearly done, Greg still has some items to put on, like the carb and the throttle cables, which are made up by hand. And

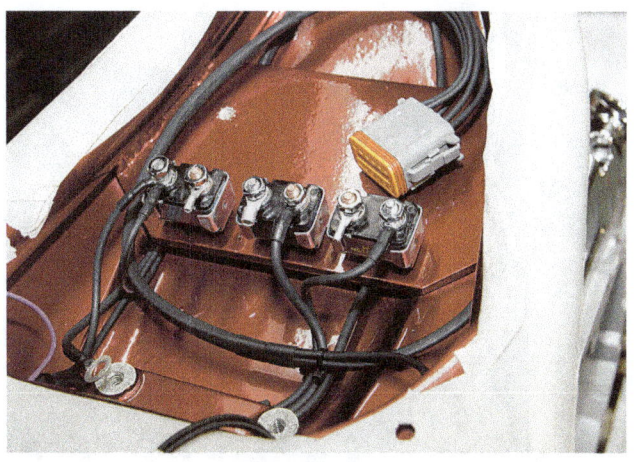

Details, details. Here you can see how the three circuit breakers are mounted, the threaded bungs for mounting the coils, and how neat all of the wiring work is.

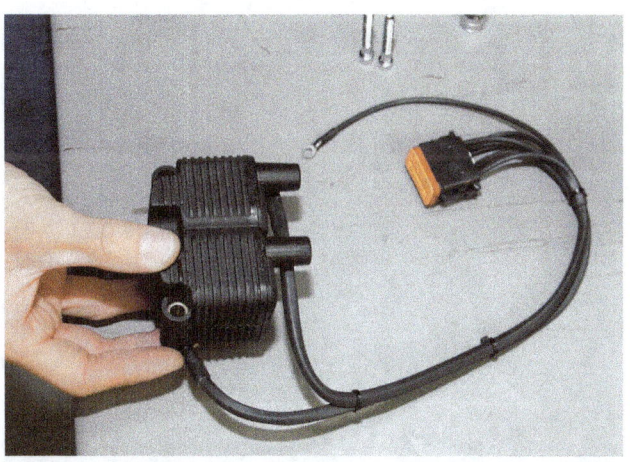

Twin Cam engines use a substantial ignition harness, which makes hiding all the wires a bit of a challenge.

Greg often uses masking tape to protect the paint in any area where he's working.

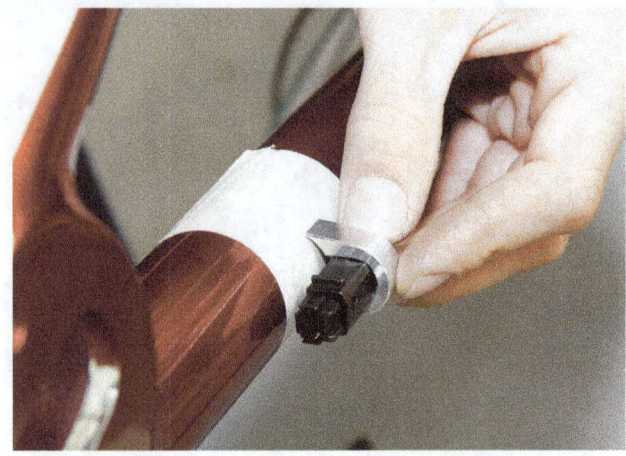

Small clamps like that shown are used throughout the bike to ensure neat routing of all the wires and cables.

Sometimes called Pro-line, the teflon brake lines are really just a braided stainless line without the braided stainless.

Mid-way through the final assembly Greg still has a lot of work to do, like attaching the carb, the starter and the rear wheel and brake assembly.

The nice thing about these brake lines is the way they can be heated and bent into a shape that will remain after the line cools.

One week later, much is accomplished, like the rear wheel and drive-side rear brake, but there's still much to do: carb, cables and a lot of wiring.

Here we can see the belt drive installed (without the cover) and the license plate bracket.

then there's the battery and starter. Then it's time to fire it up for the first time. "I usually put the tank on last," explains Greg. We have a separate tank we can use to do the initial start up. That way I don't have to take the tank off again if there's something wrong or something I have to fix right away.

Details, details, details

As you look over the nearly finished bike, you see the little P-clamps everywhere you look, These are used to keep things out of the way and arranged neatly.

Anywhere a collar or switch mounts to a handle bar with a set screw, Greg drills a little divot in the handlebar so the switch can't rotate. As Greg explains, "In the case of the switches on the handlebars, if it rotates it might sheer the wires."

The plug wires Greg uses are small diameter wires from Accel. Small enough that they can be run up inside the frame. All the wiring is connected with small connectors. This is done to keep everything super neat. Even the three wire plug on the back of the regulator is replaced with a smaller plug.

Finally, the bike is completely done. Because the owner, Larry Page, lives out of town, Donnie and crew take extra time to put some miles on the bike. As Donnie explains, "Larry lives a long way from here and we don't want him to have any trouble once the bike gets there.

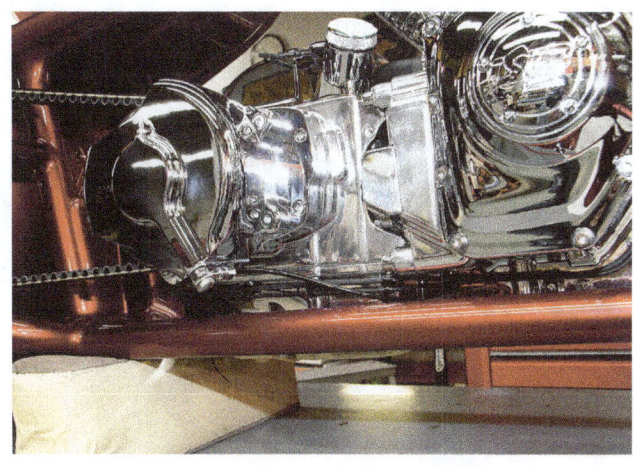

The same un-stainless line used for the brakes is used for the hydraulic clutch. Nearly all the lines run inside the frame tubes.

Here Greg does a test fit of the finished gas tank. The tank is one of the last things to go on for good, "we use another tank to start the motor the first few times."

Left side of the finished bike, clean classy and ready to road test once the first Minnesota snowfall melts.

Master builder Donnie Smith with his latest creation. One more in a very long line of custom bikes that run as good as they look.

Chapter Nine
A Dave Perewitz Bobber

Old Meets New

Though Dave Perewitz might be best known as the builder of long, stretched, 300-tire customs, he grew up building Choppers and Bobbers - the first time they were cool. For this Bobber project David started with a Rolling Thunder Hardtail frame with no top tube stretch, two inches of downtube stretch, and a 32 degree neck. The frame is manufactured from 1-1/8th inch mild steel tubing, and designed to accept a 180/200 tire with chain drive. The oil tank is a nice alu-

Something old, something new. The Bobber from Dave Perewitz is a proof that you can use new products - like an Accurate Panhead, five-speed transmission, H-D Springer fork and disc brakes - to create a very believable Bobber. Michael Keegan

lower part of the case, and then the motor is reinstalled.

To create clearance at the rear exhaust port, the boys pull the motor one more time, heat the area where the flange hits the frame with an oxy-acetylene torch, and then carefully adjust the frame tube with a hammer.

When Ron tries to set the tranny in for the first time, the fifth stud doesn't line up with the hole in the frame bracket. It turns out

The starting point, a hardtail frame, Panhead engine, five-speed tranny, rear fender from Russ Wernimont and a pair of spoked wheels.

minum piece with integral battery box, built by Fausto, of MotoXcycle of Montreal.

Though the frame came from Rolling Thunder, the Springer fork assembly is a genuine Made-in-Milwaukee item. In the best Bobber tradition, David chose fat sixteen inch tires and spoked rims for both ends. Up front, the bike rides on a 90X16 while the rear tire is stamped 200/60X16 inches.

For power, Dave picked an eighty-eight inch Panhead from Accurate Engineering, matched up to a five speed transmission. And of course the primary is an open belt, manufactured in this case by BDL.

The Mock Up Assembly

Ron Levesque and Jesse Perewitz begin the project by strapping the bare frame onto a stand. Next, they set the Panhead in place. Once the motor's in the frame, the boys discover two interference issues, one at the rear where the engine cases just touches the seat tube, and one where the rear exhaust port touches the seat tube (note the nearby photos). After taking the motor back out, Ron grinds away just a little metal on the

The Panhead is brand new, which means no metal fatigue or stripped threads. Alternator left side means a great charging system, and compatibility with modern primary assemblies. Note the 3-bolt exh. flanges.

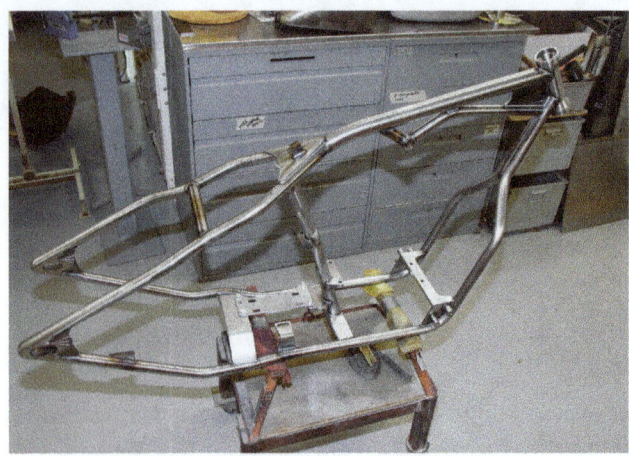

You don't have to have a big, expensive bike lift. You do need a rack that will get the bike up off the floor so everything is accessible.

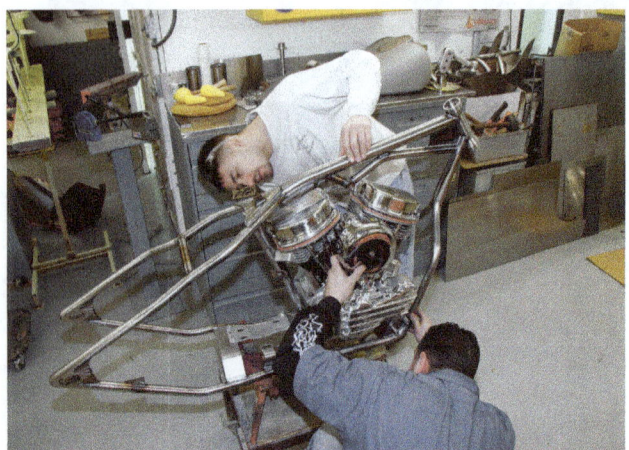

Ron (in foreground) and Jesse, start by setting the engine onto the frame mounts.

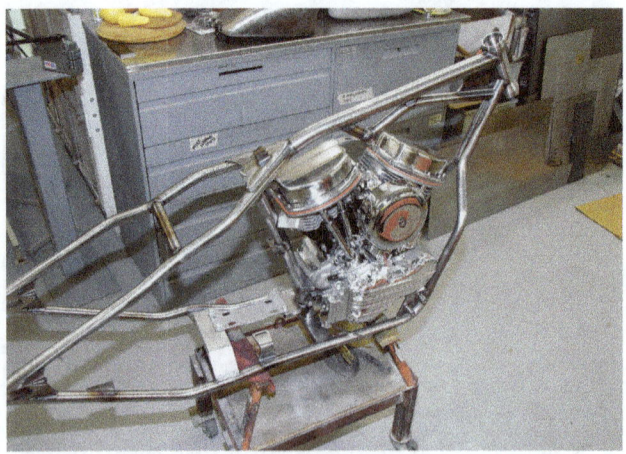

With the engine in the frame, it's time to check for any clearance issues.

The area shown here where the exhaust flange touches the frame tube.

we need an offset transmission plate to make everything line up. These are exactly the kinds of issues that crop up, and get solved, during the mock up process.

Once an offset transmission plate is bolted into the frame, the transmission drops in and all the studs drop through the bracket and frame. It now becomes obvious that a spacer will be needed between the left side engine case and the inside of the primary (check the nearby photos).

Note: many frames are now coming with the transmission plate built in, so the need for an offset plate is eliminated. When you buy your frame however, be sure to ask whether or not you need a spacer between the engine case and inner primary - the spacer is often shipped with the frame and may in fact have been lost in the assembly seen here.

PRIMARY INSTALLATION

Even the best frames may require a shim between one or two of the engine or transmission mounting points and the mount. As noted in the

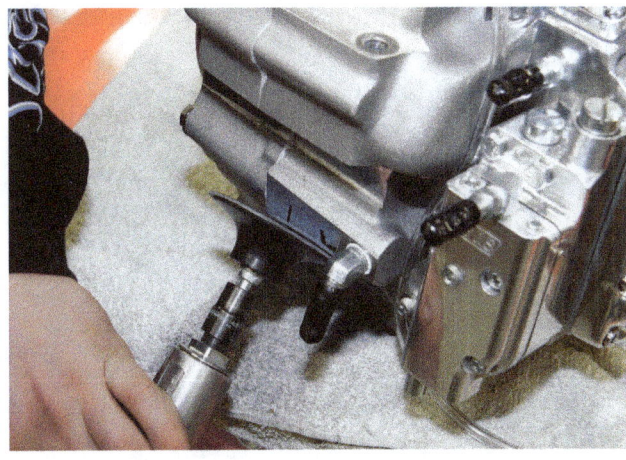

The other clearance problem is at the back of the engine, a problem Ron fixed with a little judicious grinding.

Before the fork can be installed, the bearing races must be installed (next page). The small tab is the integral fork stop, which will be eliminated.

Now the motor fits, so it's time to install the tranny mounting plate...

Ron installs and bolts up the inner primary (or motor plate) for the belt drive assembly...

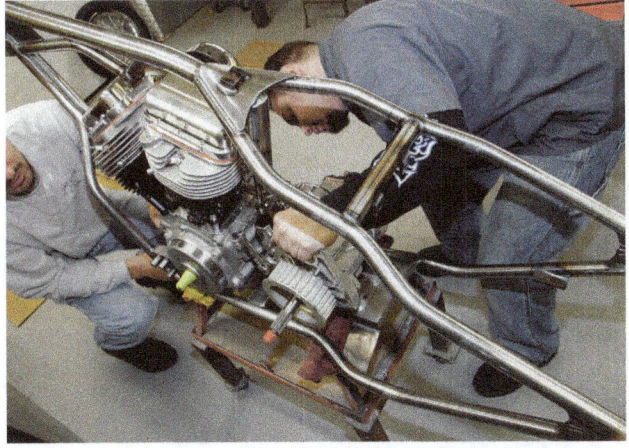

...followed by the tranny itself (note, the actual transmission will have a chain sprocket).

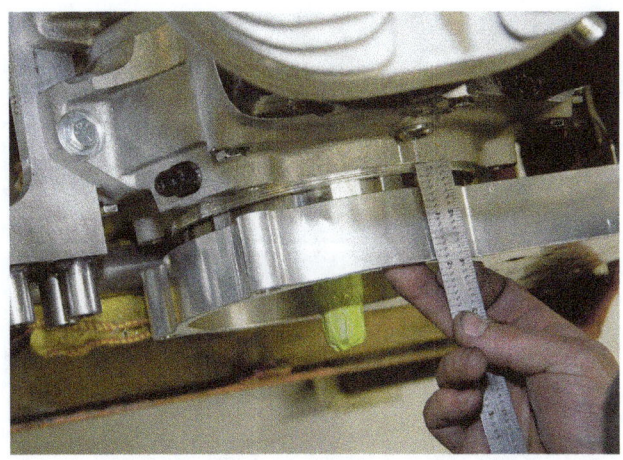

...and discovers that they need a spacer between the left side case and the inside of the motor plate.

123

To ensure the engine and transmission are aligned, Ron left the mounting nuts loose, then tightened the inner primary.

The driver shown (available at any auto parts store) is used to install the bearing races in the neck.

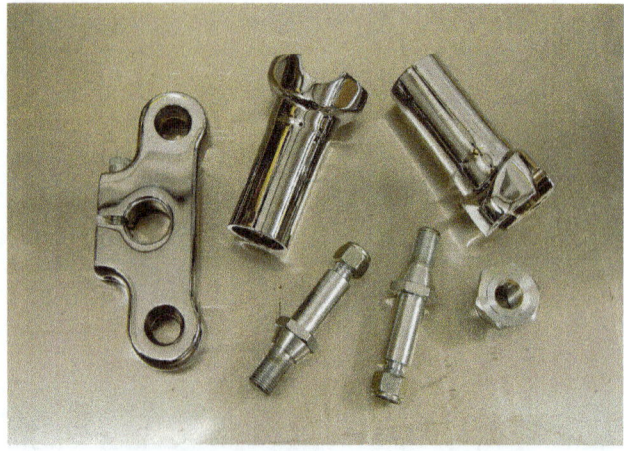

Upper tree and risers are all part of the kit that comes with the springer fork from Harley-Davidson.

other assemblies, if the engine and transmission sit square on their mounts the inner primary (or motor plate) can be tightened up and the clearance between the mounting points and the frame are checked again. This can be a tedious process, note the sequence in the 250 Softail chapter for more details.

Fork Installation

Before installing the fork, Jesse cuts off the integral fork stop tab on the bottom of the fork neck, because the Springer fork from Harley-Davidson uses its own integral stops. The next job is the installation of the bearing races in the neck. Jesse installs these with the correct driver (note the photos) which makes it easier to drive in the races without damage. The races have to be driven in until they "bottom" in the neck. It sounds obvious, but be sure the races are facing the right way, because they're hard as hell to get back out if you make a mistake.

As they install the fork, Ron comments that, "The Harley-Davidson fork kit is nice, it comes with everything, including the complete riser assembly, and it goes together really well, the threads aren't full of extra chrome like some of the other brands," (though you should still check all the threads with a tap and die set). The boys finish up the riser installation next, the Harley-Davidson risers use two standard handlebar rubbers in each one, one that comes in from the bottom and one on the top, the top rubber is followed by a steel washer, then the nut. The risers are designed for standard one-inch handle bars.

Jesse and Ron install the forward controls next, which is a pretty straight forward operation. The right side control needs to be disassembled before installation, but it's all just nuts and bolts. The JayBrake hand controls go on next, this might seem an unnecessary step, but the more you do during mock up, and the more puzzles you solve at this stage of the game, the easier the final assembly will go.

Rear Wheel Placement and Oil Tank Installation

Ron sets the wheel in place next, "this is just our first check, my ultimate goal is to get the

The upper neck bearing is packed with waterproof grease. The lower bearing comes already installed on the fork stem.

Riser studs and upper triple tree are installed next.

Upper bearing is installed prior to adjustment of pre-load ("fall away"). Top nut is used to adjust the pre-load on the tapered bearings. Though this is just the mock up, the final adjustment is explained below.

Installing the forward controls on the right involves partial disassembly.

The factory procedure is somewhat complex. You want to over-tighten the nut slightly to seat the bearings, then adjust to zero end-play and zero (or very little) actual pre-load. If in doubt, check the manual.

Brakes and handlebar controls are from JayBrake. The more you do during the mock up, the more easily the bike will go together during final assembly.

125

Little Ron hangs the rear wheel assembly in the frame for the first time.

Usually the oil tank and mounts are part of the frame kit, in this case the tank is from another shop so the mounting tabs had to be fabricated and welded on.

Instead of using the standard oil tank, Dave decided to install a nifty aluminum piece with integral battery box, built by Fausto, of MotoXcycle of Montreal.

Here you can see how Jessie sizes up the steel strap that will be used to extend the upper motor mount.

wheel in the center of the frame and the two sprockets aligned. We will get it positioned exactly in the center of the frame a little later and I will use a straight edge to see if the two sprockets are aligned. At this point it looks like we will have to use a spacer between the wheel hub and the sprocket."

The oil tank being used is not from the frame manufacturer, as Ron explains, "normally the tank and brackets would come from Rolling Thunder, but we're using a different oil tank, so we have to weld the necessary tabs on the frame."

MOTOR MOUNT, CHAIN GANG, HEADLIGHT, FENDER

The standard upper mount doesn't quite reach, so Jesse cuts it off, and extends the mount with a piece of heavy steel plate cut out on the Dake saw. Now that the oil tank and battery are sitting in the frame, it's time to figure out the chain, headlight and rear fender. Ron has the rear tire and wheel mounted in its final location, so he can safely cut a section of 530 chain to length, as

The next task if to cut the steel...

Here's the mount before being dipped in the chrome plating tank.

...Jessie checks it for length...

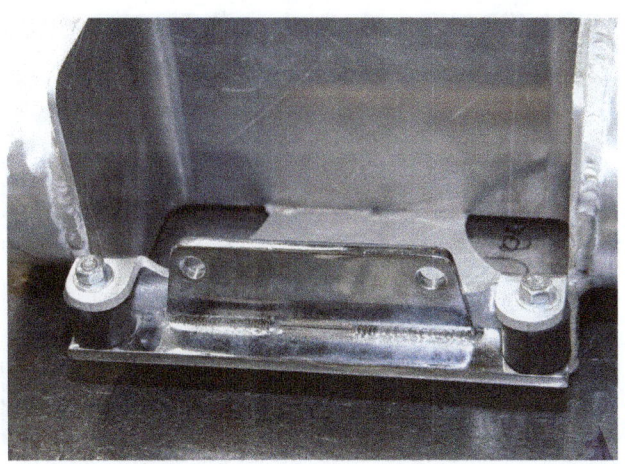

The non-standard oil tank requires a bracket as shown...

...and then tack welds it together and checks the fit again.

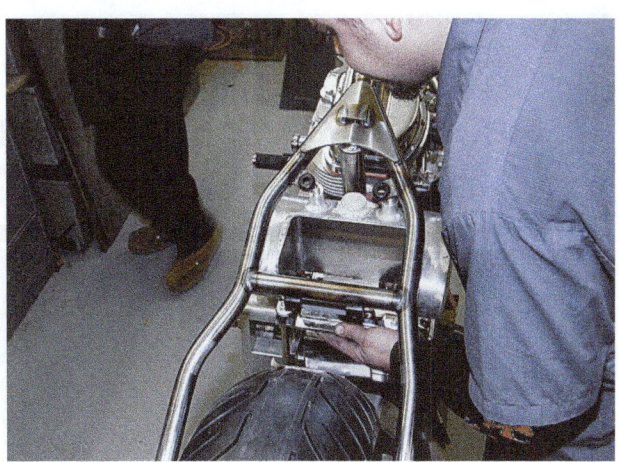

...and a test fit, or three, by Little Ron before the tabs can be welded onto the frame.

The first finished mock up for the oil tank with the battery set in place.

To shorten the chain, a small grinder is used to take the head off one pin...

...so it can be carefully driven out. Presto, a shorter chain.

shown. When the chain is installed for the last time, Ron is sure to install the master link with the closed end of the clip facing the direction of rotation.

With the chain in place, Ron tapes a series of wood blocks to the rear tire. These half-inch spacers will hold the fender up off the tire as Jesse and Ron position the fender, and then fabricate the brackets that will mount the fender to the frame. As we've explained elsewhere, the fender can't sit too close to the tire or it may rub when the tire grows at high speed.

As he sets the fender in place, the first thing Ron notices is interference between the fender and chain. Before he can get the fender close to the final position, Ron needs to cut off enough material on the left side so the chain will clear and the fender will sit straight on the bike. Ronnie uses a cut-off wheel to trim the fender. Ron and Jesse eyeball the fender position, but they can't determine the final position of the fender until the rear wheel and tire are in their final position. Like many other parts of bike building, positioning the fender is a bit of a catch-22.

FINAL REAR WHEEL POSITION

As we mentioned earlier, the rear wheel needs to sit in the center of the frame, so the first job is to find the frame's center-line, then the center of the tire, as shown by the photos.

With the wheel in the center of the frame, the boys begin the process of measuring for, and cutting, the correct spacers. Like everything else, this process is a bit of a puzzle. On the left, Ron and Jesse measure for the spacer that goes between the inside of the frame and the outside of the bearing race. They also need to use a straightedge to determine whether or not the rear sprocket should be moved out from the wheel hub (check the photos).

Two spacers need to be cut for the right side, as Ron explains, "the critical spacer is the one between the outside of the wheel bearing and the inside of the caliper carrier. You also have to cut a second spacer that fits between the outside of the caliper carrier and the inside of the frame. And you don't really know for sure exactly how every-

The spacers shown are used to position the fender up off the tire, so there's enough clearance between the fender and the tire.

Here you can see how the cut out allows room for the drive chain.

Ron sets the fender on the tire and discovers a serious clearance problem between the fender and the chain...

Centering the tire in the frame means first finding the center of the frame...

...a problem that is rectified with the careful use of a cut-off wheel, following the layout done with tape.

...as shown, with the caliper and a carpenter's rule.

1) The boys use a piece of string and a tape...

2) ...to determine where the exact center of the tire is. The bead of rubber left by the mold is not a reliable center-line.

4) A straightedge is run from the centerline of the top tube and should intersect with the center-line of the rear tire.

3) Here you can see how the center of the string is used to mark the center of the tire.

thing will fit together until it's all assembled and fully tightened."

Because the rear caliper carrier is effectively a rear wheel spacer, Ron slides the caliper over the rotor and bolts it to the caliper carrier, before he measures for the right side wheel spacers.

Ron adds a couple or warnings about the process of positioning the wheel, "If the wheel uses the old fashioned wheel bearings you have to make sure that the bearings are packed and that the end-play is set. And it's better to cut the spacer that goes between the caliper carrier and the outside of the wheel bearing a little too thin, and then use a .005 or .008 inch spacer between the carrier and the inside of the caliper mount to move it toward the outside."

The first time the boys get the wheel in the center of the frame they notice that the sprocket on the wheel is too far inboard, (note the photos). So there will have to be a spacer between the hub and the sprocket to move the sprocket out while leaving the wheel in its correct position.

Once the rear wheel is centered in the frame and the chain is tensioned, it's time to measure for rear wheel spacers.

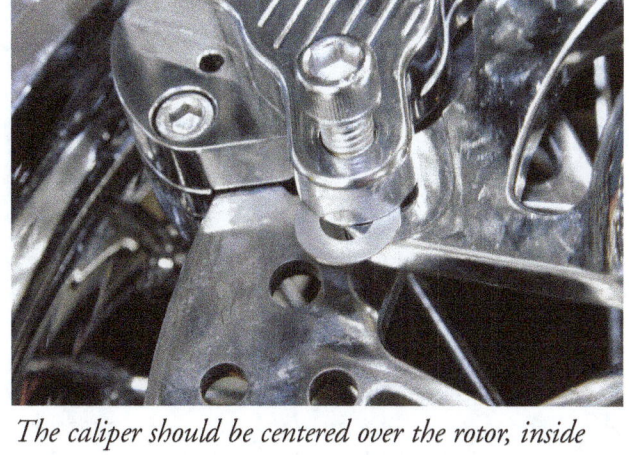

The caliper should be centered over the rotor, inside spacer is cut a little short, so the caliper can be moved slightly to the outside (and centered) with these thin, hardened shims that come with many calipers.

Note the spacer, cut and installed between the caliper carrier and the wheel bearing.

A long straightedge and a machinist ruler are used as shown...

At Cycle Fab, they have a substantial supply of wheel spacers in both 3/4 and 1-inch I.D. They were still forced to trim a spacer on the lathe.

...to determine if the alignment of the two sprockets is off, and if so, by how much.

A variety of spacers are available to move the sprocket away from the wheel hub. If possible, use one with a lip in the center to better locate the sprocket. In this case, a .200 inch spacer was needed.

Here you can get a look at the right side of the wheel with the caliper carrier and the two axle spacers, one on either side of the carrier.

With the wheel in the center of the frame and the chain running true, the crew can blow the bike apart and send the parts to the paint department.

Ron adds a .200 inch spacer between the wheel hub and sprocket. Ideally, the spacer should have a lip that the ID of the sprocket slips over, like the hub does, to make the connection between the sprocket and the hub as strong as possible. The final check of the wheel position shows the caliper to be off-center slightly to the inside, (as predicted) so a few very thin spacers are used between the caliper and the caliper carrier.

With the wheels in place and all the spacers cut, the bike can be blown apart for paint and then the final assembly. Because the Fat Bob-style tank includes a dash with the ignition switch, there is no worry about where the switch will go or whether or not a bracket needs to be fabricated during the mock up assembly. Obviously, you have to determine where the ignition switch and all major electrical components will be mounted during the mock up. And if the wires are going to be run inside the frame, it's easier to drill holes in the frame tubing before the frame is painted.

SPEAKING OF PAINT...

Once the bike is disassembled, most of the parts go to the paint area where Eric preps the frame, fender, oil and gas tank for paint. The sheet metal parts, especially the gas tank, get three layers of filler with sanding between each layer, before the final primer and sealer can be applied. A good paint job relies on great preparation.

The painted frame must be prepared before the engine and transmission can be bolted in place. Areas at risk for nicks during assembly are covered with masking tape to help protect the paint. Ron scrapes the paint off the engine and transmission mounting points so both components can bolt directly to the frame.

Now the engine and transmission, and the primary can be bolted in for the last time. Any shims used during the mock up to get the transmission to sit square on the mounts should be used during the final assembly. It's a good idea to go through the whole alignment procedure again to be sure the engine, transmission and primary are correctly aligned. Next, the fork assembly is installed for the last time and the neck bearings are adjusted.

Eric is the man in charge of prepping the parts for paint. Even the best sheet metal needs filler to create a perfectly smooth surface.

Photos from this point forward provided by Michael Keegan.

Shims used during the mock up are installed again...

After multiple coats of filler, endless sanding and a coat of primer/sealer, it's time to begin applying the Topaz paint from PPG's Vibrance line.

...but the driveline alignment should still be checked again as described in the text.

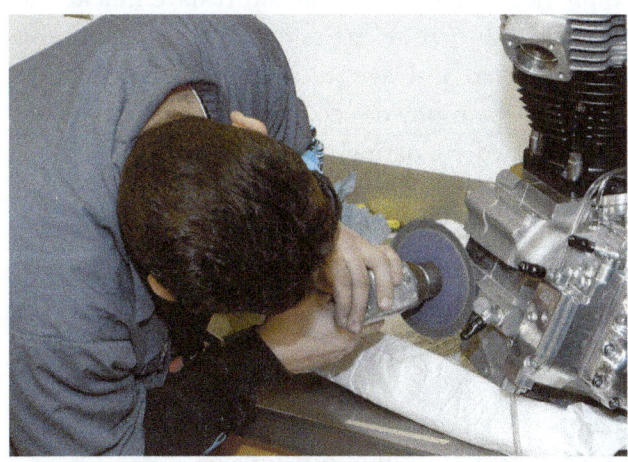

After setting the engine in for the "last time" the boys discover that the build up of paint is thick enough to create the need for a little more clearance.

Installing the Harley-Davidson Springer fork is a two-person operation.

Using very thin masking tape, Ron begins laying out the scallops on the gas tank, which has already been painted and then scuffed.

With help from Dave, Ron tries more than one layout pattern before finding just the right design.

Dave and Gary Brodour check the reassembled wheels prior to installation of the tires.

Powder coating the rims required complete disassembly of the wheels.

With the primered tank sitting on the frame, Big Ron tapes out the scallop design, which must be approved by David before the tank goes back into the paint department.

WHEEL ASSEMBLY

Bobbers need painted wheels. The guys who built Bobbers after the war didn't have much money and there wasn't exactly a chrome shop on every corner. So David disassembled these wheels and had them powder coated by Don Madden at D&T Powder Coating. Once the rims are back Dave has them assembled and trued by Gary Brodour, as shown in the nearby photo.

In the case of the final assembly, things don't necessarily follow a strict sequence. In fact, sometimes there are three or four things going on at once. The wheels are being installed while Eric paints the fender and Little Ron installs the forward controls and the shift linkage.

After checking the alignment of the engine and tranny, the primary belt drive can be installed.

Once the fork is installed and adjusted, the risers are next.

At this point the Bobber is starting to look like a motorcycle...

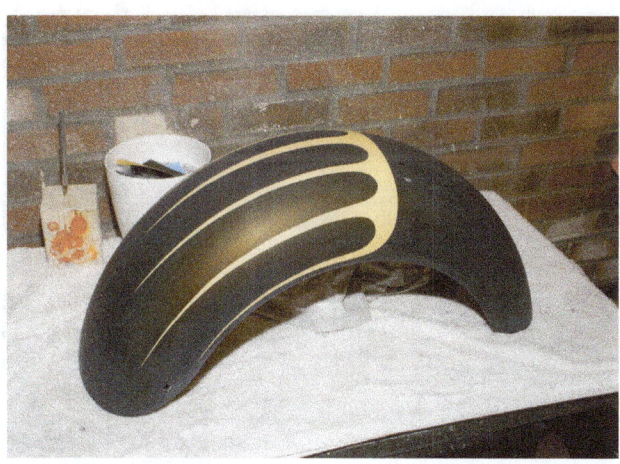

While the scallops on the tank flow straight back and almost meet, these run parallel to each other and follow the shape of the fender.

...waiting for sheet metal, wiring and plumbing.

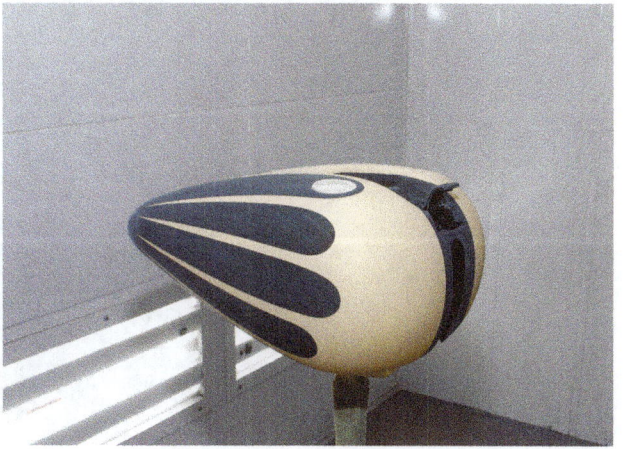

The cream color is a special PPG mix. Before being cleared, Keith Hanson will add gold-leaf pinstripes.

Installing the forward controls also means...

...is a slow and tedious process that involves plenty of bending and cutting...

...installing and adjusting the linkage to the transmission.

...before the fittings can be attached.

Routing and forming the copper oil lines...

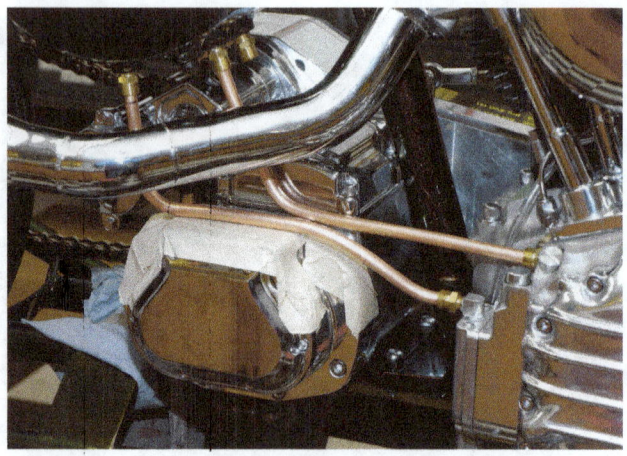
Finally the lines can be installed and tightened.

Dave wants to run the wiring inside the bars, and starts by finding the center of the bar.

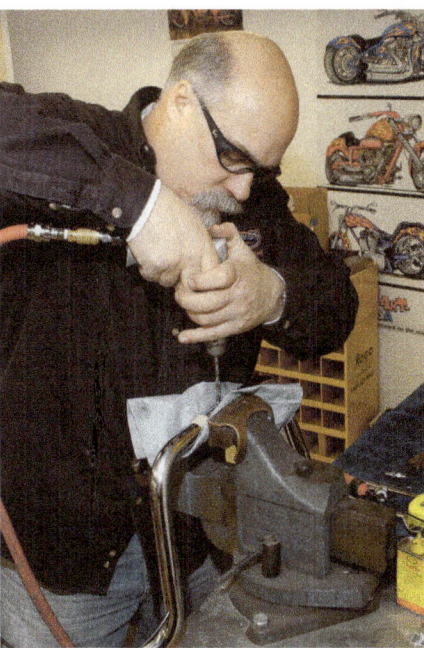

Next comes the pilot hole.

Then the hole is enlarged and the opening is smoothed out so there are no rough edges to cut the wires or harness.

Now the handlebar harness is fed through the bars, starting at the upper hole and exiting at the bottom.

With the bars installed, Little Ron feeds the main harness up through the top tube.

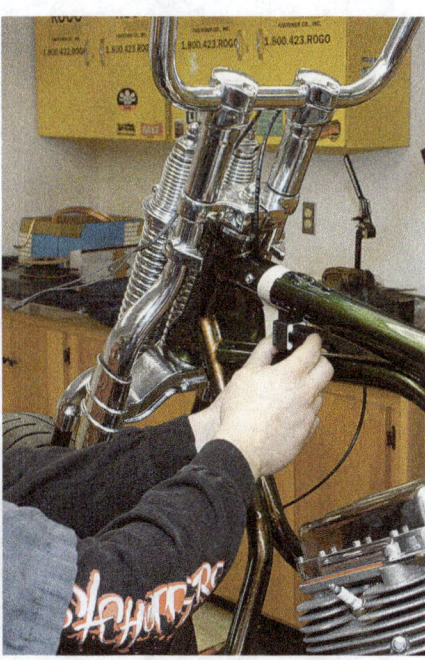

The starter relay and circuit breakers are hidden here, under the tank.

The Badlands equalizer box ensures that the LED blinkers (with minimal current draw) will trigger the flasher.

David and crew make all their harnesses from scratch. Here you see the starter relay and main circuit breaker.

The junction box for the speedo, and all the grounds, is hidden under the dash, this makes for neat, invisible wiring.

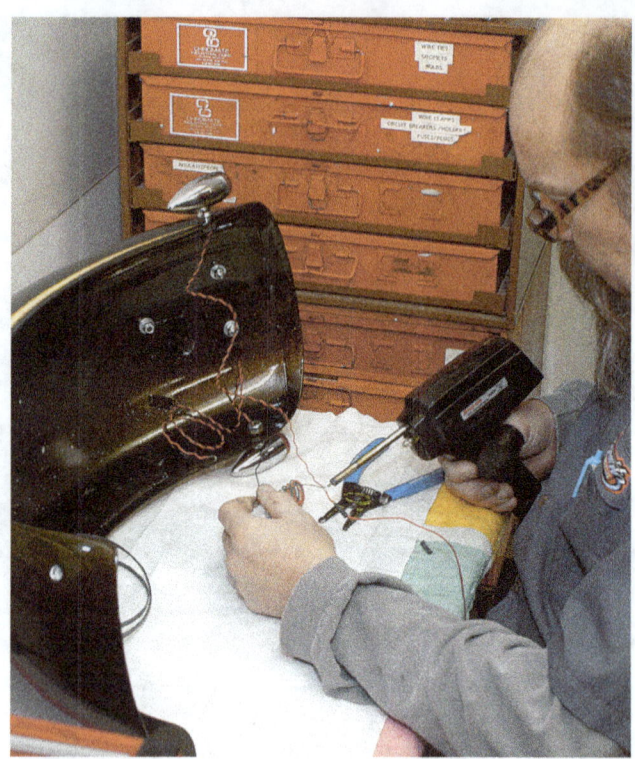

Here Ron solders up the wires for the rear harness, which will be tucked up away from the tire. Turnsignals have been converted to LEDs.

Copper Oil Lines

Lil' Ron hand shaped and fitted the copper oil lines between the oil tank and engine. First, each of the three lines is test-fitted using thin wire bent to the correct shape. These wires become templates for the copper lines.

The lines themselves are made from copper tubing purchased in a big roll at the hardware store. The fittings are from the hardware store as well. The boys report they've had no trouble with the lines cracking, "but if you were putting these lines on a rubber mounted engine you might want a flexible section between the engine and the oil tank. After the tubes are carefully cut and shaped, Ron polishes each one. The process is very time consuming, but worth it for the look.

Wiring

The entire harness with all the connections for the lights, horn, and ignition is laid out on the bench, before being installed in the bike – and pulled through the frame tubes to keep everything hidden and protected. The relays and circuit breakers are attached to the frame and hidden

Big Ron feeds all the dash wiring up through the hole at the front of the tank, while little Ron sets the tank in place.

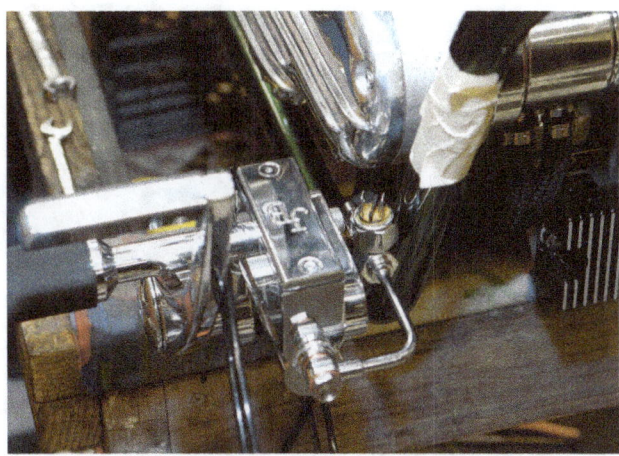

Rather than hide the brake light switch, the boys put it between the master and the frame tube, as shown, so it's nice and easy to get to.

Here Little Ron is hooking up the grounds and all the wires that go to the ignition switch.

The seat is from Danny Gray, here Dave is installing the seat springs.

You can see the base for the dash, the lights plug into the bigger holes. You can also see how the harness comes up from under the tank.

The connections for the front blinkers are made inside the headlight bucket. The lights themselves have been converted to LEDs.

139

The pipes are from Paughco, customized and then re-chromed, and finally wrapped in heat wrap.

The wires from the rear fender, taillight, and blinkers are gathered in shrink wrap to form a sub-harness, which is then connected to the main harness through, a Deutsche plug from NAMZ.

Once installed, the pipes look right at home on the new/old Bobber.

Time now to install the battery and connect the main power and ground wires.

Note the tap used to protect the frame during assembly, and the location of the oil filter.

Note how neat the wiring is, each sub harness protected by shrink wrap.

under the tank. David and crew like to build each harness from scratch, rather than buy a complete harness kit.

Because this bike will have handlebar switches, Dave gets the job of prepping the bars for wiring and hydraulic lines. The process is tedious, and requires that holes be drilled for the wires, then pull wires are carefully fed through both sides of the bars before, finally, the hires and lines can be pulled through.

Big Ron installs the rear taillight and turn signals, and routes the wires along the side of the rear fender. These wires are then run to a terminal plug, which will mate up to another, matching plug, located under the seat. Although the battery is under the seat, many of the wiring connections and junctions happen under the tank, or under the speedometer as part of the dash assembly. At this point the gas tank can be test fit again and then installed for the last time.

After a test fit of the exhaust, the pipes are wrapped and then the exhaust is installed for the last time. Before the first big road test Dave fills, bleeds, and tests both front and rear brakes, tests the brake and taillights, and mounts the headlight. All the wiring, switches and connections are double checked for clear routing, proper placement and working order. The dash cover/speedo is bolted in place and the hand-fabricated battery cover is installed. At the same time, Little Ron finishes up the wiring and installs the nicely tooled solo seat.

Now it's time for a little gas, and the first firing of the new Accurate Panhead engine. The new pipe-wrap smokes for the first few minutes as the pipes heat up. The engine is shut off and allowed to cool before being started again for progressively longer periods prior to the first road test.

The first road test is done with a degree of caution, to ensure the brakes work, that the bike tracks straight, and that there are no leaks. Once back at the shop, all fittings on the engine and brakes are checked again for evidence of seepage, and the carburetor is given a final adjustment. After one more road test, and a good cleaning, the bike is ready for delivery.

The one-off cover, is the creation of Big Ron. In addition to hiding the battery, the cover keeps the harness and battery from getting wet.

The cover looks like a natural piece of the bike once the seat is set in place.

A very clean and simple Bobber, true to the spirit of the old bikes yet assembled from all new parts.

Books from Wolfgang Publications can be found at select book stores and numerous web sites.

Titles	ISBN	Price	# of pages
Advanced Airbrush Art	9781929133208	$27.95	144 pages
Advanced Custom Motorcycle Assembly & Fabrication	9781929133239	$27.95	144 pages
Advanced Custom Motorcycle Wiring - *Revised*	9781935828761	$27.95	144 pages
Advanced Pinstripe Art	9781929133321	$27.95	144 pages
Advanced Sheet Metal Fab	9781929133123	$27.95	144 pages
Advanced Tattoo Art - *Revised*	9781929133822	$27.95	144 pages
Airbrush How-To with Mickey Harris	9781929133505	$27.95	144 pages
Barris: Flames, Scallops and Striping	9781929133550	$24.95	144 pages
Bean're - Motorcycle Nomad	9781935828709	$18.95	256 pages
Body Painting	9781929133666	$27.95	144 pages
Building Hot Rods	9781929133437	$27.95	144 pages
Colorful World of Tattoo Models	9781935828716	$34.95	144 pages
Composite Materials 1	9781929133765	$27.95	144 pages
Composite Materials 2	9781929133932	$27.95	144 pages
Composite Materials 3	9781935828662	$27.95	144 pages
Composite Materials Step by Step Projects	9781929133369	$27.95	144 pages
Cultura Tattoo Sketchbook	9781935828839	$32.95	284 pages
Custom Bike Building Basics	9781935828624	$24.95	144 pages
Custom Motorcycle Fabrication	9781935828792	$27.95	144 pages
George the Painter	9781935828815	$18.95	256 pages
Harley-Davidson Sportster Hop-Up & Customizing Guide	9781935828952	$27.95	144 pages
Harley-Davidson Sportser Buell Engine Hop-Up Guide	9781929133093	$24.95	144 pages
How Airbrushes Work	9781929133710	$24.95	144 pages
Honda Enthusiast Guide Motorcycles 1959-1985	9781935828853	$27.95	144 pages
How-To Airbrush, Pinstripe & Goldleaf	9781935828693	$27.95	144 pages
How-To Airbrush Pin-ups	9781929133802	$27.95	144 pages
How-To Build Old Skool Bobber - 2nd Edition	9781935828785	$27.95	144 pages

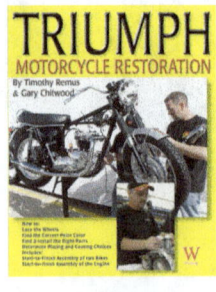
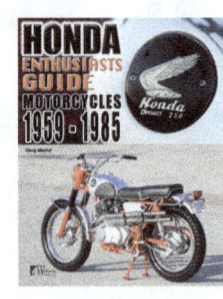

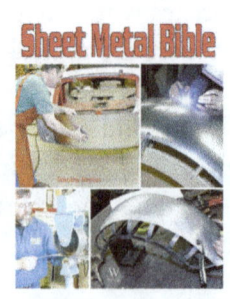

Books from Wolfgang Publications can be found at select book stores and numerous web sites.

Titles	ISBN	Price	# of pages
How-To Build a Cheap Chopper	9781929133178	$27.95	144 pages
How-To Build Cafe Racer	9781935828730	$27.95	144 pages
How-To Chop Tops	9781929133499	$24.95	144 pages
How-To Draw Monsters	9781935828914	$27.95	144 pages
How-To Fix American V-Twin	9781929133727	$27.95	144 pages
How-To Paint Tractors & Trucks	9781929133475	$27.95	144 pages
Hot Rod Wiring	9781929133987	$27.95	144 pages
Into the Skin	9781935828174	$34.95	144 pages
Kosmoski's *New* Kustom Paint Secrets	9781929133833	$27.95	144 pages
Learning the English Wheel	9781935828891	$27.95	144 pages
Mini Ebooks - Butterfly and Roses	9781935828167	Ebook Only	
Mini Ebooks - Skulls & Hearts	9781935828198	Ebook Only	
Mini Ebooks - Lettering & Banners	9781935828204	Ebook Only	
Mini Ebooks - Tribal Stars	9781935828211	Ebook Only	
Pin-Ups on Two Wheels	9781929133956	$29.95	144 pages
Pro Pinstripe	9781929133925	$27.95	144 pages
Sheet Metal Bible	9781929133901	$29.95	176 pages
Sheet Metal Fab Basics B&W	9781929133468	$24.95	144 pages
Sheet Metal Fab for Car Builders	9781929133383	$27.95	144 pages
SO-CAL Speed Shop, Hot Rod Chassis	9781935828860	$27.95	144 pages
Tattoo Bible #1	9781929133840	$27.95	144 pages
Tattoo Bible #2	9781929133857	$27.95	144 pages
Tattoo Bible #3	9781935828754	$27.95	144 pages
Tattoo Lettering Bible	9781935828921	$27.95	144 pages
Tattoo Sketchbook / Nate Power	9781935828884	$27.95	144 pages
Tattoo Sketchbook, Jim Watson	9781935828037	$32.95	112 pages
Triumph Restoration - Pre Unit	9781929133635	$29.95	144 pages
Triumph Restoration - Unit 650cc	9781929133420	$29.95	144 pages
Vintage Dirt Bikes - Enthusiast's Guide	9781929133314	$27.95	144 pages
Ult Sheet Metal Fab	9780964135895	$24.95	144 pages
Ultimate Triumph Collection	9781935828655	$49.95	144 pages

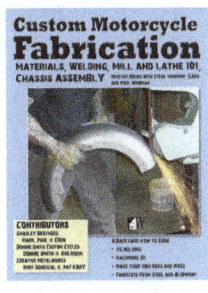

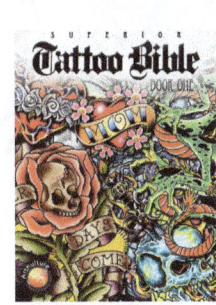

Sources

Accurate Engineering
128 Southgate Road
Dolhan, AL 36301
334.702.1993
www.accurate-engineering.com

Arlen Ness
6050 Dublin Blvd.
Dublin, CA 94568
925.479.6350
www.arlenness.com

Baker Drivetrain
9804 E. Saginaw
Haslett, MI 48840
Toll Free: 1.877.640.2004
Fax: 517.339.4590
www.bakerdrivetrain.com

BDL
1959 North Main St.
Orange, CA 92865
Phone: 714.685.3333
Ans./ Fax: 714.685.3339
www.beltdrives.com

Cyril Huze Custom, Inc.
Tel: 561.392.5557
Fax: 561.392.9923
www.cyrilhuze.com

Donnie Smith Custom Cycles Inc.
10594 Radisson Rd. NE
Blaine, MN 55449
763.786.6002
Fax: 763.786.0660
www.donniesmith.com

Dougz
LaCrosse, WI
608.783.3684
www.dougz.com

Jammer Cycle Products
1.800.597.6467
www.jammerclub.com

Kustomwerks
1200 South Park Dr.
Kernersville, NC 27284
Inquiries: 336.996.8690
www.kustomwerks.com

Lee's Speed Shop
12450 Highway 13 So.
Savage, MN 55378
952.233.2782
www. Leesspeedshop.com

Motorcycle Works
Frank
203 W. Dennis
Olathe, KS 66061
913.768.6888

Perewitz Cycle Fabrication
910 Plymouth St.
Bridgewater, MA 02324
508.697.3595
www.perewitz.com

Primo Belt Drives
Rivera Engineering
12532 Lambert Road
Whittier, CA 90606
562.907.2600

S&S Cycle, Inc.
14025 County Hwy. G
Viola, Wisconsin 54664
608.627.2080
www.sscycle.com

Ultima Products
www.ultimaproducts.com

Zipper's Performance Products
6655-A Amberton Drive
Elkridge, Md 21075
410.579.2828
Fax: 410.579.2835

www.ingramcontent.com/pod-product-compliance
Lightning Source LLC
Chambersburg PA
CBHW082125230426
43671CB00015B/2809